Winslow Homer
Artist and Angler

WINSLOW HOMER
Artist and Angler

Patricia Junker with Sarah Burns

WITH CONTRIBUTIONS BY
William H. Gerdts
Paul Schullery
Theodore E. Stebbins Jr.
David Tatham

AMON CARTER MUSEUM, FORT WORTH, TEXAS, AND FINE ARTS MUSEUMS OF SAN FRANCISCO

Thames & Hudson

This book is published in conjunction with the exhibition
Casting a Spell: Winslow Homer, Artist and Angler.

Fine Arts Museums of San Francisco
California Palace of the Legion of Honor
December 7, 2002 – February 9, 2003

Amon Carter Museum
Fort Worth, Texas
April 11 – June 22, 2003

Casting a Spell: Winslow Homer, Artist and Angler is co-organized by the Amon Carter Museum and
the Fine Arts Museums of San Francisco. The presentation of the exhibition in San Francisco is
made possible by support from The Bernard Osher Foundation, The Lunder Foundation, and the
Ednah Root Foundation.

The exhibition catalogue is generously supported by Burgess and Elizabeth Jamieson.

First published in the United States of America in hardcover in 2003 by
Thames & Hudson Inc., 500 Fifth Avenue, New York, New York 10110

First published in the United Kingdom in 2003 by
Thames & Hudson Ltd, 181A High Holborn, London WC1V 7QX

Library of Congress Catalog Card Number 2002102599

ISBN 0-500-09307-5

British Library Cataloguing-in-Publication Data
A catalogue record for this book is available from the British Library

Printed and bound in Belgium

PHOTOGRAPHERS' CREDITS: © Bruce Curtis: figs. 29, 34; Matt Flynn: fig. 32; Katya Kallsen: cats. 38, 51;
Allan Macintyre: fig. 56; Benjamin Magro: cat. 18; Melville McLean: figs. 26, 29, 43, 57, cats. 13, 36;
Richard Walker: fig. 120

FRONTISPIECE: Winslow Homer, *St. John's River, Florida,* 1890. The Hyde Collection Trust,
Glens Falls, New York. Cat. 21

Lenders to the Exhibition

The Adirondack Museum, Blue Mountain Lake, New York

Amon Carter Museum, Fort Worth, Texas

Arizona State University Art Museum, Nelson Fine Arts Center, Tempe

The Art Institute of Chicago

Brooklyn Museum of Art, New York

The Cummer Museum of Art and Gardens, Jacksonville, Florida

The Currier Gallery of Art, Manchester, New Hampshire

Dallas Museum of Art, Texas

Fine Arts Museums of San Francisco

Harvard University Art Museums (Fogg Art Museum), Cambridge, Massachusetts

Henry E. Huntington Library and Art Gallery, San Marino, California

The Hyde Collection Trust, Glens Falls, New York

The James W. Glanville Family Partnership

Collection Karen A. and Kevin W. Kennedy, courtesy James Graham & Sons Gallery, New York

Mrs. William S. Kilroy Sr.

James and Frances McGlothlin

The Metropolitan Museum of Art, New York

Museum of Art, Rhode Island School of Design, Providence

Museum of Fine Arts, Boston

National Gallery of Art, Washington, D.C.

Portland Museum of Art, Maine

San Antonio Museum of Art, Texas

Sterling and Francine Clark Art Institute, Williamstown, Massachusetts

Graham D. Williford

Yale University Art Gallery, New Haven, Connecticut

Anonymous private collections

Foreword

It is testimony to the appeal of the enigmatic Winslow Homer and his art that so much scholarship continues to be focused on his life and career. In recent years Homer has been the subject of landmark retrospective exhibitions—the survey of his watercolors produced by Helen Cooper in 1986 and the comprehensive exhibition mounted by Nicolai Cikovsky Jr. and Franklin Kelly in 1995—and seminal monographic studies on discrete aspects of this multifaceted artist's work. Given all that we have learned about Homer, it might seem inconceivable to many that there could remain a significant body of his work that has not received scholarly treatment, and yet that has been the case with his works that depict angling. In collaboration with Sarah Burns, Patricia Junker began a study of this little-understood area of Homer's art in 1999. Over the next years she joined her passions for the art and for the sport to bring us this exhibition of a subject that fascinated the artist throughout his life and inspired some of the most experimental watercolors in the last two decades of his career.

This book accompanies an exhibition of splendid paintings—kaleidoscopic views of trout ponds, brilliantly colored trophy fish, and evocative transcriptions of a sportsman's days on teeming rivers and lazy creeks. The selection of pictures presented in our galleries offers visitors to our respective museums a brief but memorable glimpse into Homer's world, the domain of the Victorian sportsman, and the arena of nature. We are grateful to the lenders for making this presentation possible, one that we like to think fulfills Homer's own express desire to have these particular paintings seen and appreciated as a unified, interconnected body of work. Also, we thank those who have lent their financial support to the exhibition: in San Francisco, the exhibition has been funded in part by The Bernard Osher Foundation, The Lunder Foundation, and the Ednah Root Foundation; in Fort Worth, the Amon G. Carter Foundation continues to be a major force in American art scholarship through its support for the Amon Carter Museum and the museum's diverse programs.

Although the exhibition itself can be enjoyed for only a brief period, this book preserves what we have learned in bringing these pictures together. We are grateful to the curator and to the other authors for their pioneering research and for the fresh insights they offer here. We especially thank Burgess and Elizabeth Jamieson for generously underwriting the publication, thus making possible such a thorough and richly illustrated overview of Homer's angling subjects and the sporting art of his contemporaries.

HARRY S. PARKER III
Director
Fine Arts Museums of San Francisco

RICK STEWART
Director
Amon Carter Museum

Acknowledgments

Good company in a journey makes the way to seem the shorter.

Venator, the hunter, to Piscator, the angler,
in Izaak Walton, *The Compleat Angler*, 1653

Were it not for finding thoughtful walking companions to encourage his discourse, Izaak Walton's Piscator, the author's alter ego in *The Compleat Angler*, might never have clarified his own thinking on the art of angling. This project, too, had its genesis in the wide-ranging conversations I enjoyed with both Homer scholars and anglers at times that seemed more like recreation than solemn dedication to scholarly pursuits. I must acknowledge, first, the collaboration of Sarah Burns, the Ruth N. Halls Professor of Fine Arts at Indiana University. She helped conceive of this study over the course of the year she was a scholar in residence at Stanford University and a regular visitor to the American Art Department at the M. H. de Young Memorial Museum in San Francisco, where the project took shape.

As we considered an exhibition, we immediately turned for advice to Abigail Booth Gerdts, director of the Lloyd Goodrich and Edith Havens Goodrich/ Whitney Museum of American Art Record of Works by Winslow Homer, and she kindly identified for us the works of art that we might include. Ms. Gerdts made our way shorter and easier than it otherwise would have been, as many of the angling pictures have not been widely exhibited or published. This project is a testament to her generosity.

There followed over time wonderful, enlightening conversations with other scholars who joined the project as collaborators. Our catalogue authors are eminent among those who have shaped our understanding of Homer's art: William H. Gerdts, Professor Emeritus of Art History, The Graduate Center of the City University of New York; Theodore E. Stebbins, Jr., Distinguished Fellow and Consultative Curator, Harvard University Art Museums; and David Tatham, Professor of Fine Arts, Emeritus, Syracuse University. Throughout our research, writing, and planning we have been guided by Paul Schullery, a leading authority on the history of fly fishing in America.

Even while our idea for the exhibition was evolving, it won immediate support from my former colleagues at the Fine Arts Museums of San Francisco. I must thank Harry S. Parker III, Director of Museums, and Steven A. Nash, Associate Director and Chief Curator, for their enthusiasm for and commitment to the project. They inspired the Museums' devoted friends of American art, Mr. and Mrs. J. Burgess Jamieson, to support my early research travel that moved the exhibition from mere wishful thinking to a solid plan. The Jamiesons have continued in their remarkable generosity by funding this publication. The Ednah Root Foundation, which underwrites all programs of the American Art Department at the Fine Arts Museums, deserves particular mention here. In addition, the exhibition in San Francisco has been made possible by funding from The Bernard Osher Foundation and The Lunder Foundation.

When I had the opportunity to move to the Amon Carter Museum, my new colleagues embraced the idea of collaboration with the Fine Arts Museums. I have enjoyed enthusiastic support for my efforts from Rick Stewart, Director, and Bob Workman, Deputy Director, both of whom bring to the project their American art expertise as well as their broad institutional vision. Ruth Carter Stevenson, the museum's founder, president, and inspiration, has been a great friend, facilitating our work in many ways. Her daughter, Karen J. Hixon, a trustee of the Amon Carter Museum, has also taken a personal interest in the exhibition that has helped at key points to spur it onward. The Amon G. Carter Foundation, which generously supports the Amon Carter Museum, is at the core of all we do.

At both institutions, a large team has overseen the gathering of objects, the mounting of the exhibition, and the planning of education programs that are integral to an exhibition's reception. The logistics of the project have been overseen in San Francisco by Kathe Hodgson, who served as Exhibitions Coordinator through much of the planning process, and by Krista Davis, who succeeded her in that position; they were assisted by Daniell Cornell, Associate Curator of American Art. At the Amon Carter Museum many administrative

tasks fell to Wendy Haynes, Exhibition Manager.

In San Francisco I wish to acknowledge Barbara Boucke, Development Director, and Anne-Marie Bonfilio, Corporate Relations Manager; Therese Chen, Head Registrar, and Steven Lockwood, Associate Registrar; Sheila Pressley, Director of Education, and the Museums' large, dedicated docent corps; Barbara Traisman, Senior Media Relations Officer; and Bill White, Exhibitions Designer, and his talented crew. Ron Rick, Chief Designer, developed the exhibition graphics and, as an avid fly fisherman, provided much inspiration as well. Jane Glover in the American Art Department contributed significant research assistance.

For their work on the exhibition in Fort Worth, I would like to thank Claire Barry and Isabelle Tokumaru, our Senior and Associate Paintings Conservators respectively, based at the Kimbell Art Museum; Melanie Boyle, Director of Development and Membership, Lucy Hyden, consultant, and Pam Graham, Outreach Support Coordinator, who with Bob Workman have handled fund-raising for the exhibition; Keely Edwards, Graphic Design Coordinator; Sam Duncan, Associate Librarian; Lori Eklund, Director of Education, Laura Matzer, Public Programs Coordinator, and Libby Cluett, School and Youth Programs Coordinator, who have developed the varied education offerings; Will Gillham, Director of Publications; Jeff Guy, Director of Finance and Operations; Rebecca Lawton, Assistant Curator of Paintings and Sculpture; Trish

Matthews, Executive Assistant to the Director; Tim McElroy, Installation and Design Coordinator; Jane Myers, Chief Curator; Carol Noel, Public Relations Coordinator, and her assistant, Ann Rickenbacher; Helen Plummer, Curatorial Associate in Photography; Jane Posey, Curatorial Administrative Assistant; John Rohrbach, Associate Curator of Photography; Paula Stewart, Archivist; Melissa Thompson, Registrar, and Courtney De Angelis, Associate Registrar; and Lisa Thornton, Technical Assistant. Karin Strohbeck, Library and Archives Assistant, deserves particular mention for bringing important sources to my attention and for obtaining rare material for me via interlibrary loan. I thank Amon Carter Museum docents Alan Laureyns and Dr. and Mrs. John Richardson for their advice and many kindnesses throughout the project. We are all grateful to Jan and Maurice Holloway for helping to underwrite the museum's education programs for the exhibition.

This publication has had a dedicated team of its own. Ann Karlstrom, Director of Publications and Graphic Design at the Fine Arts Museums of San Francisco, has overseen its production. Fronia W. Simpson, copy editor, shaped the essays with her extraordinary sensitivity and diplomacy and thoroughly engaging interest in the topic. Susan Dwyer, Vice President at Thames & Hudson publishers, has enthusiastically supported the book. Michael Sumner is responsible for its handsome design; he was assisted by Melody Sumner Carnahan. Sarah Alexander, Louise Chu, and Sue Grinols provided production assistance in San Francisco. I wish to acknowledge the tremendous help provided me at the Amon Carter Museum by Miriam Hermann, Publications Assistant, who secured reproduction rights; and Rynda Lemke and Steven Watson, museum photographers.

Beyond the two collaborating museums, our work on the exhibition has benefited from the help of lenders, dealers, librarians, friends, and museum colleagues. For their help with research I wish to acknowledge: David Barquist, Yale University Art Gallery; Margaret Conrads, The Nelson-Atkins Museum of Art; Melissa De Medeiros, Knoedler Archive; Joseph Ditta, The New-York Historical Society; Linda Ferber, Brooklyn Museum of Art; Vincent Giroud, Beinecke Library, Yale University; Jonathan Harding, Century Association; Eleanor Jones Harvey, Dallas Museum of Art; Elizabeth Harvey and Lai Jun Wong, Brooklyn Public Library; Barbara Johnson; David Ligare; Beth Miller, Yale Center for British Art; David McNeilly; Ellen Miles, National Portrait Gallery, Smithsonian Institution; J. Sam Moore; Emily Ballew Neff, The Museum of Fine Arts, Houston; Kimberly Orcutt and Stephanie Mayer, Harvard University Art Museums; Richard C. Randt; Sue Welsh Reed, Museum of Fine Arts, Boston; Nicolas Ricketts, The Strong Museum; Steven John Ross, The University of Memphis; Cynthia Sanford, Brooklyn Historical Society; Marc Simpson, Williams College Graduate Program in the History of Art; Gary Smith; Gary Tanner, Yoshi Akiyama, and John Price, The American Museum of Fly Fishing; Jeanette Toohey, The Cummer Museum of Art and Gardens; Judith Walsh, National Gallery of Art; Prosser M. Watts Jr.; H. Barbara Weinberg, The Metropolitan Museum of Art; Lucie Wellner; and Caroline Welsh, The Adirondack Museum.

I wish also to acknowledge the anglers who helped inspire this study, especially Margaret Thomas and her parents, William and Suzanne Thomas; and the painter James Prosek, who by his own art offered me insight into Homer's inspiration.

Our research travels took us to Winslow Homer's favorite fishing locales, and our efforts were guided by individuals with intimate knowledge of those regions. For their assistance to Mr. Stebbins and Professor Gerdts with the history of Adirondack fishing, of artists painting in the Adirondacks, and of the North Woods Club, we wish to thank Jim Meehan and Tracy Meehan of The Adirondack Museum; Warder Cadbury; and Theodore S. Wickersham. In locating material on Quebec, Professor Tatham was assisted by Jim Burant at the National Archives of Canada. Anglers Erroll Barron, Robert J. Demarest, and Steve Schullery helped me in planning my research in Florida. In my work on early Enterprise, Florida, and the Brock House I was guided by Spring Dautel; Rita Gillis, West Volusia Historical Society; and Mr. and Mrs. Samuel A. Vickers. In my researches in Homosassa, I was aided by Kathy Turner Thompson, Citrus County Historical Society; and by Duncan, Wilma, and Kathy Foulkes MacRae, who have maintained as their home the Homosassa Inn, where Homer stayed. In Maine, where Winslow Homer lived the last two decades of his life, we have been greatly assisted by Laura Latman of the Bowdoin College Museum of Art, keeper of the Homer family archive; and Doris Homer and Charles Willauer, who have maintained the Homer family properties at Prout's Neck and have for many years warmly welcomed Homer scholars and enthusiasts into what was the artist's studio-home there.

We wish to express our deep gratitude to the lenders of Homer paintings. Homer's angling pictures are prize catches indeed, and this project could not have been possible in any form without the generosity of so many institutional and individual owners of these beautiful paintings, most of which are delicate watercolors. We thank the directors and staffs of the museums that granted us loans from their collection. Many dealers negotiated loans on our behalf, and for their help I wish to thank Warren Adelson and Susan Mason, Adelson Galleries, Inc.; Lillian Brenwasser, Kennedy Galleries, Inc.; Charles Credaroli; Stuart Feld and Gregory Hedberg, Hirschl & Adler Galleries, Inc.; Debra Force; Maria Friedrich, Graham & Friedrich; Frederick Hill, Berry-Hill Galleries, Inc.; Dara

Mitchell and Valerie Westcott, Sotheby's; David Nisinson; Paul Provost and Eric Widing, Christie's; Cameron Shay, James Graham & Sons; John Surovek, John Surovek Gallery; and Richard York, Richard York Gallery. Other colleagues who graciously assisted with loans are Julie Broadus, Lisa Cantor, Molly Dolle, Linda Echols, Barbara Goering, Mrs. Wellington Henderson, Mrs. Peter McBean, Debbie McBrearity, Meg Perlman, Bertha Saunders, and William Truettner, Smithsonian American Art Museum.

Finally, I extend special thanks to individuals who have supported me personally through this effort. I am grateful for the friendship of Burgess and Elizabeth Jamieson, who have always taken a keen interest in my work and helped it forward. My husband, David—fellow angler and ever joyful companion—participated in nearly every aspect of this project from its early planning to its culmination. Everything that I undertake is made better by his thoughtful consideration, big-hearted help, and good wishes.

Patricia Junker
Curator of Paintings and Sculpture
Amon Carter Museum

"To Make You Proud of Your Brother"
Fishing and the Fraternal Bond in Winslow Homer's Art

Sarah Burns

As every student of Winslow Homer knows all too well, the painter was notoriously difficult to approach, guarding his privacy and hoarding his words like some social skinflint. In the circle of his family he lowered his defenses, but in all his life he had only one supremely intimate, bosom friend: his brother Charles Savage Homer Jr. (1834–1917), who was his elder by two years.[1] Reportedly inseparable as boys, the brothers nurtured and sustained their bond up to the very hour of Winslow's death in 1910. In 1884, not long after his mother's death, Winslow had drawn up his will, leaving his entire estate to Charles. This Charles now inherited, along with a desire to keep his brother's privacy inviolate.

When Homer's first biographer, William Howe Downes, began to gather information soon after the artist's burial, he found that both Charles and Arthur (1841–1916), the youngest of the three Homer siblings, imposed stringent limits on what the critic was allowed to see and to print. Tactfully, the frustrated Downes wrote in his acknowledgments, "With admirable loyalty his brothers have scrutinized every personal detail with sole regard to what he would have been likely to approve, and the family habit of reserve in such matters is strong. The best things are those which do not get into print." Downes suggested, however, that readers might enjoy the privilege of reading between the lines.[2]

There is much about the two brothers' relationship that we will never know. Information can be gleaned from Homer's letters, which allow us to piece together certain particulars of the siblings' interactions and modes of exchange,[3] and from oral testimony collected by Downes and other early chroniclers. Homer's paintings, notably those depicting anglers, also offer opportunities to understand how highly he valued brotherhood. Indeed, we can read these paintings between the lines, figuratively speaking, as images that bear witness to the lifelong sympathy that united Winslow and Charles. Further, the angling scenes offer insight into how the broader culture of fraternal society underwrote and nurtured the painter's enterprise. In this essay, accordingly, I seek to deepen our sense of Homer as artist, angler, and brother.

Regarding Homer's childhood, very few scraps of recollection exist. Beyond the fact that he was by all accounts devoted to his older brother, we know that the boys enjoyed "fishing, boating, and other rural sports dear to the heart of boyhood."[4] Charles and Winslow attended grammar and middle schools in Cambridge, Charles going on to graduate in 1855 from the Lawrence Scientific School at Harvard, and Winslow—several months earlier—to an apprenticeship at John H. Bufford's lithography shop in Boston. After graduation, Charles began his career as a chemist at the Pacific Mills in Lawrence, Massachusetts, and Homer, having endured two years of menial artistic labor at Bufford's, set out on a career as a freelance illustrator, first in Boston and then, by 1859, in New York. But in some measure, he was always dependent on Charles.

FIG. 1
Charles Savage Homer Sr., ca. 1870. Photographer unknown. Bowdoin College Museum of Art, Brunswick, Maine. Gift of the Homer family, 1964.69.181.4

had set out with splendid, brass-bound trunks but returned—two years later—with a satchel tied up with string.[5] Hardly had the patriarchal prodigal returned than he was off again in May 1852, spending two more years away in London and Paris, seeking in vain to get a California mining lease from the powerful landowner John C. Frémont. During this time, apparently, his wife and sons had to manage on their own, with little or no financial support from Charles Sr.

Charles Sr.'s prolonged absences were not particularly uncommon in the world of mobile, striving, middle-class fathers. In the nineteenth century, home and work became increasingly separate and distant from one another, and the workday longer. Because of this, fathers tended to spend less time with their children. One observer in 1842 noted that "Paternal neglect" had become epidemic.[6] Mothers accordingly assumed greater power on the domestic front, and this was no doubt the case in the Homer family. The teenaged Charles likely stepped into a quasipaternal role to which, as eldest, he had a claim. Parents routinely delegated authority to the eldest child, who was expected to be leader, guide, and model to younger siblings.[7]

So close in age to Winslow, Charles could hardly have assumed anything resembling full-blown paternal authority. No sooner had he become a wage earner, though, than he began to shoulder the full burden of supporting his family. From the late 1850s or early 1860s, as Philip Beam has written, Charles Sr. was "destined never again to support himself." Thus, in 1858, the Homers moved to Belmont and took up residence in a house taken for them by Charles Jr., whose annual salary by then was $4,000. At that point Winslow was at least partly self-supporting, but he remained indebted to his brother in various ways.[8]

Homer family lore attributed Charles's intervention with Winslow's determination to pursue his goal of becoming a painter rather than settle for a

One key to the Homer family dynamics and the strength of Winslow's attachment to Charles may lie in Charles Savage Homer Sr.'s role as absentee father. A hardware merchant and would-be entrepreneur, the senior Homer (fig. 1) sold his business and left Boston in 1849 for the gold fields of California, dreaming like thousands of others of untold riches. This venture proved a complete disaster. A family story recounted that Charles Sr.

[page 12]
DETAIL: CAT. 2
Crossing the Pasture, 1871–1872.
Oil on canvas, 26 ¼ × 38 ⅛ in.
Amon Carter Museum,
Fort Worth, Texas (1976.37)

CAT. 5
Fishing, 1879. Oil on canvas, 7 ½ × 9 ¼ in. Museum of Art, Rhode Island
School of Design, Providence. Bequest of Isaac C. Bates (13.935)

career in illustration. According to this tradition, Homer placed two of his early Civil War oil paintings at a dealer's and vowed that if they did not sell he would give up painting and accept a position on the staff at *Harper's Weekly.* On the sly, Charles purchased both works, providing the encouragement Winslow needed. Lloyd Goodrich adds that Winslow, having discovered the truth sometime later, "swore roundly and refused to speak to his brother for weeks." This story has a mythic ring, and in fact has recently been questioned. Whether true or not, it is emblematic of the relationship in its stress on Charles's status as brother-benefactor.[9]

As an increasingly well-connected professional,

Charles was also instrumental in linking his brother with potential buyers. During the 1860s Charles had risen to management level at the Pacific Mills, where by 1864 he was overseer of the chemical department. In 1870 he left Pacific Mills to join the firm of Lawson Valentine (1828–1891), a varnish manufacturer who, like the Homer family, had Cambridge roots. Having been in various partnerships, Valentine formed his own company in 1867, with a manufacturing plant in Brighton, Massachusetts. In 1872 this factory burned down and Valentine moved the business to Brooklyn, maintaining offices across the river in New York City. Valentine became one of Winslow's most important patrons in the 1870s as

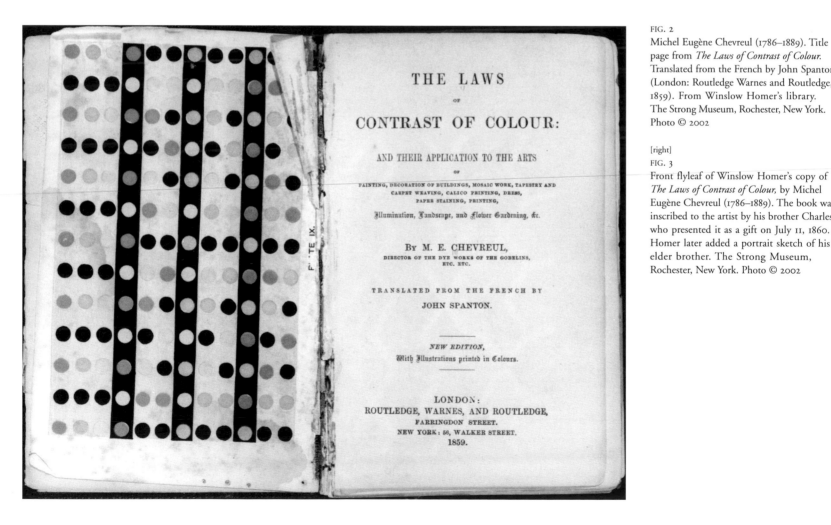

FIG. 2
Michel Eugène Chevreul (1786–1889). Title page from *The Laws of Contrast of Colour.* Translated from the French by John Spanton (London: Routledge Warnes and Routledge, 1859). From Winslow Homer's library. The Strong Museum, Rochester, New York. Photo © 2002

[right]
FIG. 3
Front flyleaf of Winslow Homer's copy of *The Laws of Contrast of Colour,* by Michel Eugène Chevreul (1786–1889). The book was inscribed to the artist by his brother Charles, who presented it as a gift on July 11, 1860. Homer later added a portrait sketch of his elder brother. The Strong Museum, Rochester, New York. Photo © 2002

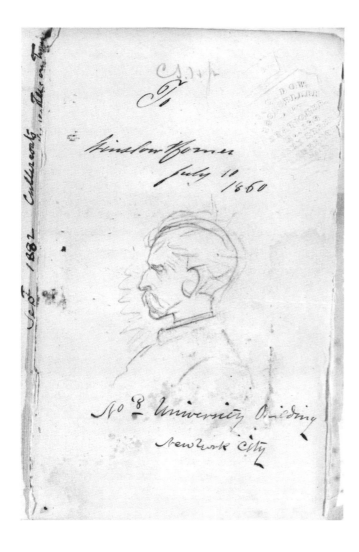

Harvard rowing crew and another rower in a single scull. Knowing Homer's fondness for visual jokes and puns, it is tempting to think that he included the Harvard crew as a covert reference to his brother's alma mater. The name of the river functions as surrogate for Charles himself, by that time perhaps already associated with Valentine's enterprise.

Charles's position as an industrial chemist was important to his brother in more ways than one. There was the pleasurable and profitable relationship with Lawson that Charles helped foster, of course. But there was also his expertise in the chemistry of color, which must have been the primary focus of his job in the textile industry, where the formulation of dyes was all-important. It was undoubtedly through on-the-job experience that Charles came across one of the most influential nineteenth-century treatises on color, Michel Eugène Chevreul's *De la loi du contraste simultané des couleurs,* first published in French in 1839. Although this book was widely used by painters in the later nineteenth century, its original purpose was utilitarian.

Chevreul, a noted chemist, became director of the dye plant of the Gobelins tapestry works in Paris. Investigating complaints about instability and fading in dyes used for Gobelins yarns, Chevreul discovered that surrounding colors played a critical part in determining any individual color's appearance. *De la loi du contraste simultané des couleurs* grew out of rules for Gobelins weavers that Chevreul deduced based on his observations.[12] The first English edition appeared in 1854, just when Charles was about to embark on his career as chemist for the Lawrence textile works. In 1860 Charles gave Winslow a copy of the 1859 edition (fig. 2), and Winslow inscribed a profile portrait of his brother on the front flyleaf (fig. 3). The book became Homer's lifelong guide, governing his understanding and application of color theory to his painting. Late in life, he told his friend John W. Beatty, "It is my Bible."[13]

well as a close friend to both Homer brothers. From the early 1870s, Winslow visited the Valentine family in their summer house in Walden, New York, and later at their new estate, Houghton Farm, in Mountainville, also in New York. There he painted genre scenes of idyllic rural life, including the charming *Fishing* (cat. 5) derived from studies made at Houghton Farm. In the course of the decade, Valentine bought several dozen works from the artist.[10]

At some point between 1867 and 1872, Winslow designed a wood-engraved view of the Valentine Company buildings as seen from the opposite bank of the Charles River.[11] On the water are a four-man

FIG. 4
Charles Savage Homer Jr., 1880. Watercolor on paper, 20 ½ × 15 in.
Private collection, courtesy John H. Surovek Gallery, Palm Beach, Florida

The story of this exchange exemplifies the way in which Charles and Winslow complemented each other to near perfection. Charles was situated on the business end of the color business and later, when he worked for Valentine, dealt on an industrial scale with high-quality varnishes. Winslow, occupying the aesthetic pole on this color continuum, was nonetheless dependent on the chemicals industry for the very materials he used, as well as for the origin of his own color theory.[14] As complementary personalities, too, Winslow and his brother were mirror images of each other, in the sense that a true mirror image reverses whatever is reflected there.

Philip Beam recounted that all who knew Charles described him as a "prince" and a "wonderful fellow." He was tall, handsome, and robust (fig. 4), becoming portly in later life. Socially adept and comfortable in large groups, he was a "witty after-dinner speaker." He lived in high and lavish style, with a large apartment in New York, a home in his wife's birthplace, West Townsend, Massachusetts, and the commodious summer house at Prout's Neck, Maine, where after 1884 Winslow maintained his own studio-home on the grounds of the family compound. Charles was notably prosperous and successful. When he died in 1917, his estate was worth about $200,000 and included large stock holdings in a variety of companies. Charles had a full complement of servants and in the early twentieth century an automobile and driver. His wife, Martha (Mattie), became a socialite much given to elaborate teas and dinner parties. Charles's expansiveness extended as well to acquisition: he was "an omnivorous collector" who "filled his West Townsend house to overflowing." In many ways, it would seem, Charles Jr. was an improved and far more successful version of his flamboyant sire.[15]

If Charles expanded, Winslow by contrast contracted, literally and figuratively. Winslow, as many acquaintances reported, was small, wiry, and reticent (fig. 5). He was addicted to systems and methodical order. James Edward Kelly, an aspiring painter working in the art department of *Harper's Weekly*, portrayed Homer in his unpublished memoirs as a "slim, erect, alert" man "dressed to perfection" in a "black cutaway coat and steel-gray trousers" that had "the set and precision of a uniform." When Kelly visited Homer in his Tenth Street studio, he found everything "in perfect order, spick and span looking, like himself." Indeed, Homer was so compulsively neat that "during the intervals of his talk, if there was anything out of order, he would shift it to its place; a thread or a piece of paper on the floor would bring him to a standstill until he could pick it up." This obsession extended to all aspects of his life. According to Beam, the artist "preserved his cheques, tied up in chronological order, for decades."[16]

Although his reclusiveness was more myth than fact, certainly he held himself far more in reserve than did his older brother. Kelly reported that before admitting a caller, Homer would crack the door open, blocking the gap with his body until he decided whether or not to permit entry. At Prout's Neck, his guarded behavior was legendary. In part this arose from the need to fend off interruptions during working hours, but as Beam suggested, Homer "came to make a fetish of privacy" beyond practical requirements. He was equally compulsive when it came to property lines and on one occasion "put up a fence between himself and . . . his neighbor to the east, even though the two were perfectly friendly." Such patterns make it clear that Homer was a man with an overwhelming need to police boundaries: bodily, personal, and spatial.[17]

Although there is abundant evidence that within his family circle Homer let down his guard and opened the door of his selfhood more than a crack, still he and Charles were dramatically different in behavior and outlook. Yet they shared an intense emotional bond, and this theme —of brotherly interdependence—is fundamental

FIG. 5
Winslow Homer, ca. 1880. Photograph by Napoleon Sarony (1821–1896), New York. Bowdoin College Museum of Art, Brunswick, Maine. Gift of the Homer family, 1964.69.179.3

CAT. 2
Crossing the Pasture, 1871–1872. Oil on canvas, 26 ¼ × 38 ⅛ in.
Amon Carter Museum, Fort Worth, Texas (1976.37)

to understanding Homer's recurrent delineation of boys and men, harmoniously paired.

Crossing the Pasture (cat. 2) gives us entrée into Homer's figuration of brotherhood and everything that it connoted for him. Exhibited at the Century Association in 1872 as *Two Boys Going Fishing,* the painting shows the pair in the middle of a wide, rocky pasture, backed by green mountains. On the right, in the distance, are a farmhouse and a grazing cow, on the left, a stone wall and a red bull alert to the intruders' presence in his field. Their body language speaks eloquently of the relationship they share. The older boy stands between his younger brother and the bull. Dressed in a stiff tan jacket and pants, with a hat of the same shade pulled low over his eyes, he shoulders a switch cut from a tree. Younger and smaller, the other boy shrinks close to his brother's side, his right hand perhaps gripping the tail of the tan jacket. He wears a soft brown cap, a soft white shirt, and knee pants. He scissors his bare shins and feet together and reaches across with his other hand to help carry the bait bucket. The differences are subtle but significant. The younger boy's body is closed, self-protective, diffident. With his naked feet, he seems more vulnerable than his brother, shod in thick leather boots. The older boy, erect and vigilant, stands or steps sturdily, legs open, elbow crooked and fingers clenched around the switch, the other arm hanging straight down, hand wrapped around the bucket's handle next to his little brother's. He is the very image of the extrovert, whereas the small boy's body language eloquently signals his introversion.

Crossing the Pasture offers an ideal vision of sibling relations, the elder boy guiding and shielding the younger. It is not autobiographical, yet elements or traces of personal experience are part of the mix. Indeed, it is difficult to look at this painting without thinking back to Homer's youth, when in the absence of the adventurous, harum-scarum father, Charles began rehearsing for the role that he would

continue to play in his younger brother's life: protector, supporter, and confidante. Homer never sold this painting. After 1901 it hung in one of the ground-floor rooms at Kettle Cove, a cottage Homer had built on the Prout's Neck property with the intention of occupying it "to die in," although in the end he rented it out and never moved there himself. While it does not necessarily follow that the painting held some sentimental value for its creator—Homer being disposed to regard the bulk of his work as commodities—it still seems significant that this was one of the few that he kept all his life.[18]

In certain ways Winslow's dependence on Charles did not lessen even with advancing maturity. Charles was always willing to prop his brother up during periods of sluggish cash flow, and Charles's money underlay the acquisition of the land at Prout's Neck, where Homer moved permanently in 1884. Although Charles Savage Sr. actually transacted the purchase and built the family home, the Ark (fig. 6), nothing would have been possible without Charles's backing. Winslow, who remodeled the carriage house as studio and living quarters, made it his permanent

FIG. 6
The Charles Savage Homer house, called the Ark, and Winslow Homer's studio home, Prout's Neck, Maine, ca. 1884. Photographer unknown. Bowdoin College Museum of Art, Brunswick, Maine. Gift of the Homer family, 1964.69.177.25

address barely two months after his mother died. From that time, although he traveled widely, the center of his life and work was Prout's Neck. His father lived in the Ark (and wintered in Boston), and Charles and Mattie spent the summers there as well.[19] It is from this point that we can better trace the interactions of the two brothers, since Mattie began to save their correspondence beginning in 1883. The fact that Homer was unmarried and Charles and Mattie childless probably played a part in perpetuating the brothers' intimacy. Their loyalties undivided, they remained emotionally available to each other. Mattie, as an extension so to speak of Charles, was in some senses an honorary brother and a good friend to whom Winslow wrote in much the same tone he used with her husband.

By all accounts, fishing constituted the brothers' greatest and most enduring tie, and their best times together seem to have been on numerous camping and fishing excursions in the wilderness. Charles was as avid an angler as Winslow himself, and here a spirit of competition ruled. Charles recollected that Winslow "did not go in for expensive or elaborate tackle, but he usually caught the biggest fish."[20] The brothers also fished together at Prout's Neck, and a photograph taken about 1900 (fig. 7) shows the aftermath of a successful foray there. Old men by now, they stand facing each other, Winslow smiling and of course impeccably dressed, portly Charles more rumpled. In his left hand Winslow holds a gaff and a dangling brace of sizable fish. Both men grasp a horizontal fishing rod, Charles with two fists and Winslow with one, down by the butt. Between their hands, and exactly in the center, four fat flounder hang from this makeshift bar. It is not clear which one of them caught the flounder, although the rod—the only one in the photograph—appears to belong to Charles. The picture is tantamount to a graphic diagram of their relationship as brothers of the rod and creel. Charles's two-fisted grip on the rod hints at a tug-of-war and friendly sibling rivalry. At the same time, the perfectly centralized flounder suggest an even rate of exchange, brother to brother. Or is Winslow, holding his lesser catch off to the side, conceding first place to Charles? The photograph is a geriatric variation on the theme first essayed in *Crossing the Pasture*. Although one is no longer dependent on the other in quite the same fashion, at the same time they remain connected, the segment of rod almost like the band of flesh that joined the famous twins Chang and Eng.

Homer expressed his emotional dependence in a letter to brother Arthur shortly after Charles and Mattie embarked on a voyage to Europe. "I have never seen anyone off before, that I cared anything about & found it hard," wrote Winslow, "& I was

FIG. 7
Winslow Homer (right) and his brother Charles Savage Homer Jr., with their day's catch, Prout's Neck, ca. 1900. Photographer unknown. Bowdoin College Museum of Art, Brunswick, Maine. Gift of the Homer family, 1964.69.153.2

glad when the steamer was off but New York seems empty now to me." He took himself off to the North Woods Club in the Adirondacks for fishing and repose and later wrote to Charles, now back in the United States, that he was working very hard on two oil paintings. He boasted that these were "great works" but in the next sentence revealed a hint of anxiety: "Your eye being fresh from European pictures, great care is required to make you proud of your brother." Homer might have been joking in his deadpan way, knowing full well that his brother *was* proud of him. But probably the desire to measure up to his older brother's expectations—a vestige of boyhood still very much a part of his emotional makeup—played a role. For his part, Winslow was equally proud of Charles. Downes recounted that on one occasion, when Winslow found himself engulfed by a group of female fans, he admonished them to remember "that my brother here is quite as distinguished in his line of work as I am in mine."[21]

In the letter just cited, Winslow mentioned that he had made watercolor studies of both subjects, Adirondack hunting scenes, and rather than put them on the market intended to present the two of them to Charles along with "the one that I made expressly for you." Winslow's gifts to Charles communicated an extraordinary affection that he may have been incapable of expressing any other way. Beam noted that over the years Winslow gave Charles "scores of watercolors, especially those which depicted scenes they had known together." The number of watercolors Winslow actually gave Charles is unknown. Since Charles inherited Winslow's entire estate, many of the angling watercolors could have come to him after his brother's death. Yet the anecdotal tradition does suggest that Winslow may have been as generous to Charles as Charles was to him. Charles and Mattie for their part regularly sent presents to Winslow: boxes of cigarettes, a heavy silver pencil with multicolored leads, bottles of wine.[22]

FIG. 8
The Homer brothers' cabin, Tourilli Fish and Game Club, Province of Quebec, Canada. Photographer unknown. Bowdoin College Museum of Art, Brunswick, Maine. Gift of the Homer family, 1964

For Winslow, obsessed with his sales and his bank balance, these gifts of his art were supreme gestures of love and no doubt bids for Charles's approval. At least two of the watercolors were trophylike displays of fish, such as a "fine sketch of a black bass taken in the boat five minutes after he was caught" (cat. 44, ill. p. 63). Winslow intended the sketch for Charles's "fish room" at the house in West Townsend. *Thornhill Bar* of 1886 (cat. 7, ill. p. 167) and *Two Trout* (cat. 17, ill. p. 64) also hung on the walls of this specialized den, shrine to a shared passion.[23]

Other watercolors, some perhaps owned by Charles, were scenes of angling in the Adirondacks and Quebec, places the brothers had often fished, sometimes together, sometimes solo or with other friends. These paintings mark the deep significance of place in the two brothers' enjoyment of each other's company. There were special sites, even special structures, sacred to their communion.

Their log cabin (fig. 8) at the Tourilli Fish and Game Club in Quebec was one such sanctuary. The club, situated at a wide pool in the Tourilli River, was, as Goodrich recounted, in "deep forest, miles from any settlement, and reached by a blazed trail." It was not sufficiently isolated for Winslow and Charles, however: "In a still more remote spot on the lake the brothers had a log cabin built." Here, plentifully supplied with whiskey, rum, and tobacco, they would stay for several weeks at a time. So cherished was this cabin (and its associations) that Homer built a replica for Charles in the woods at Prout's Neck, hiring a French-Canadian carpenter to ensure authenticity. "Here the two brothers could retire for a smoke and a talk."[24]

Camp Fire (cat. 6) suggests the flavor and intimacy of this exclusively male, brotherly ritual. An Adirondack scene reportedly based on a spot where the artist and his party bivouacked one night, the painting shows two sportsmen relaxing in the rosy glow of the flames. Vivid sparks fly up into the darkness, and beyond, deep brown shadows obscure the forest interior. In a makeshift hut decorated with fishing gear sprawls one of the anglers, asleep or in reverie. His companion (identified as Charles himself in family tradition) sits on the platform in the corner nearest the fire, peacefully ruminating. They are silent and do not look at each other, yet there is a sense of unspoken communication in their enjoyment of this shared experience. Far from menacing, the dark woods seem to shelter and sequester the adventurers from all contact with the world.[25]

This was the kind of experience Charles and Winslow sought to revisit in their replicated log cabin as well as the real one up in Canada. They may also have been intent on revisiting a much earlier past. Indeed, the log cabin facsimile and the brothers' ritualized retreats there strongly evoke the image of a boys' clubhouse and the clannish fraternity of what the historian Anthony Rotundo has dubbed "boy culture." Club formation, writes Rotundo, was one of the "great passions" of nineteenth-century boys. In small towns and big cities these groups met in cellars or attics or other liminal places and pursued their common purpose of "nurture and athletics." Bonded by group loyalty and dedicated to exuberant hedonism, boys rigidly excluded outsiders and staked out antagonistic positions against the "civilized" values of the domestic sphere. Withdrawing into their own exclusive solitude, Winslow and Charles temporarily became boy brothers again, escaping from Mattie's continuous socializing and the "tea fights" that Winslow in particular detested. The fact that Winslow even required his family to use a system of secret, coded knocks when they came to his studio further suggests that he never completely abandoned the boy culture of yore. Even more tellingly, he loved gags and pranks of all kinds, at the age of fifty-nine dressing up as the Devil to scare his father out of bed.[26]

On a larger scale, middle-class and elite male culture also carried that distinctive, clubbing mode of fraternization into adulthood. In the nineteenth century, fraternal organizations such as the Odd Fellows proliferated, introducing men to a world of initiation and secret ritual. These orders, in Mark Carnes's view, provided solace from the psychic pressures of new social and institutional relationships, while easing accommodation to the emergent economic order of capitalism. Beyond the secret societies, clubs in the nineteenth century played an increasingly active role in organizing masculine experience. Private, limited in membership, and closed to women (except for infrequent, designated Ladies' Days), clubs offered men the opportunity to pursue pleasures and freedoms unavailable in their ordinary domestic or public, commercial spheres. They frequently facilitated business and professional relationships, but more important, they enabled the formation of environments "in which peers would find themselves comfortable and at home in the company of kindred spirits."[27]

CAT. 6

Camp Fire, [1877]/1880. Oil on canvas, 23 ¾ × 38 ⅛ in. The Metropolitan Museum of Art, New York.
Gift of Henry Keney Pomeroy, 1927 (27.181). Photograph © 1995 The Metropolitan Museum of Art

FIG. 9
Winslow Homer and friend Albert Kelsey in Paris, 1867. Photographer unknown. Bowdoin College Museum of Art, Brunswick, Maine. Gift of the Homer family, 1964.69.185a

From the beginning of his professional life, Winslow moved in such circles of male fellowship. He won election to the Century Association in 1865 and regularly attended until late in the 1870s. In 1877 he became a member of the Tile Club, a group of New York artists, initially limited to twelve, who met on Wednesday evenings to design decorative tiles and to enjoy an uninhibited good time, eating, drinking, carousing, and telling jokes. The art critic Earl Shinn, who attended as a guest in 1878, noted that on this occasion the illustrator F. Hopkinson Smith told stories in "Negro and Irish" dialect, and that everybody, including Homer, danced a "comic breakdown."[28]

Beyond the clubs, Homer's social circle was predominantly masculine as well. This was hardly unusual in the nineteenth century, when separation of male and female spheres helped foster intimate male ties, especially among adolescents and young adults. But for Homer such friendships, in the absence of marriage, may have been even more significant. Certainly as a young man he had a number of close comrades. An illuminating picture emerges from the diary of the painter Alfred C. Howland (1838–1909), who sailed for France in June 1860. Homer and several other young men accompanied him to the ship and gave him a rousing sendoff. "How I love these fellows!" Howland wrote. "If they were only going with me, life would seem a perfect bliss."[29] Evidence of another close relationship survives in the photograph of Homer and Albert Kelsey, his studio-mate in Paris (fig. 9). Homer, in a natty suit, sits on a tall, fluted column. Hands laced together, Kelsey props himself against Homer's back with an air of easy familiarity. On the back of the card is the inscription, "Damon and Pythias," a reference to the ancient story of friends so dear that when Pythias was condemned to die Damon offered to take his place.[30] In the late 1860s and through the 1870s, Homer continued to travel and lodge with artist friends during summer months spent in search of new subject matter.

Later, of course, the sporting clubs came to be central to Homer's art and his angling, the North Woods Club in the Adirondacks from 1889 and the Tourilli Fish and Game Club in Quebec from 1893, when he and Charles became members. Like the urban clubs, these societies were private and restricted, accessible only to those with means and connections. While they did not offer the sumptuous home comforts often found in urban venues, they were rugged but hardly primitive. Both the North Woods Club and the Tourilli Club had well-appointed lodges, excellent food, and other expensive amenities.[31] Although women were sometimes present, the atmosphere and attractions catered to masculine tastes. Homer's pictures of angling were recollections of and reflections on that fraternal world of carefully ritualized wilderness experience: the silent woods, the glassy lakes, the foaming rapids, the waterfalls, the fragile canoes, the skilled sportsmen, the rough-hewn guides, the graceful cast, the cunning lure, the leaping fish, the harmonious community of men.

And indeed, while anyone might respond to the beauty of his angling scenes, only true initiates—club members—could understand them. The critic Orson Lowell made this plain when reviewing a show of Homer's Quebec watercolors at M. Knoedler & Company gallery in 1898. Lowell claimed to have seen the show with an experienced angler able to appreciate the rightness of every detail, from the overcast "fishing skies" to the "nose" indicating the sex (male) of a hooked fish. In one scene, an angler was executing a cast. The effect was "good, but only a fisherman could understand what all that line in the air means." Lowell hoped "sincerely . . . that the unbroken set may find a permanent place in some sportsmen's clubhouse," since nowhere else would it enjoy the ideal audience it deserved.[32]

The Tourilli Club and the idyllic lakes and rivers of Quebec may have constituted the supreme

fishing experience for Charles and Winslow. The fact that the log cabin they occupied became a precious retreat even in replication supports this conjecture. Their bond is invisible yet palpable in Charles's Kodak snapshot of his brother in a canoe, in the middle of a still lake (fig. 10). Reflected in the satiny water, Winslow sits upright in the stern, paddle poised. On the shore, unseen, is Charles holding the camera and aiming with care to align Winslow perfectly with the vertical axis of the circle. His brother is the center of the composition and of the universe they share.[33]

FIG. 10
Winslow Homer in a canoe, probably 1890s. Photograph probably by Charles Savage Homer Jr. Bowdoin College Museum of Art, Brunswick, Maine. Gift of the Homer family, 1964

CAT. 40
Entering the First Rapid, Grand Discharge, 1897. Watercolor
over graphite on paper, 13 ½ × 20 ½ in. Private collection

Homer's canoe, real enough in the photograph, is also the container, vessel, and symbol of masculine community in this watery wilderness. While several of the Quebec watercolors show sportsmen fishing from rocks, many more depict fishermen in canoes, threesomes occasionally, but more often pairs. Whatever the grouping, each man has a role essential to the success of the enterprise. In *A Good Pool, Saguenay River* (cat. 30, ill. p. 48), a French-Canadian and an Indian guide paddle while the angler hooks a fine trophy fish. A similar trio appears in *Under the Falls, the Grand Discharge, Lake St. John, P.Q.* (cat. 37, ill. p. 146). In these two paintings, there are obvious signs of class and ethnic difference, although in the boat all are at least temporarily on the same level, working toward the same goal.

When two men occupy the canoe, however, it is more difficult to distinguish between them; they are equal players, each dependent on the other for survival. The *Two Men in a Canoe* (cat. 36, ill. p. 143) glide across the surface of a smooth, shining lake like the one on which Homer paddles in Charles's snapshot. Lavender-gray haze envelops the landscape and allows us to see the canoeists as little more than slightly darker silhouettes. One paddles and one casts his line. Guide and sportsman, perhaps, yet at the same time perfectly balanced, and perfectly in harmony.

Finally, in two of the 1897 watercolors, there is flawless reciprocation as men guide their canoes through dangerous waters. We see them from behind in *Canoe in the Rapids* (cat. 38, ill. p. 150), their paddles synchronized, both intent on the course, acting in concert. *Entering the First Rapid, Grand Discharge* (cat. 40) shows the vessel angling toward us from the left, the two paddlers tensed in readiness for surging, treacherous currents. Their paddle strokes mesh in precise counterpoint; they act as one, piloting their craft with delicacy and skill. With their mustaches, round-brimmed hats,

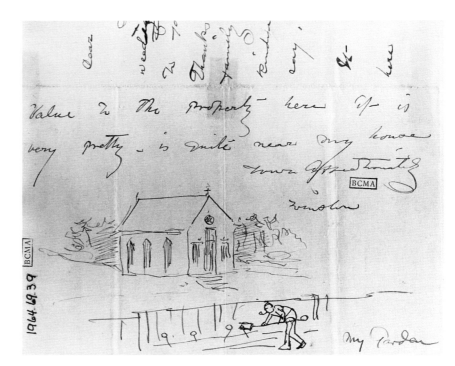

FIG. 11
Sketch of St. James Episcopal Church, Prout's Neck, Maine, from Homer's letter to his sister-in-law Martha (Mattie) Homer (Mrs. Charles Savage Homer Jr.), June 19, 1885. Bowdoin College Museum of Art, Brunswick, Maine. Gift of the Homer family, 1964.69.39

open-necked shirts, and suspenders, they might be woodsmen, or sportsmen incognito. They resemble each other sufficiently to be taken for brothers, and indeed the image reads as a metaphor for the kind of brotherly affection and interdependence that was the underpinning of Winslow's emotional life and probably of Charles's as well.

The jaunty pipe in the mouth of the boatman in the stern could be a clue to a layer of personal meaning in this painting. Homer was a pipe smoker (as was Charles), and in one letter to Mattie in 1885 (fig. 11) he cartooned himself digging in his garden, pipe jutting from his lips. The figure in the watercolor is not by any measure a self-portrait; among other things, he is young and has a full head of hair. Yet the pipe seems to work as a bit of signature play, a tip to those in the know that Homer has deposited a sign of himself in his picture. This would mark him (that is, his surrogate or alter ego) as the little brother, the second-born, always ranked behind the first. The latter, as here, always leads the way and stands between his brother and imminent danger. Yet at the same time, they constitute an indissoluble team, two individual, equal, and separately functioning parts of a whole. Neither can make it through the rapids without the other.

In a low-key, Victorian, Yankee fashion, Charles and Winslow were the Theo and Vincent van Gogh of the American nineteenth century. Charles lent critical emotional and financial support to his brother throughout their lives, and his love and approval, especially after the death of their mother, were critical to Winslow's well-being. On no one else (except his mother) did Winslow bestow such affection, and no one else was the recipient of such artistic generosity, represented by the paintings that Winslow gave Charles over the years. Although Charles, prosperous and gregarious, presumably had an extensive social circle, the best times of his life may have been in Winslow's company, whether in the remote wilderness of Canada or the log-cabin sanctuary at Prout's Neck. On the margins in most accounts of Homer's career, Charles was a great deal more central. He was the silent partner in Winslow Homer's enterprise, and more than any others, the angling paintings survive to tell us of this enduring relationship.

NOTES

1. Homer did not become particularly close to his younger brother, Arthur, until later in life.

2. William Howe Downes, *The Life and Works of Winslow Homer* (1911; reprint, Mineola, N.Y.: Dover, 1989), vi.

3. The Homer Collection, Winslow Homer Papers and Family Memorabilia, are deposited in the Bowdoin College Museum of Art, Brunswick, Maine. Gift of the Homer family, 1964.

4. Downes, *Homer,* 24. Downs here gives the bare-bones account of Charles's education. Gordon Hendricks, *The Life and Works of Winslow Homer* (New York: Harry N. Abrams, 1979), 19, provides a few more details.

5. Downes, *Winslow Homer,* 24.

6. Rev. John S.C. Abbott, "Paternal Neglect," *Parent's Magazine* 2 (March 1842): 148. Mark C. Carnes, *Secret Ritual and Manhood in Victorian America* (New Haven: Yale University Press, 1989), 110–113, discusses the issue of absentee fathers in antebellum society.

7. See, for example, James Abbott, *The Rollo Code of Morals* (Boston: Crocker & Brewster, 1841), 83–95. This good-conduct book precisely outlines the rules of brotherly responsibility.

8. Philip Conway Beam, "Winslow Homer's Father," *The New England Quarterly* 20, no. 1 (March 1947): 58; Hendricks, *Homer,* 35.

9. Downes, *Winslow Homer,* 47, reports the story of the alleged purchase without identifying Charles. Lloyd Goodrich, *Winslow Homer* (New York: Macmillan, 1945), 18–19, names Charles as the buyer. Lucretia Giese, "Winslow Homer: Painter of the Civil War," Ph.D. diss., Harvard University, 1986, 278–280, casts doubt on this tale. It was a vintage legend, however. A nephew, Charles Lowell Homer, recorded the same story in a biography of his uncle, Homer Collection, Bowdoin College Museum of Art.

10. On Valentine's collection, see John Wilmerding and Linda Ayres, *Winslow Homer in the 1870s: Selections from the Valentine-Pulsifer Collection,* exh. cat. (Princeton: The Art Museum, Princeton University, 1990). For a sketch of Valentine's character, see Lyman Abbott, *Reminiscences* (Boston: Houghton Mifflin, 1915), 340–347. Hendricks, *Winslow Homer,* 132, discusses Valentine's business and Charles's role in securing Valentine's patronage of his brother. On the Brooklyn factory and its operations, see "Varnish Making," *The Manufacturer and Builder* 9, no. 11 (November 1877): 256.

11. There is currently no information about the whereabouts of this print. My thanks to David Tatham for telling me about this image and providing a Xerox copy.

12. See Albert B. Costa, *Michel Eugène Chevreul, Pioneer of Organic Chemistry* (Madison: State Historical Society of Wisconsin, 1962).

13. John W. Beatty, "Recollections of an Intimate Friendship," in Goodrich, *Winslow Homer,* 223. For more on Homer's use of Chevreul, see Kristin Hoermann, "A Hand Formed to Use the Brush," in Marc Simpson et al., *Winslow Homer: Paintings of the Civil War* (San Francisco: The Fine Arts Museums of San Francisco and Bedford Arts, Publishers, 1988).

14. Philip Conway Beam, *Winslow Homer at Prout's Neck* (Boston: Little, Brown, 1966), 204, writes that at Prout's Neck the self-sufficient Homer ground his own pigments. However, I have found no record of this practice in his earlier career.

15. Most information on Charles comes from Beam, *Winslow Homer at Prout's Neck*; the book is a rich source of recollections and anecdotal information about Charles Jr. On Charles's lifestyle, see 49–53, 199. Other studies contribute little new information or impressions. The value of Charles's estate is estimated in "C. S. Homer Leaves All to Wife," *New York Times*, September 22, 1917, 16, col. 5.

16. James Edward Kelly, "Harper's and Old Franklin Square," Kelly Papers, Archives of American Art, Smithsonian Institution (hereafter AAA), microfilm reel 1877, frames 166 and 169; Beam, "Winslow Homer's Father," 56 n. 8.

17. Beam, *Homer at Prout's Neck*, 187, 200. See 174–208 for anecdotes about Homer's belligerence to callers.

18. Downes, *Winslow Homer*, 115–116.

19. For an account of the Homer family's activities at Prout's Neck, see Beam, *Homer at Prout's Neck*, 25–84; and Patricia Junker, "Expressions of Art and Life in *The Artist's Studio in an Afternoon Fog*," in Junker et al., *Winslow Homer in the 1890s: Prout's Neck Observed*, exh. cat. (New York: Hudson Hills Press, in association with the Memorial Art Gallery of the University of Rochester, 1990), 34–65.

20. Downes, *Winslow Homer*, 112.

21. Homer to Arthur Benson Homer, June 17, 1891; Homer to Charles Savage Homer Jr., October 15, 1891, Homer Collection, Bowdoin College Museum of Art; Downes, *Winslow Homer*, 166.

22. Beam, *Homer at Prout's Neck*, 50. The two hunting watercolors were *Guide Carrying a Deer* (1891; fig. 39), and *Sketch for "Hound and Hunter"* (1892; fig. 45). Homer mentioned the gifts referred to above in letters to Charles Savage Homer Jr., December 27, 1893, to Mattie (Martha French) Homer, December 25, 1895, and December 27, 1891, Homer Collection, Bowdoin College Museum of Art. After Mattie's death, in 1937, the Macbeth Gallery exhibited a group of paintings from her estate and elsewhere. The catalogue introduction noted that in the early years Winslow had benefited from his brother's patronage, and that "[o]ccasionally in his later career . . . Charles added to his collection a water color that he particularly liked, and some others he received by gift from his appreciative brother." Macbeth Gallery, *Winslow Homer: Water Colors and Early Oils from the Estate of Mrs. Charles S. Homer and Other Sources* (May–June 1938), n.p. There were fifty-seven of Winslow's watercolors in Mattie Homer's estate; see "Inventory of collection of Mrs. Charles Savage Homer Jr., compiled by Arthur P. Homer, 1938," Homer Collection, Bowdoin College Museum of Art. I am grateful to Abigail Booth Gerdts for alerting me to the problems of sorting out the watercolors Winslow gave Charles during his lifetime from those Charles inherited with his brother's estate.

23. Homer, letter to Charles Savage Homer Jr., June 21, 1900, Homer Collection, Bowdoin College Museum of Art.

24. Goodrich, *Winslow Homer*, 146–147; Beam, *Homer at Prout's Neck*, 187.

25. For a detailed discussion of *Camp Fire*, see David Tatham, *Winslow Homer in the Adirondacks* (Syracuse, N.Y.: Syracuse University Press, 1996), 75–80. Natalie Spassky et al., *American Paintings in the Metropolitan Museum of Art*, vol. 2, *A Catalogue of Works by Artists Born between 1816 and 1845* (New York: The Metropolitan Museum of Art, 1985), 467, argues that the seated man resembles Charles in Homer's two watercolor portraits.

26. E. Anthony Rotundo, *American Manhood: Transformations in Masculinity from the Revolution to the Modern Era* (New York: Basic Books, 1993), 39–53; Beam, *Homer at Prout's Neck*, 186–187, 197.

27. Mark C. Carnes, "Middle-Class Men and the Solace of Fraternal Ritual," in Carnes and Clyde Griffen, eds., *Meanings for Manhood: Constructions of Masculinity in Victorian America* (Chicago: University of Chicago Press, 1990), 51; Leonard Harry Ellis, "Men among Men: An Exploration of All-Male Relationships in Victorian America," Ph.D. diss., Columbia University, 1982, 346–347, 363. Also see Mary Ann Clawson, *Constructing Brotherhood: Class, Gender, and Fraternalism* (Princeton: Princeton University Press, 1989).

28. Earl Shinn, "Account of Activities of the Tile Club," Earl Shinn Papers, AAA, microfilm reel 3580, frame 1470. On the Tile Club, see Ronald G. Pisano, *The Tile Club and the Aesthetic Movement in America* (New York: Harry N. Abrams, 1999).

29. Alfred Howland, diary entry, June 1860, quoted in Goodrich, *Winslow Homer*, 11.

30. Nineteenth-century American and British men often referred to their close friendships in classical or biblical terms. Damon and Pythias as well as David and Jonathan were particularly current. See David Deitcher, *Dear Friends: American Photographs of Men Together, 1840–1918* (New York: Harry N. Abrams, 2001), 60; and Jeffrey Richards, "'Passing the Love of Women': Manly Love and Victorian Society," in J. A. Mangan and James Walvin, eds., *Manliness and Morality: Middle-Class Masculinity in Britain and America, 1880–1940* (New York: St. Martin's Press, 1987), 112.

31. On amenities at the North Woods Club and the Tourilli Club, see Tatham, *Winslow Homer in the Adirondacks*, 102–107; and Frank Sleeper and Robert Cantwell, "Odyssey of an Angler," *Sports Illustrated* 25 (December 1972): 71.

32. Orson Lowell, "New York Letter: Water Colors by Winslow Homer," *Brush and Pencil*, June 1898, 131–134.

33. During the same trip, Winslow also took a Kodak photograph of two men in a canoe. One of them might be Charles, but since the faces are obscured it is impossible to say for sure. Homer Collection, Bowdoin College Museum of Art.

Pictures for Anglers

Patricia Junker

ON JANUARY 19, 1890, WINSLOW HOMER WROTE from his studio home at Prout's Neck, Maine, to his New York dealer, Gustave Reichard, in eager anticipation of his next show of watercolors, his first in four years. He was soon to send thirty-three works, he wrote, which were to be shown simply, in wide mats and narrow, polished white frames, "cheap frames," he admitted, "but the watercolors will show well." He had a clear idea how to market these new pictures:

If you could get the address of the members of the Adirondack Club or any other sporting club so as to have things already to send out invitations it would be well. If you approve of the following notice for publication in the Sporting papers we will have it in: To Fly-fisherman and Sportsman—On exhibition February 5th to 12th a small collection of water colors taken in the North Woods, by Winslow Homer N.A. and treating exclusively of fish and fishing. Reichard & Co., 226 Fifth Ave.[1]

Although a few of the paintings in the group represented deer hunting with hounds, the great majority of works did indeed depict fish and fishermen, and Homer sensed a particularly receptive audience for these, perhaps seeing the show as a fitting prelude to the opening of the angling season, as winter anglers headed south to Florida and others prepared for outings to come in the spring.

The new series had been painted in 1889, conceived during two extended visits to the North Woods Club, a private hunting and fishing preserve in the Adirondacks, near Minerva, New York. Homer had fished the waters there before, but not for fifteen years, so far as can be documented. He had been introduced to the place by his New York painter friend Eliphalet Terry in 1870, when the property was still simply "Baker's clearing," land farmed by the Reverend Thomas Baker and his wife and daughters, who took in boarders as the sportsmen's rush to the Adirondacks began in the years after the Civil War.[2] Homer and Terry had fished there again in 1874, before the Bakers sold the property to the moneyed sportsmen who wished to establish a private club there. The Adirondack Preserve Association was founded on Baker's clearing in 1887, and Homer was elected to membership soon after, in 1888. He took full advantage of the privilege at his first opportunity the following year. The newly founded North Woods Club, as the association came to be known, certainly suited him, for his stay there in the spring and early summer of 1889 extended to nine weeks, and he returned to the club that fall for another stay of seven weeks. Thereafter he would visit regularly in the spring or fall, nearly every fishing season to the end of his life.

Homer's new enthusiasm for the place had an extraordinary effect on his art in 1889. The sensations he had been gathering to that point from his initial sporadic encounters with the North Woods came together at this juncture with such intensity as to reveal to Homer new subject matter and new worlds of color, light, and movement. Where before he had been inspired to create occasional anecdotal illustrations of Adirondack camp life, character studies of the region's wizened woodsmen, or charming idylls of country boys earnestly whiling away a summer's day at the favorite fishing hole (cat. 4), now his vantage point had changed and his focus on the sport of angling was intense. In 1889 Homer painted in the North Woods, not as a contemplative observer of others engaged in outdoor life, but as an avid angler, wholly absorbed in nature and in his sport, delighting in capturing the brilliant color of leaping trout, the calligraphic arabesque of an angler's backcast, and the prisms of color seen within just a few square inches of a shallow trout pool. His first extended stay at the North Woods Club also afforded him the pleasure of intensive dedication to painting in watercolor in the out-of-doors, something he had not done since his stay in the English fishing village of Cullercoats in 1882–1884. At this time, Homer's skills and enthusiasm as angler and watercolorist were perfectly in sync, and he produced a stirring group of angling scenes.

Homer's exhibition advertisement, just as he had written it, appeared in the display ads in the back pages of *Forest and Stream* on February 20, 1890. The exhibition of North Woods watercolors, which opened at Gustave Reichard and Company on February 14, 1890, and ran at least through the end of the month, did not receive critical notice, however, in either of the leading New York angling journals, *Forest and Stream* or *American Angler*, though both magazines occasionally reported on art exhibitions of interest to sportsmen. But even without significant help from the most popular sporting weeklies, Homer's exhibition of hunting and fishing subjects proved an extraordinary commercial and critical success, the first validation of his work in watercolor since he had shown his studies of English fisherfolk to wide acclaim more than six years earlier, in December 1883. Thirty of Homer's thirty-three watercolors quickly sold, and

all of the leading New York newspapers and art journals gave lengthy, enthusiastic notice to the Reichard gallery exhibition.

This new series was widely regarded by the critics as an unprecedented conceptual and technical achievement for Homer. These works were marvelous in their depiction of animated nature and filled with vitality, a vitality different even from the boldness of the fluid and richly hued watercolor seascapes Homer produced at Gloucester, Massachusetts, in 1880 or from the emotionally charged energy of his subsequent watercolors of solid North Sea fishermen and -women. Every element seemed alive and unfixed in these paintings. The writer for the *New York Commercial Advertiser* thrilled to "the movement of the waters, the elusive scintillations of the gaudily scaled fishes, and the constantly changing tints of the growth along the lakes and rivers."[3] New animated subjects—leaping and fighting fish, the lively light-filled surface of a still pond, the rush of a rapid trout stream (cat. 9), and the elegant flight of a well-cast fly line—capitalized on Homer's unconventional virtuosity in watercolor, his vigorous shorthand style and vivid color sense that seemed perfectly suited to "impressions" of fleeting moments in nature. "These paintings are devoted to hunting and fishing scenes, and are marked, nearly all of them, by the artist's best qualities," noted the critic for the *Art Interchange*, defining those qualities in this way:

Many of his summary renderings of woodlands and water are admirable examples of painting the essentials and omitting the incidents. . . . There are two or three studies of fish hanging against tree trunks, and many in which the finny beauties are leaping finely out of the water in pursuit of the glittering bait or because they are already cruelly hooked. The painter's command of his materials in this rendering of color, texture, and glint, is only equalled by the artistic sense which enables him so skilfully to suggest motion. . . .[4]
Similarly, the writer for the *Evening Post* enthused

CAT. 4

Waiting for a Bite, 1874. Oil on canvas, 12 × 20 in. The Cummer Museum of Art
and Gardens, Jacksonville, Florida. Bequest of Ninah M.H. Cummer (C.119.1)

CAT. 9
Casting in the Falls, 1889. Watercolor over graphite on paper, 14 × 20 in.
Dallas Museum of Art, Texas. Dallas Art Association Purchase, 1961 (1961.11)

about the instinctive "impressionistic" quality he found in Homer's Adirondack watercolors, which seemed to him more purely sensual and more authentic than the seemingly objective, analytic studies of light and life created by Homer's French contemporaries:

There is a directness and simplicity, an individuality and character in the water-colors that is expressibly refreshing. The painter seems to have been pleased or interested in this or that effect in nature, to have noted it, and to have at once set to work to realize it in pictorial form. The effect is seized in its largest sense, and the salient points are emphasized. Detail is not much insisted upon. Mr. Homer's water-colors, in fact, are impressions. But Mr. Homer has not found it necessary to copy Manet or Monet, or Renoir or Degaz [sic]; he has means of his own, very simple means, artistic rather than scientific, and he uses them frankly. Truth is his first principle; to give the main facts with the least trouble the next. His results are delightful.[5]

Likewise, the writer for *The Art Amateur* found such closely focused and hyperkinetic angling subjects perfectly suited to Homer's proclivity for "bold effects of color, extreme breadth and facility of treatment and that science of abstraction on which this artist has based his powerful style."[6]

As exhilarating as these brilliant and facile studies from nature might have been to connoisseurs of watercolor painting, color and brio were not the only extraordinary qualities of these Adirondack watercolors of Homer's. The critics also recognized that they represented an exceptional level of engagement with nature and sport. These watercolors were "the fresh and individual notes from the sketchbook of an angler," as Charles de Kay wrote of them in the *New York Times*.[7] They offered a mesmerizing look at worlds of color and life found within the confines of a trout pond, an exotic realm of nature that was the exclusive province of the serious sportsman. Caught up in a painting of leaping rainbows (fig. 12), de Kay described the kaleidoscopic

view that the angler-artist enjoyed when he trained his eye on even the smallest patch of lake, awaiting the rise of the fish:

Two trout leaping together from the flat disks of the lily at the same dragonfly—and missing it—form a picture that sportsmen will delight in. They belong to the most brilliant variety of that game fish, and sweep through the air like tropical birds, with their brilliant spots and ruddy fins fully displayed. The surface of the lake is wrought with a rare sense of color. Lily leaves overturned by the wind show their pink and violet undersides, and one feels, rather than distinctly sees, the background of sombre forest.[8]

For all their so-called impressionistic manner of execution, Homer's new Adirondack scenes so naturally conveyed an angler's visual experience that they brought out the fisherman in the art critic for the *New York Herald-Tribune*, who delighted in

FIG. 12
Leaping Trout, 1889. Watercolor over graphite on paper, 13 ⅞ × 19 ⅞ in. Museum of Fine Arts, Boston. William Wilkins Warren Fund. © Museum of Fine Arts, Boston

describing the fine points of each painting with a knowing eye. "There are those who are unfortunate enough to care nothing for Walton's art," he wrote, invoking the name of angling's most beloved defender, the early-seventeenth-century English angler-philosopher, Sir Izaak Walton (1593–1683). But clearly this critic, like Homer, was not among them; in fact, the writer's deep appreciation for the details of the paintings suggests the angling notes embedded within these pictures that can be read by informed viewers:

The fish which he paints are the Adirondack trout, which we fear would be considered unworthy game by fishermen on Canadian rivers. But Mr. Homer teaches us again that "it is not all of fishing to fish," and the artist's trout are not to be estimated according to their weight. Some studies illustrate the varied coloring of trout according to age or the character of the water or the conditions of the lighting. There are troutlings with the bars still on their sides, leaping high in the air. There is a trout jumping at the stretcher fly which is nearly as white in this light as the fresh-run sea trout of Canada or the silver trout of Dublin Lake. Another drawn into the light by a fluttering red ibis, exhibits iridescent, purplish tones which are perfectly truthful. . . . One of the finest of the smaller studies is a picture of a wrathful fisherman who has dropped a red ibis upon the cool dark water of a lake only to bring up a sunfish [cat. 18, ill. p. 112], *or in New England parlance, a "pumpkin seed." With a quick movement the fisherman tries to snatch away his fly, forgetting that the suddenness of his action may cost a broken tip if the "pumpkin seed" has hooked himself.*[9]

It seems inevitable that dramatic angling pictures should issue from the brush of so avid an angler as Homer. The wonder is that they did not come sooner in his art. From his angling holidays of 1889 came a new fascination with painting sporting subjects, a fascination that would engage him for the rest of his life. But why had the joys of angling and the deep mysteries of the trout pond not penetrated his painter's psyche earlier? The answer to this question lies in part in what we know of Homer's experience as an angler to 1889 and in what we can learn of his appreciation for the market for sporting pictures as it was developing in the 1880s.

ART IN THE SERVICE OF SPORT

In his introduction to *The Compleat Angler,* Izaak Walton declared that "as no man is born an artist, so no man is born an angler," but both talents seem to have come naturally to Homer.[10] He was perhaps endowed with his mother's feeling for watercolor painting, as she distinguished herself to some degree by the delicate bird and botanical renderings that she painted throughout her life.[11] Though principally self-taught, Homer honed his predilection for drawing with a reportorial eye by making illustrations for the pictorial weekly magazines, first in his native Boston and then in New York, where he settled in 1859. Early on, in Boston, he received some training

FIG. 13
Man Fishing, between 1847 and 1854. Pencil sketch on front paste-down endpaper of the book *Boy's Treasury of Sports, Pastimes, and Recreations,* page dimensions 6 ½ × 4 3/16 in. From Winslow Homer's library. The Strong Museum, Rochester, New York. © 2002

Rising to the Fly, 1861. Watercolor on paper, 6 ⅜ × 9 ¾ in. Museum of Art,
Rhode Island School of Design, Providence. Given anonymously (48.156)

in the rudiments of painting from the French-born artist Frederic Rondel (1826–1892), and, as the Homer scholar David Tatham has shown, in the heady environment of Boston and Cambridge a naturally curious Homer would have encountered influential men of science and art who likely fed a fundamental urge on Homer's part to paint and draw the natural world from direct observation— men like the Harvard naturalist Louis Agassiz (1807–1873), whom Homer likely knew, and William Morris Hunt (1824–1879), a Paris-trained Boston painter and teacher and an early advocate of painting in the open air in the French manner. Possibly through Hunt's lectures or through John La Farge (1835–1910), Hunt's pupil, who became Homer's good friend, Homer also might have encountered the teachings of the modern French realist Gustave Courbet (1819–1877), who would have reinforced the artistic self-reliance that Homer possessed from the outset: "every artist should be his own teacher," so Courbet wrote late in 1861 in a widely disseminated treatise that perhaps inspired Homer to find his way as a painter.[12]

A childhood sketch of an angler (fig. 13) suggests that some of Homer's earliest flights of artistic fancy may have involved the subject of fishing. Just how he acquired this interest and developed into a serious angler is not clear. Fishing seems to have been a favorite boyhood pastime of the Homer boys, Charles, Winslow, and Arthur, in rural Cambridge, Massachusetts, where they grew up. Charles and Arthur told their brother's first biographer, William Howe Downes, that Winslow would rise well before dawn to make a two-mile trek to Fresh Pond to fish

FIG. 14
A group of artists on the bank of the East Branch of the Ausable River, October 5, 1874. Photographer unknown. The Adirondack Museum, Blue Mountain Lake, New York. A nattily dressed Homer is seated in the second row, second from left, smoking a pipe. The fishing party included the painters J. Francis Murphy (1853–1921), Calvin Rae Smith (1850–1918), Hendrik-Dirk Kruseman Van Elten (1829–1904), and, in the foreground at far right, Roswell Shurtleff (1838–1915), who appears as *The Angler* in Homer's oil (cat. 3).

before beginning his day's work as an apprentice in the Boston lithography shop of John H. Bufford.[13] Probably the first serious angler to enter the Homer boys' lives was their uncle Arthur W. Benson, their mother's favorite younger brother, after whom she named her third son, Arthur Benson Homer. Benson had made his fortune in the shipping business in New York before Arthur Benson Homer was born in 1841. A man of extraordinary means and influence in the social and cultural institutions of Brooklyn, where he settled, Benson was remembered at his death in 1889 first and foremost as an inveterate angler. He died in his skiff at his favorite fishing locale, Lake Monroe, at Enterprise, Florida, having suffered a heart attack after casting his fly line. "He never failed to be on the water on a fine day," the *Brooklyn Daily Eagle* stated in reporting on Benson's death, characterizing him as a man possessed with a passion for fishing "akin to that which animated the gentle Izaak Walton."[14] Benson even won the admiration of the eminent angler Charles Hallock (1834–1917), founder and publisher of *Forest and Stream,* who penned a fond tribute to the single-mindedness of his well-known angler friend in his sporting paper a full seven years after Benson's death.[15] Benson seems to have remained close to Homer's mother. She and her husband, Charles Savage Homer, at times lived near Benson in Brooklyn Heights, quite possibly because her wealthy and generous brother looked after them as their own fortunes ebbed and flowed. They were in fact living in Brooklyn Heights when Henrietta Benson Homer died in April 1884. Charles and Winslow Homer traveled on occasion to Enterprise to fish with their uncle, who wintered at the famed Brock House hotel there every season until his death.[16]

An amusing if somewhat awkward brush and ink sketch of 1861 showing a pair of leaping speckled trout (cat. 1) testifies to Homer's early experience with the sport of dry fly fishing and his easy appreciation of the dramatic potential of angling subjects. When he sketched this, Homer was already a successful and accomplished illustrator, and the small monochromatic study, executed in a deft, shorthand, almost calligraphic brush style, shows a desire on Homer's part to give bold, graphic representation to a true-to-life experience that he and all fly fishermen knew but could never record—that exhilarating split second when a trout leaps wholly out of the water to take an artificial dry fly. As lively as the composition is, the trout are generalized and flat, and their actions seem exaggerated; the whole looks contrived, almost decorative, rather than observed. At this early stage

in his career, Homer's absorption in his favorite sport was perhaps not yet so deep that he could thoroughly comprehend and describe its nuances. Anglers, rather than game fish, would constitute his sporting subjects for the next two decades.

In January 1870 Homer exhibited a painting entitled *Trout Fishing* at the Century Association in New York, the distinguished club of artists, writers, and intellectuals that had elected Homer to membership in 1865.[17] Presumably he was fishing often, probably on his summer sketching trips, beginning in the spring of 1870, when he fished the small ponds and trout streams on the Baker property

FIG. 15
The Painter Eliphalet Terry Fishing from a Boat, 1874. Watercolor over graphite on paper, 9 ¾ × 12 ⅞ in. The Century Association, New York

with Eliphalet Terry. In 1874 Homer was fishing in the Adirondacks again, traveling to Baker's clearing with Terry that spring, and then, in September, going to Keene Valley, on the Ausable River, this time with other artist friends (fig. 14), including Roswell Shurtleff, whom Homer had known in Boston and who regularly fished there. With Terry and Shurtleff, Homer was in the company of serious anglers and would have learned from them the fine points of the modern practice of fly-fishing, even if he had not mastered them on his own. At each venue he painted portraits of his angler friends engaged in their sport—Terry in an Adirondack guide boat, landing a fish, his rod severely bent as he attempts to bring him to the net (fig. 15); and Shurtleff, fishing in the rapids below a waterfall (cat. 3), demonstrating perfect modern angling form and technique, his casting arm bent at the elbow as he stops his strong, upward stroke abruptly so as to flex the rod and achieve a powerful backcast as he prepares to send the line forward. Both men use the new lightweight, multipiece, flexible bamboo fly rod and reel, tackle that in Homer's day was rapidly transforming fly-fishing into the active and highly technical sport we know today, and Homer's otherwise stiff and posed studies of Terry and Shurtleff are infused with an energy that derives quite simply from the artist's portrayal of the tension in fly rods under load. Homer was not the first to seize on this conceit to convey pictorially the dynamics of angling, but he was the rare artist who appreciated the subtlety of the gesture and made it appear convincing. Other less sophisticated artists were inclined to exaggerate the rod's bend under tension, to the point where, as one exasperated critic writing in *Forest and Stream* put it, a serious angler had to wince when he encountered such an aberration in pictures: "You can't stand it. Something is going to give or break or snap while you are even looking on, and fearful lest you may hear the profanity, you turn your head away."[18]

With his portraits of Terry and Shurtleff as vigorous modern-day anglers, Homer's serious interests in the sport and the aesthetics of fly-fishing were now beginning to show. The picturesque aspects of angling as outdoor recreation had occasionally captured his imagination up to this time: *The Fishing Party,* a wood engraving of 1869 (fig. 30, ill. p. 75), depicts fashionable women of leisure rather delicately approaching a gentle trout stream; and *Camping Out in the Adirondack Mountains,* drawn for *Harper's Weekly* in 1874 (fig. 35, ill. p. 85), presents curious denizens of the wilderness, hunting and fishing guides. *Camp Fire* (cat. 6, ill. p. 25), a magnificent, large canvas conceived in Keene Valley in 1877 and exhibited in 1880, shows modern sportsmen, though in this instance the still camp scene provides something of an excuse to explore the dramatic nocturnal light effects of the glowing and popping fire. But Homer saw beyond the opportunities that the newly popular sport of angling afforded for exploring amusing and colorful Victorian-era outdoor types; he appreciated that fly-fishing epitomized individual skill and craft, worthy subjects for a heroic art.

What aspirations he had for these portraits of Terry and Shurtleff fishing is not clear, however. Neither painting seems to have been done simply as a portrait for a friend. But neither was publicly exhibited, so far as documentation shows. The watercolor of Terry was the basis for an oil painting begun months later, which stayed in Homer's studio for decades.[19] And the impressive oil painting of Shurtleff seems to have remained with the artist also, possibly until 1882, at which time Homer may have given it away to an acquaintance.[20] Perhaps he felt constrained or unsatisfied by the heavy oil medium as he sought to give expression to the almost imperceptible flight of a delicate fly line, for Homer would never again paint a fly fisherman in oil.[21] It is possible that variants on the Terry and Shurtleff portraits were the angling pictures *Fly Fishing* and *Pull Him In!* that Homer showed

CAT. 3
The Angler, [1874]. Oil on canvas, 23 ½ × 16 in. Private collection

CAT. 20
Netting the Fish, 1889–1890. Watercolor over graphite on paper, 14 × 20 in.
The Art Institute of Chicago. Gift of Annie Swan Coburn to the Mr. and
Mrs. Lewis L. Coburn Memorial Collection (1933.526). All rights reserved.

with the American Society of Painters in Water
Colors at the National Academy of Design in
February 1875, his first major showing of watercolor
paintings, when he submitted an extraordinary thirty-
four sheets on a variety of subjects to demonstrate
his versatility and virtuosity in the medium.[22] These
early efforts at depicting the modern sportsman
clearly informed Homer's much later *Netting the
Fish* (cat. 20), a monochromatic wash study created
around 1889 as the basis for an etching (cat. 19).

If Terry and Shurtleff taught Homer something
about modern fly-fishing and served him as models
of the modern sportsman, their own paintings
offered him no such instructive insight into
the possibilities of modern sporting art. Terry's
obsession with angling led him early on to make a
specialty of the traditional trophy still life (fig. 16),
a favorite genre with sportsmen who relished an
accurate rendering of a trophy fish, that is, one
which conveyed the size and weight of a prize

CAT. 19
Fly Fishing, Saranac Lake, 1889/1890. Etching and aquatint on paper, plate 17 ½ × 22 ⅝ in.
Amon Carter Museum, Fort Worth, Texas. Purchase with funds provided by the Council
of the Amon Carter Museum (2002.3)

catch.[23] And Shurtleff, who on occasion contributed angling notes to the weekly *American Angler,* published and edited by his good friend William C. Harris (1830–1905), was apparently more inclined to write about his contests with game trout than he was to paint them; so far as his extant works attest, he preferred to make studies of the picturesque woodland scenery around the "lodge in the wilderness" that he built in Keene Valley after 1882.[24] A rare example of Shurtleff's angling art is the simple

graphic title design—hackneyed in its use of rod and net and rustic twig lettering—he created for the cover of *American Angler* in the late 1890s, in its last years of publication.[25]

Others of Homer's contemporaries, however, were painting sporting pictures for sportsmen long before Homer painted for that audience, and they were popularizing new pictorial conventions that Homer would later adopt and transform. Samuel A. Kilbourne, Gurdon Trumbull, Wakeman Holberton

FIG. 16
Eliphalet Terry (1826–1896), *Silver Trout*, 1872. Oil on canvas, 14 × 25 in.
The Century Association, New York

(1839–1898), and Walter Brackett (1823–1919), names long forgotten today, were all specializing in angling subjects by the early 1870s. And though they necessarily painted the familiar trophy pictures, too, they also redirected the angling art genre away from the "catch" and toward the essential thrill of the sport, the contest between man and fish. They were among the first artists to attempt depictions of leaping and fighting game fish, and they attracted attention with their novel compositions. Though stilted and almost comical to modern eyes, especially in comparison with Homer's transcendent achievements, to many of their fellow anglers, their pictures were an appealing departure from dead fish still-lifes. As an enthusiastic angler, Homer must have taken note of the productions of these artists, perhaps registering their innovative pictorial strategies even as he himself essayed other themes. Homer might have seen Holberton's *A Leap for Life* in the exhibition of the American Society of Painters in Water Colors at the National Academy of Design in March 1873 or admired the fighting

game fish pictures (fig. 17) exhibited by Trumbull at Snedecor Gallery in New York the following year, in March 1874.[26]

Surely the review of Trumbull's exhibition in *Forest and Stream* would have resonated with Homer, an artist who aspired to a fundamental realism in his subjects and an angler who craved the excitement of playing a fish. The reviewer, probably Hallock himself, the paper's founder and publisher, disparaged the traditional fish trophy pictures as he introduced Trumbull's artistic breakthrough:

The fish seen in what are called genre *pictures are well known to our collectors. Here fish are only accessories, and are introduced simply with an idea of producing effects of light or color as are the ruddy copper kettles worked up into Flemish pictures. We know, too, of fish in the ordinary routine pictures, as either hung from a nail by a string, or, if varied a little, lying on the grass with the ever constant wicker work creel, the fish all dead, or, if portrayed alive, lazily disporting in the water with about the same effect as when we see a gold fish phlegmatically moving in an aquarium.*
Trumbull's specimens, however, a trout and a bass, were "the two most remarkable pictures of fish ever yet produced by an American artist," the writer said. These were painted fish endowed by the artist, he believed, with life and spirit:

Until the grand productions of Mr. Gurdon Trumbull, we never saw any pictures of fish where the artist attempted to produce that absolute spring for life, that mad frenzied terror, that startling degree of vital energy and electric force which a fish has when struck with the line. . . . If painters have with their highest and happiest aspirations endeavored to portray animals in action . . . before Mr. Trumbull, not one has ever thought of giving to canvas the impressions of a life belonging to another organization. . . . The trout has the hook, has made his mad rush, has snapped the frail tackle, and is over the fall with a plunge and a swirl, and you see him flash through the green water. So truthful is it, so rapid is the movement of the trout, that one expects the next moment to see him disappear and leave nothing but the pouring flood, with its flecks of white foam, within the gilt frame of the picture. . . . The bass is quite as surprising as a picture. Who that has caught this game fish does not know that he is an angry fish, and fights to the death? The artist has caught precisely the energy of the fish. Finally, the review recognized the experienced sportsman that lay behind these productions: "The amount of patient, discriminating labor which has been put into these pictures no one can tell. How many fish must Mr. Trumbull have captured himself, and had escape from him before he caught in his brain the form, the manner, of the objects he has painted?"[27] It was understood by any angler who admired Trumbull's fighting fish pictures that the artist had to be not just an accomplished painter—a fish portraitist, as it were—but a dedicated angler, too, who knew fish and fish behavior. A skilled artist can re-create the form and color of a still object, but only an experienced angler can reenvision brief, transitory encounters with living fish.

Homer's growing interest in fly-fishing through the 1870s and 1880s precisely parallels the growth of the sport itself, a fact that helps to explain in part the path his art would take. It was in the 1870s that fly-fishing in America developed from a strongly regional activity, with anglers tied to local waters and long-standing local angling traditions, into a popular national pastime.[28] With the great increase in mobility and leisure in the decades after the Civil War, as railroads made once-remote wilderness areas accessible to sportsmen, the country's anglers became peripatetic, testing their skills in waters from Canada south to Florida and into the American West. These were also years of a great boom in tackle making and marketing, when the well-known name of Orvis became firmly established in American sport for manufacturing and marketing tackle to anglers across the nation.

FIG. 17
Gurdon Trumbull (1841–1903), *Black Bass*, 1872. Oil on canvas, 17 ½ × 25 ⅛ in. Florence Griswold Museum, Old Lyme, Connecticut. Gift of the Hartford Steam Boiler Inspection and Insurance Company

The rise in angling tourism and the new lucrative trade in angling products led to the founding of popular weekly magazines devoted to the sport— *The American Sportsman* appeared in 1871, followed by *Forest and Stream* in 1873 and *American Angler* in 1881. These important magazines addressed the various scientific, technical, commercial, and cultural concerns of anglers, and they attracted an ever-larger national readership through the end of the nineteenth century.

The new illustrated sporting magazines played an important role in bringing visual art to sportsmen, and whatever regular and direct contact Homer had with contemporary sporting art in the 1870s and 1880s probably came chiefly through these publications. It is not unreasonable to assume that Homer likely felt that irrational attachment to

CAT. 30
A Good Pool, Saguenay River, 1895. Watercolor over graphite on paper, 9 ¾ × 18 ⅞ in.
Sterling and Francine Clark Art Institute, Williamstown, Massachusetts (1955.1492)

angling magazines that seems to possess most avid anglers. And there among the weekly angling notes and seasonal features on the exceptional fishing in Canada, the Adirondacks, and Florida—the favorite destinations of the angling tourist in the 1870s and 1880s—he would have found an array of engaging illustrations. These ranged from detailed renderings of the form and distinguishing features of each species of game fish and instructional aids for the discerning angler to plates designed to accompany the dramatic or humorous firsthand accounts of angling experiences that regularly appeared. Even the advertisements for tackle could be superb examples of sport illustration. Photography entered the pages of these sporting journals in the late 1880s, just as soon as the portable camera was readily available to amateurs. As they marked the appearance of the silver jubilee number in 1898, the editors of *Forest and Stream* cited "the addition of the camera to the sportsman's outfit" as one of the tremendous and far-reaching changes in the sport that had significantly transformed the magazine in its twenty-five years.[29]

As an illustrator himself, Homer must have been fascinated by the images that appeared in these publications, appreciative of the insight and skill they required, struck by their humor, and intrigued by the notion of a meaningful visual dialogue between sportsmen and artists. He seems to have found source material here as well, as he occasionally did in the popular graphic arts: Homer's highly dramatic *A Good Pool, Saguenay River,* of 1895 (cat. 30), for example, must owe its design to the funny exaggerated perspective favored by illustrators of angling stories (fig. 18), with the fighting game fish leaping in the immediate foreground to emphasize its size and might and the angler but a small detail in the far distance.

As the readership for the illustrated sporting weeklies steadily grew in the 1870s, publishers recognized that they had an audience of devoted sportsmen to support other publishing projects, many of them aimed toward the new highly technical angler. Following on refinements in color lithography, an array of beautifully printed volumes appeared over the next two decades that elevated sporting illustration to a very high level of artistic quality. No serious, informed sportsman with any curiosity and visual sense could have been unaware of these landmark colorplate works of ichthyology and sporting art, each heavily promoted in the sporting magazines. Homer, we know, found source material here as well.

Until 1878, when Charles Scribner and Sons began to release in installments the first-of-its-kind *Game Fishes of the United States,* anglers had no good color reference work on American game fish. This new authoritative text, by the young ichthyologist G. Brown Goode (1851–1896), classified twenty species of game fish, those which "by reason of their cunning, courage, strength, beauty, and the

FIG. 18
Unknown artist, *As it Appeared to Him,* from "The Story of a Summer's Exile," an account of a fishing trip to Quebec, in *American Angler,* February 9, 1884

FIG. 19
After Samuel A. Kilbourne (1836–1881), *Speckled Trout,* 1878.
Lithograph by Armstrong and Co., Lithographers, Boston, 16 × 20 in.
From *Game Fishes of the United States,* 1879–1881. Private collection

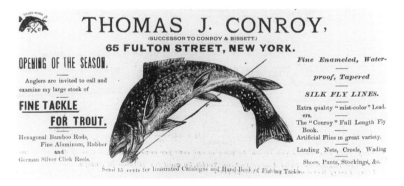

FIG. 20
Advertisement for Thomas J. Conroy, outfitter, New York,
from *American Angler,* April 5, 1884. The fighting fish is derived
from Samuel A. Kilbourne's *Speckled Trout,* 1878 (fig. 19).

sapidity of their flesh, are sought for by those who angle for sport with delicate fishing tackle," as Goode defined them. He described their anatomical features, habits, and geographic distribution. The beauty and sport of American fishes were under-appreciated, Goode said, "save among naturalists and anglers, for others seldom see them until their lifeless bodies are displayed in the markets." The accompanying folio plates, exceptional color lithographs produced by the Boston firm of Armstrong and Company after paintings by Samuel A. Kilbourne, were splendidly designed to do for American game fish what John James Audubon (1785–1851) had done decades earlier for the country's native birds, showing them life size, as living entities, in all their resplendent, evanescent glory. "Mr. Kilbourne's paintings will open up a new world of delight to many who have never dreamed of the loveliness of the denizens of our own streams and bays," Goode enthused.[30] Kilbourne's compositions, showing colorful fighting fish from an angler's point of view, set a new standard of naturalism and authenticity in sporting art and quickly came to epitomize the visual delight and exhilarating sport that defined angling. Kilbourne's realistic flopping, fighting *Speckled Trout* (fig. 19) became a ubiquitous image in Homer's day, for it was copied by other graphic artists (fig. 20) and eventually adopted by the Charles F. Orvis Company as its signature trade sign.[31]

In 1879, in response, no doubt, to the Goode-Kilbourne work, the indefatigable angling businessman-journalist William C. Harris, publisher of the weekly *American Angler* and a host of technical books and angling guides, set out to create an even more comprehensive study of American game fish, one with even more color illustrations, all certifiably true to life. With the little-known painter J. L. Petrie, Harris tramped across the continent through the 1880s to catch and paint from life examples of all the game fish known in America, expanding the scope of his work into western waters. Harris's ambition was extraordinary. He envisioned a publication with two thousand illustrations of fish drawn from life. In twelve years of seasonal work on the project, Petrie created for Harris eighty-five paintings in oil, and eighty were reproduced as folio-size color lithographs for *The Fishes of North America that are Caught on Hook and Line,* which began to appear in installments in 1891.[32] Testifying to the unimpeachable accuracy of the fish represented, Harris explained to subscribers, "I have taken the fishes reproduced in this work on my own rod, and laid them before the artist in the freshness of their coloration. This method enables me to vouch for the accuracy of form and color in the lithographs presented."[33] He described at length how the fish studies were produced, including in his text an engraving made, he said, from a photograph of the artist and writer at work on the Gallatin River in Montana (fig. 21). "The artist is painting a Montana grayling, and the author has just left the stream and is watching the progress of the work," so he described the amusing illustration showing Petrie at his easel positioned at the river's edge, taking down the colors of the fish Harris has just reeled in, before they fade away. Harris proudly trumpeted the fact that the systematic study of these fishes and the careful transcription of their appearance, which required examination of multiple specimens of each species, owed much to his own skills as an angler and to his enviable good fortune in reaching unfished waters:

It may interest the angler to state that within fifteen feet of the easel I caught fifty to sixty grayling, trout (black spotted) and whitefish, without moving five feet either up or down stream. These fish were all taken with the artificial fly, and at the first few casts the water was made to foam by the rising fish jostling each other and eagerly jumping for the feathers. It cannot be doubted that the artist had a wealth of material to work upon.[34]

FIG. 21
After J. L. Petrie, *How the Work Was Done. Painting the Montana Grayling on the banks of the Gallatin River, Montana.* Photomechanical reproduction, 12 × 18 in. From *The Fishes of North America that are Caught on Hook and Line,* 1891–1898. Princeton University Library, Princeton, New Jersey

Harris worked tirelessly to promote the series through his publications, by using sales agents in the field, and by appealing directly to angling clubs to attract subscribers. But the expense of the enterprise proved his financial undoing. In his prospectus, Harris estimated that the total cost of the project would run to more than $45,000, with $25,000 encompassing the cost of the plates, which required as many as fifteen colors to reproduce the full range of hues and subtle modulation of tones seen in living fish. In the spring of 1897, just before his *American Angler* ceased publication in 1898, Harris began to advertise for sale the collection of Petrie paintings that represented for him a personal, decade-long voyage of piscatorial discovery. "Our actual working time covers a period of 972 days, and the cost, allowing for a small per diem sum for my time when at work with the artist, has been $25,639.00," Harris wrote in his advertisement, but added, "I will sell them for a much smaller amount."[35]

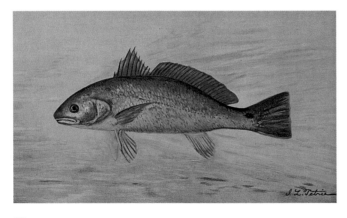

FIG. 22
After J. L. Petrie, *The Rainbow Trout (Salmo irideus). Weight 1 lb. Specimen caught in Spokane River, Washington,* by William C. Harris

FIG. 23
After J. L. Petrie, *The Ouananiche or Winninish (Salmo salar ouananiche), Specimen (Weight 1 lb.) Caught and painted at the Grand Discharge, Province of Quebec, Can.,* © *1897* by William C. Harris

FIG. 24
After J. L. Petrie, *The Red Drum, or Channel Bass (Sciæna ocellata), painted at Aransus Pass (Gulf of Mexico), Texas,* © *1898,* by Wm. C. Harris. All lithographs by George H. Walker & Co., Boston, Massachusetts, 12 × 18 in. From *The Fishes of North America that are Caught on Hook and Line,* 1891–1898. Princeton University Library, Princeton, New Jersey

Petrie was not the artist Kilbourne was (and quite possibly, not an angler, either), and aside from their color effects, which are admirable, the lithographs after Petrie's paintings (figs. 22, 23, 24) are not exciting works of art. Still, as authentic color notes, the plates must have intrigued the anglers of Homer's day.

We cannot point to any direct connection between Homer's stunning, up-close impressions of leaping and fighting game fish and the highly literal productions of Kilbourne and Petrie. But the Kilbourne and Petrie plates were widely popular. They appeared as Homer was developing into a serious angler and venturing into angling subjects in his art, and because both portfolios immediately became standard authorities on the fine points of fish anatomy, color, and behavior, Homer might have referred to them. These publications were owned by serious anglers and were available in sportsmen's clubs, so Homer might have had easy access to them, too.

We can see, however, that Homer admired the sumptuous elephant folio-size *Sport, or Fishing and Shooting,* published in 1889 by Arthur Corbin Gould (1850–1903), founder and publisher of *Shooting and Fishing,* another popular illustrated weekly.[36] This collection of carefully produced color lithographs was Gould's effort to set a new standard for sporting art. "With all the literature, there has been but little in the way of illustration which satisfied the sportsman," Gould wrote in his introduction to *Sport.* "In fact, so poorly has this work been done," he continued, "that devotees to rifle, rod, and gun have frequently asserted that there were no correct pictures representing American sports. Even the work of the best artists, which satisfied from an artistic standpoint, when submitted to sportsmen, rather pained than pleased, for their incorrectness made such pictures forever unsatisfactory."[37] With this in mind, Gould commissioned illustrative work in watercolor from the best artists in the field of

FIG. 25
After Frederic Remington (1861–1909), *Goose Hunting*, 1889. Chromolithograph by Forbes Lithograph Manufacturing Co., Boston, 18 × 24 in. From *Sport, or Fishing and Shooting.* Library, Amon Carter Museum, Fort Worth, Texas

[below]
FIG. 26
Wild Geese in Flight [Under the Lighthouse], 1897. Oil on canvas, 34 1/16 × 50 1/8 in. Portland Museum of Art. Portland, Maine. Bequest of Charles Shipman Payson, 1988 (1988.55.2)

sporting art, work that was then "submitted to the careful examination of many practical sportsmen . . . and not until pronounced correct in detail was it considered suitable for reproduction."[38] He included hunting scenes by Frederic Remington and Arthur Burdett Frost (1851–1928), who remain two of the most celebrated names in the genre, and angling subjects by the more obscure late-nineteenth-century specialists Henry Sandham (1842–1912) and Sherman Foote Denton (1856–1937).

Homer somehow knew Gould's volume, which was produced in an edition of 350 copies, printed for subscribers. The integrity of these sporting art images collected by Gould, all vetted by active sportsmen, would have made them especially worthy and reliable models for other artists, Homer included. In 1897 he turned to Remington's *Goose Hunting* (fig. 25) in Gould's *Sport* and used the composition as the basis for his oil *Wild Geese in Flight* (fig. 26), set on the dunes at Prout's Neck. For his eerily spare composition, Homer edited out Remington's hunters and thereby changed the meaning of the subject entirely. He focused not on the prowess of the

hunter, but on the fragility of the hunted.[39] One could argue that with *Wild Geese in Flight,* Homer did not so much copy Remington's work as respond to it.

Holding sporting art up to the close scrutiny of discriminating sportsmen is risky business, but in 1890, when Homer unveiled his first significant body of interconnected sporting subjects, he did not shy away from the challenge. He had become a proud member of the brotherhood of anglers and would have derived immense satisfaction from their embrace of his work. The effectiveness of Homer's plan to appeal directly to anglers with his first show of North Woods watercolors is somewhat difficult to assess, however. It is not easy to identify any of the first owners of these paintings as noted sportsmen. In fact, the most enthusiastic purchasers of the new works were men recognizable first and foremost as passionate collectors of contemporary art, men who were already keen admirers of Homer's work: Thomas B. Clarke and William T. Evans III, both of whom made multiple acquisitions from the Reichard gallery show.[40] Still, all but three of the watercolors quickly sold, so Homer clearly had found an audience for these new pictures.[41]

Spurred by the success of his 1890 show of Adirondack watercolors, Homer produced other series of angling pictures over the next decade: Florida scenes in 1890; more Adirondack subjects in 1892 and 1894; Quebec series in 1895, 1897, and 1902; and more Florida angling pictures in 1904. Moreover, intermittently in the years after 1900, Homer sent angling pictures to M. Knoedler & Company—his dealer after 1898—expressly to appeal to eager fishermen in the spring. This compulsion to paint his angling experiences surely testifies to Homer's almost mystical absorption in his favorite sport—in the primordial contest between man and fish. But it also suggests the high value that Homer placed on this particular painting challenge and the high regard that he had for men who appreciated the fine art of angling, just as he did. And by 1890 that audience had grown significantly in size and sophistication, giving rise to a whole genre of art dedicated to celebrating the high drama of rod and field sports. Sporting art was engaging American sportsmen as never before, and Homer's fascination with such subjects followed to some degree the increasing popularity of this developing genre in the 1880s and 1890s. That he elevated sporting art to a surpassing level of conceptual complexity and technical invention has obscured whatever connections exist between Homer's art and the sporting scenes of his contemporaries. Nevertheless, instructive connections to late-nineteenth-century sporting art can be made in Homer's art, connections that reveal just how rigorous and meaningful the challenge of painting for fellow anglers was for him.

NOTES FROM THE SKETCHBOOK OF AN ANGLER

Angling is an intensely visual sport, which is not to say, however, that it offers up its thrills to the casual observer. Its visual delights are of the subtlest kind: a mere ripple in the surface of a pond tells when a fish is present and feeding, and sport derives from the almost imperceptible action of the finest silk (in Homer's day) or synthetic fly line. An expert angler has the skill to make himself invisible to fish, the highly elusive object of his desire. Focus, discipline, and patience are the sport's hallmarks, not easy attributes to pictorialize. As one thoughtful late-nineteenth-century angler aptly put it, the aesthetics of angling are not readily apparent or easily appreciated by anyone but anglers:

Angling is replete with attractive elements, but it is a genuine inborn love for the sport that impells its devotees to give time and money that they might indulge that love. There is no chance for display as there is in shooting or riding or rowing. Be one never so skillful,

CAT. 45

Fish and Butterflies, 1900. Watercolor over graphite on paper, 14 ½ × 20 ¹¹/₁₆ in.
Sterling and Francine Clark Art Institute, Williamstown, Massachusetts (1955.775)

CAT. 11
A Good One, 1889. Watercolor over graphite on paper, 12 ¼ × 19 ½ in.
The Hyde Collection Trust, Glens Falls, New York (1971.68)

his skill is not known outside his craft. The expert with shotgun or rifle or oars commands the applause of the crowd, while the angler, no less proficient in his chosen recreation, must content himself with doing his work quietly and alone. He never performs for outside effect. He has no audience to applaud him. His sport is quiet and gentle, lacking in everything showy and impressive to the vulgar, but he knows there is something to admire and applaud in the manipulation of forty feet or more of line.[42]

Angling is not a spectator sport per se. The drama is played out before a far smaller audience—principally the angler and his prey, or perhaps extending at times to the angler's guide and fishing companions. Angling does not lend itself easily to heroic art. Homer's love of the sport moved him instinctively to paint it. But surely he understood that he was painting for a very specific audience when he took for subject matter the almost indescribable fine points of angling.

Homer understood, as all anglers do, that there is more to fishing than catching fish. His fishing subjects are immensely varied. Often they show the "quiet and gentle" aspects of the sport: a guide sitting silently, eyeing the riveting ring of light that is a fish's rise; a lone angler playing his line, creating an elegant backcast seen from a distance against the red dawn sky; or the noiseless interplay of a small perch and a monarch butterfly (cat. 45). He marks the distinctive characteristics of the various fishing waters, each demanding different skills and knowledge on the angler's part: still Adirondack ponds or small, rippling streams; the dense and placid swampy coves of Florida's St. John's and Homosassa Rivers; the wild waters of the Saguenay and the teeming Grand Discharge in Quebec. He pays tribute to those who appreciate and excel in the sport, especially the local fishing guides whom he knew and admired. Many of his paintings are glimpses into their solitary world and are profound expressions of a complete absorption

in nature: he shows them studying the water, casting to a rise, or resting, communing silently with the clouds, trees, or water.

The serial nature of Homer's work was different from that of angling artists whose purpose was to create a comprehensive documentary record of fish; his was a near cinematic approach especially appropriate to the enormously varied experience of fishing—an approach that set him apart from other sporting artists of his day. Critics had recognized this immediately with the first exhibition of Homer's Adirondack watercolors. Painting in series, Homer avoided the stultifying effect of too much information in any one scene, something the more literal-minded angling artists could not seem to appreciate. The writer for the *New York Sun* had aptly described Homer's singular vision, his artistic breakthrough in the sporting art genre, this way in 1890:

Not the least part of [the paintings'] significance sprang from the fact that they so well exemplified the difference between pictorial and illustrative work. Most of them represented scenes in the struggles between fly fishers and their prey on the lakes and streams of our Northern forests. It was as curious as delightful to see how the keen artistic instinct of the painter had never once permitted him to show us such a struggle in the inclusive way that an illustrator would rightly have selected. An illustrator would have portrayed it as a whole, concentrating attention neither on the man, nor the fish, nor the landscape. But Mr. Homer gave us now the most beautiful landscape, with the boat a scarcely noticeable feature; now the figure of a fisher emphasized in some typical attitude, while his prey was merely hinted at; and now the prey itself, some great rosy-speckled trout leaping through the air at the seductive shining fly. Of course, there was always a background of water and shore, and as a background it was always delightfully conceived and handled. But the main theme was always accented; there was always a centre of interest and an harmonious setting for it.[43]

There is an unmistakable interconnectedness among the various scenes within each of Homer's angling series—from the Adirondacks, Florida, and Quebec respectively—that makes each series read as a kind of angler's diary, part travelogue, part adventure story, and part philosophical reflection. In the Adirondack pictures he shows us the look of the piney woods, the small and gamey brook and rainbow trout resident in the cold ponds and streams, and the skills of the native guides with rod and gun (cat. 11, ill. p. 56). In the Florida scenes he re-creates the heavy, sultry, tropical atmosphere, the easygoing hours on still and shallow waters, and the surpassing fighting nature of the largemouth black bass, the region's most sought-after and celebrated freshwater game fish.

A journalistic quality is particularly strong in Homer's Quebec series. The paintings describe sites seen en route to and from the fabled fishing grounds of the Laurentides and Lake St. John, the Grand Discharge, and the Saguenay River. They convey the rigors of canoe trips, from shooting the rapids to portaging around them (cat. 47). They show the skill required to fish there, with anglers casting long distances across wide waters into rapids that are inaccessible by canoe (cat. 48, ill. p. 152). They further record Homer's deeply personal reflections on the physical strength and introspection of his French-Canadian fishing guides (cats. 31, 32, ill. p. 60, 61). When he exhibited his first group of Quebec pictures—both Tourilli Lake and Lake St. John scenes—at the St. Botolph Club in Boston in the fall of 1895, the paintings were offered for sale.[44] But by 1897, after another productive painting season in the region, Homer had become keen on preserving the unity of what was now an extensive Quebec series. He decided to exhibit them as a discreet group: "Of Life and Scenes in the Province of Quebec (Canada)," a selection of twenty-seven watercolors, was first shown at the Carnegie Institute in Pittsburgh in February and March 1898 and then

moved to M. Knoedler & Company in New York in April.[45] Homer also wished to sell the paintings as a single body of work. To his friend and patron Thomas B. Clarke, Homer wrote in 1897 of his plans for these Quebec watercolors, "I shall show them in New York in March when I may or [may] not offer them for sale. My idea is to keep them in one collection for some Institution to buy the lot."[46] Similarly, to John W. Beatty, director of the Carnegie Institute, he said as he proposed the exhibition of his Quebec pictures for Pittsburgh, "they are not for sale. I shall keep the collection to-gether until later."[47] Writing of the paintings when they were on view at the Knoedler gallery in 1898, Orson Lowell, in the journal *Brush and Pencil,* confirmed the wisdom in Homer's plan: "The pictures might all have been made between catches while upon a fishing trip, and, taken altogether, form a most interesting account. While each picture is complete in itself, it is as a collection that they should be seen; I sincerely hope that the unbroken set may find a permanent place in some sportsmen's clubhouse."[48]

A few of Homer's angling pictures were painted with angler friends in mind, sometimes as records of an outing. For instance, to James Ernest G. Yalden, Homer's close friend and occasional fishing companion at the North Woods Club, he presented a painting of trophy trout, perhaps Yalden's own, handsome catches, each about twelve inches long (cat. 22, ill. p. 62).[49] A different kind of trophy picture is the quick watercolor study of a brilliant blue and yellow bass Homer painted while fishing at the North Woods Club in the late spring of 1900 (cat. 44, ill. p. 63) and sent to his brother Charles: "Tell Charlie I have a fine sketch of a black bass taken in the boat five minutes after he was caught," Homer wrote to his sister-in-law Martha, "I present it to him for his fish room at W.[est] T.[ownsend]."[50] Homer knew that Charles would appreciate the challenge that his brother had met in creating a color study of the fish as it appeared in life. And the

CAT. 47
Canoes in Rapids, Saguenay River [Against the Shoal], 1902.
Watercolor over graphite on paper, 13¼ × 21¾ in. Private collection

CAT. 31
The Guide, 1895. Watercolor over graphite on paper, 13 ½ × 19 ⅝ in.
The James W. Glanville Family Partnership

mention of a fish trophy room in the house at West Townsend, Massachusetts, suggests that Charles's passion helped to feed Homer's enthusiasm for painting angling pictures; Homer's *Two Trout* (cat. 17, ill. p. 64) also had a place there.[51] Early in 1905 Homer painted a charming watercolor of a spotted sea trout (cat. 53, ill. p. 84) for Mrs. Richard Austin Watts, wife of a Michigan man Homer befriended and fished with that winter in Homosassa, Florida. Watts family history holds that this fish does not record Mrs. Watts's own catch, though it is inscribed to her. Rather the painting, an extraordinarily facile rendering, was Homer's playful offering to Mrs. Watts on his return from the day's fishing, since she had not accompanied the two men but had stayed back on shore and darned Homer's socks.[52]

But most of Homer's angling pictures were intended for the community of anglers at large, who must have represented for Homer the kind of informed viewer for his pictures that he longed for.

CAT. 32
The Guide, 1895. Watercolor over graphite on paper,
16 ¼ × 14 in. Private collection

CAT. 22
Two Trout, 1891. Watercolor over graphite on
paper, 18 ⅞ × 13 ⅜ in. Inscribed lower right:
To J. Ernest Yalden/with compts of Winslow Homer/1891.
Private collection

Homer felt that he knew the audience and market
for these pictures. In part this may have been due
to the remarkable success of his Adirondack watercolors in 1890 and the possibilities this suggested
for other series on the angling theme. In 1897, for
example, as he considered the best way to unveil
his latest Quebec watercolors, his next significant
angling series after the Adirondack works, he
thought about how to create a stir among potential
patrons; he approached John W. Beatty with the
idea of a tightly focused exhibition of the series at
the Carnegie Institute, suggesting the particular
appeal that the pictures would have: "You will find
that the men of Pittsburgh will like these things
and the women will be curious to know what the
men are liking," Homer wrote to Beatty, "and first
thing you know you will have an audience."[53]

There is some evidence that for Homer the
impetus to paint angling pictures came as well from
his dealers, who perhaps recognized an enthusiastic
niche market for such sporting art. To Knoedler
in late March 1903 Homer wrote: "Watercolors
received—also your request for Fishing subjects in
Adirondacks—As I shall go up for the Spring fishing
I will take my sketch block—& will give you a full
line of goods for next season—."[54] Yet he did not.
There are no known Adirondack angling pictures
after 1902, although he fished there every subsequent
spring through 1906 and in 1908 and 1910 as well.[55]

Homer's Quebec watercolors had been critically
acclaimed, but they did not sell well.[56] In the 1890s
he produced angling pictures at other venues, too,
in Florida and in the Adirondacks. By 1901 he had
unsold angling pictures on hand. There began successive efforts on Homer's part to reach anglers with
these works. "I send you by the American ex today
—six watercolors of fishing subjects," he wrote to
Knoedler on April 15, 1901, "They may be of interest
to the fishermen now turned loose for spring
season. . . . If you know any fishermen call their
attention to them."[57] In late March 1905 he did the

same, sending twenty-eight watercolors to Knoedler —various Adirondack, Quebec, and Florida works. However, by then Homer's enthusiasm for the effort had clearly waned: "these things are put out only on account of the fishing season & are mostly old & of little account," he wrote on March 31, in a letter accompanying the pictures.[58] These are surprising words to us today since the list of watercolors shipped included extraordinary things: the glittering *Mink Pond* of 1891 (fig. 56, ill. p. 113), the dramatic

Fishing the Rapids, Saguenay River, of 1902 (cat. 48, ill. p. 152), and the magnificent pair of black bass (figs. 98, 99, ill. p. 178–179) painted in Florida in 1904.[59] Perhaps it was the artist's frustration speaking—frustration over the scant sales of his watercolors. But if he could speak dismissively of his work one day, he could be defensive on another, writing on April 11 to Knoedler, "I write to assure you that all these things now sent although slight were made in a serious manner."[60]

CAT. 44

Bass, [1900]. Watercolor over graphite on paper, 13¾ × 21 in. Arizona State University Art Museum, Nelson Fine Arts Center, Tempe, Arizona. Gift of Oliver B. James (53.138)

CAT. 17
Two Trout, 1889. Watercolor over
graphite on paper, 19 ½ × 13 ¼ in.
Private collection

Whatever doubts Homer may have developed over time about the value or validity of his angling scenes, it is clear from extant commentary that he did not fail a discerning audience of anglers. "That is certainly a great point in favor of the pictures: they interest not only the painter and student, but the more exacting fisherman, stickler as he is for all the little things that make a fishing picture right," Lowell had noted in 1898 in praising Homer's Quebec works.[61] Authenticity was the single most important criterion for the angler-critics who scrutinized Homer's paintings, and they consistently recognized—indeed, reveled in—the authenticity of experience that Homer unfailingly conveyed in his angling watercolors, even with exceedingly spare economy of means.

In April 1890 Homer and Reichard allowed *Harper's Weekly* to illustrate one of his new leaping trout watercolors (cat. 13, ill. p. 81) in an impressive, photomechanical reproduction which bore the title *A Perilous Leap* (fig. 27). While the illustration served to promote the artist's latest work, it also helped to establish Homer as a keenly observant and highly skilled sportsman-artist, for it was accompanied by an angler's full and poetic description of a trout on the full jump, one that attests to the authenticity of Homer's depiction and pays tribute to Homer's powers of observation and transcription:

It is of evenings, just as the sun is setting and the breeze ruffles the lake, the trout are prone to jump. Perhaps the coming obscurity causes insects to move less rapidly. Now comes the fitting opportunity for the trout. From the mirrored surface of the lake out flashes ingots of silver and suddenly they take the golden reflections of the setting sun and are bedecked with jewel. They blaze with emerald and ruby tintings. Here, there, everywhere the trout are springing; near the lily-pads, and away out from shore, and the little splashings and gurglings of the water are musical. You cannot fail seeing these airy prismatic forms describing

FIG. 27
A Perilous Leap—From the Painting in Water Color by Winslow Homer. Photomechanical reproduction from *Harper's Weekly*, April 12, 1890. Private collection

their arches in the air, and hearing the cadences their actions set, as it were in harmonics.

You are not then prone to take heed of how many inches trout can jump. Scientific considerations are chased away by the poetry of the lake and the many mysteries found there. Mr. Homer Winslow [sic] catches trout and so seizes just that inspiration. A jumping trout imprints on an artist's brain a passing episode, a tiny rainbow, that comes and goes within a brief second of time.[62]

In 1898 Lowell had walked through Homer's exhibition of Quebec pictures at M. Knoedler & Company with an angler friend who could not contain his enthusiasm for their "technical excellencies." "He has bored me with his fish talk before now," Lowell wrote, "[but] upon that afternoon the heroic dose of it was most enjoyable. . . . And what trouble I had keeping his voice down! He seemed bent on talking in his out-door, fishing wilderness tones. Now I know all about it." Lowell's friend appreciated the pictures' authentic gray "fishing

FIG. 28
Ouananiche Fishing, Lake St. John, Province of Quebec, 1897. Watercolor over graphite on paper, 14 × 21 in. Museum of Fine Arts, Boston. Warren Collection. William Wilkins Warren Fund. © Museum of Fine Arts, Boston

skies"; he commented on the perfect rendering of the sensuous form of a birch-bark canoe; he saw shadows falling blue on a tree trunk "in a fine outdoor way." Amazingly, in the briefest outline of a leaping ouananiche, the angler-critic also claimed that he could see by the length of the nose that Homer had here represented a male fish (fig. 28).[63]

No testimony on the authenticity of Homer's angling art is more full or meaningful than that offered by George Van Felson of Quebec. Van Felson was a founder of the Tourilli Fish and Game Club and a renowned expert on Canadian game fish, and thus he brought to his judgment of Homer's art an extraordinary level of experience and expertise as an angler and fish culturist. Homer had come to know Van Felson at the Tourilli Club, where he and his brother Charles were also members, and the three men developed a close friendship. In July 1902 Homer presented to Van Felson one of his watercolors of a leaping trout. We know Van Felson's response to Homer's picture because in 1930 he wrote to M. Knoedler & Company about the circumstances of the gift and his assessment of the painting's quality. "During the summer of 1903, Winslow Homer, on his way to the Tourilli Fish and Game Club, called to see me and wished to know how I appreciated the Painting," Van Felson recounted, "and I told him 'perfect.'" Homer replied, or so Van Felson said, "I thought so myself, Georges, but wanted to know if you found it so." There seems to have been a significant element of deference to Van Felson's piscatorial knowledge in Homer's presentation of a fish picture to his Canadian angler-friend. Van Felson then elaborated on the quality of the painting:
Homer, who was passionately fond of fishing, gives in his picture "the Trout" as it emerges from the water, such a conception he had visionized [sic] while fishing the waters of the Tourilli Fish and Game Club. The rivers and streams are from the Mountains: Clear, rapid, and cool. The trout therein are of a superior

quality and most brilliantly colored. When emerging from the water, they have a gloss, or sheen, that fades away a few moments after being landed.

Homer often mentioned this fact to me and visionized [sic] this condition, [and] hence reproduces a True to Life Conception *of the Trout in Life.*

To my knowledge, most fish are painted as seen still. Such is the case in hundreds of Fish Pictures with scenery.

This is the only Picture of a Trout True to Life in America and possibly in the World.[64]

Homer valued the critical judgment of informed viewers and would have been heartened by the testimony of Lowell's angler friend and of Van Felson, men who understood the fine points of angling that he was depicting and appreciated the breadth of angling experience that his paintings represented. If he looked to the sporting papers for endorsement of his efforts, however, he was disappointed, for surprisingly, commentary on Homer's art never appeared there. But after Homer died on September 29, 1910, the editors of *Forest and Stream* did pay a brief tribute to him on the journal's front page. They called him, quite simply, "perhaps the best known painter of outdoor scenes and life of his time."[65] Obviously they had followed his work. He was not unworthy of their sporting paper; his angling pictures simply transcended sporting art. That focus which made Homer such a penetrating observer of the angler's sport also made him a brilliant colorist, sensitive draftsman, and versatile and inventive painter. Homer's angling pictures capture a world that exists on the periphery of conventional living, a world of nature—fleeting, mysterious, and beautiful.

NOTES

1. Winslow Homer, Prout's Neck, Maine, to Reichard & Co., New York, January 19, 1890, William T. Evans Papers, Archives of American Art, Smithsonian Institution, Washington, D.C. (hereafter AAA), microfilm reel number 4054, frames 69–72. The exhibition also included two much earlier Adirondack subjects in oil: *The Two Guides,* 1877 (Sterling and Francine Clark Art Institute, Williamstown, Mass.), and *Camp Fire* (cat. 6, ill. p. 25); see "Three Interesting Exhibitions," *New York Sun,* March 3, 1890, 4. The advertisement ran in *Forest and Stream* 34, no. 5 (February 20, 1890): 99.

2. The authoritative study of Homer's experience at the North Woods Club is David Tatham, *Winslow Homer in the Adirondacks* (Syracuse, N.Y.: Syracuse University Press, 1996). Also see Tatham, "Winslow Homer at the North Woods Club," in *Winslow Homer: A Symposium,* ed. Nicolai Cikovsky Jr. (Washington, D.C.: National Gallery of Art, 1990), 114–130.

3. "The Fine Arts," *New York Commercial Advertiser,* February 15, 1890, 9.

4. "Art Notes," *Art Interchange* 24, no. 5 (March 1, 1890): 66.

5. "Art Notes," *New York Evening Post,* February 19, 1890, 6.

6. "Picture Exhibitions and Sales," *The Art Amateur,* April 22, 1890, 93.

7. [Charles de Kay], "Water Colors by Winslow Homer, N.A.," *New York Times,* February 18, 1890, 4.

8. *New York Times,* February 18, 1890, 4.

9. "Mr. Homer's Water Colors. An Artist in the Adirondacks," *New York Herald-Tribune,* February 26, 1890, 6.

10. Izaak Walton, *The Compleat Angler; or, the Contemplative Man's Recreation. Being a Discourse on Rivers, Fish-Ponds, Fish, and Fishing* (1653), ed. John Burton, with an introduction by John Buchan (Oxford and New York: Oxford University Press, 1982), 8.

11. Examples are in the collection of the Bowdoin College Museum of Art, Brunswick, Maine. Henrietta Benson Homer exhibited with the Brooklyn Art Association in successive exhibitions over a four-year period from March 1873 through December 1877, always flower studies; see Clark S. Marlor, ed., *A History of the Brooklyn Art Association with an Index of Exhibitions* (New York: James F. Carr, 1970), 230.

12. Tatham, *Winslow Homer in the Adirondacks,* 43–48.

13. William Howe Downes, *The Life and Works of Winslow Homer* (1911; reprint, New York: Dover Publications, 1989), 28. Also see Tatham, *Winslow Homer in the Adirondacks,* 44–45.

14. Benson's passion for angling is detailed at length in the news report on his death at Enterprise, Florida; see "Died in a Boat. How Arthur W. Benson Passed Away," *Brooklyn Daily Eagle,* December 30, 1889, 4.

15. Charles Hallock, "Two Ancient Anglers," *Forest and Stream* 46, no. 8 (February 22, 1896): 156–157.

16. Gordon Hendricks revealed the close relationship between Homer's mother and her brother, Arthur W. Benson; see Hendricks, *The Life and Work of Winslow Homer* (New York: Harry N. Abrams, 1979), 94, 96. A Homer family Bible in the possession of the Maine dealer Marvin Sadik bears this entry on Henrietta Benson Homer's death: "Died April 27th 1884 at 173 Henry St., Brooklyn, N.Y. Buried May 1/84 at Mt. Auburn. Lot 563—Lily Path." I am grateful to David Tatham for this information. The registers of the Brock House hotel record the visits of Winslow and his father in February 1886 and Charles Homer Jr. in March 1888, visits that overlap with their uncle's stays there. The Brock House registers are in the collection of the West Volusia

Historical Society, De Land, Florida. I am grateful to Rita Gillis, Assistant Director of the society, and to Spring Dautel for compiling entries on Benson's stays at the Brock House and the Homers' visits there.

17. The dates of Homer's membership are given in *The Century Yearbook/2000* (New York: The Century Association, 2000), 421. I am grateful to Jonathon Harding, curator of the Century Association collection, for his help with my research at the club. This particular submission to the Century show for January 1870, a painting that is unlocated, is documented in James L. Yarnall and William H. Gerdts, comps., *The National Museum of American Art's Index to American Art Exhibition Catalogues, from the Beginning through the 1876 Centennial Year,* 7 vols. (Boston: G. K. Hall & Co., 1986), vol. 3, no. 45079.

18. Charles Cristadoro, "The Rod in Picture," *Forest and Stream* 42, no. 12 (March 19, 1894): 233.

19. The painting is *Playing a Fish,* 1875, now in the Sterling and Francine Clark Art Institute, Williamstown, Massachusetts. Homer reworked the painting in the 1890s; for a discussion of the changes, see Tatham, *Winslow Homer in the Adirondacks,* 54–55.

20. When Lloyd Goodrich examined the painting in 1986 for the New York dealer Joan Michelman, he noted that attached to the stretcher was an old card inscribed, not in Homer's hand, "presented to Thos. J. Miller by Winslow Homer, New York 1882." I am grateful to the current owner of the painting for sharing Goodrich's notes with me.

21. In a letter to M. Knoedler & Company dated September 31, 1905, Homer asked for the return of a Quebec watercolor of an angler casting into rapids, identifiable as *Fishing the Rapids, Saguenay* (cat. 48, ill. p. 152), because he wished "to refer to it in a picture that I have now on hand and propose to paint," possibly referring to a new work in oil. See Homer, Scarboro, Maine, to M. Knoedler & Co., September 31, 1905; original in Knoedler library, copy AAA, microfilm reel number NY59-5, frames 579–581. At this same time he was probably beginning work on the oil version of *Shooting the Rapids, Saguenay River* (fig. 77), which proved to be a problematic work for Homer and remained unfinished at his death.

22. The two watercolors have not been located. See *Catalogue of the Eighth Annual Exhibition of the American Society of Painters in Water Colors,* exh. cat. (New York: National Academy of Design, 1875), nos. 64, 84. For a thorough discussion of Homer's submissions to the exhibition and critical reaction to them, see Margaret C. Conrads, *Winslow Homer and the Critics: Forging a National Art in the 1870s,* exh. cat. (Princeton, N.J.: Princeton University Press in association with the Nelson-Atkins Museum of Art, 2001), 65–73.

23. See the exhibition record for Eliphalet Terry compiled by Yarnall and Gerdts, vol. 5, nos. 88816–88834.

24. Shurtleff's summer home is described and pictured in Lizzie W. Champney, "The Summer Haunts of American Artists," *The Century* 30 (1885): 858–859.

25. Among Shurtleff's published angling notes is his lively account of fighting a rainbow trout printed by Harris in "An Angling Coincidence: The Rainbow Trout," *American Angler* 25, no. 10 (October 1895): 293–294. For a brief account of Shurtleff's painting in Keene Valley, see Patricia C.F. Mandel, *Fair Wilderness: American Paintings in the Collection of The Adirondack Museum* (Blue Mountain Lake, N.Y.: The Adirondack Museum, 1990), 104–105. Another outline of his career is found in his obituary, "R. M. Shurtleff Dead," *New York Times,* January 7, 1915, 13. Shurtleff's *American Angler* title design is signed, "R.M.S."

26. See *Catalogue of the Sixth Winter Exhibition, Comprising the Sixth Annual Exhibition of the American Society of Painters in Water Colors,* exh. cat. (New York: National Academy of Design, 1873), cat. 168.

27. "In the Picture Galleries," *Forest and Stream* 2, no. 7 (March 26, 1874): 105.

28. The growth of fly-fishing beginning in the 1870s is thoroughly explicated by Paul Schullery in his chapters "The Victorian Fly Fisher," part two of his *American Fly Fishing: A History* (New York: Lyons & Burford Publishers, 1987), 61–141. This brief overview draws from Schullery's history.

29. "Our Jubilee Number, 1873–1898," *Forest and Stream* 50, no. 26 (June 25, 1898): 501.

30. G. Brown Goode, introduction to *Game Fishes of the United States* (1878–1881; facsimile ed., New York: Winchester Press, 1972), n.p. For a summary of the high-quality color lithographic work of Armstrong and Company as specialists in color prints on sporting subjects, see Peter Marzio, *A Democratic Art: Chromolithography, 1840–1900* (Boston: David R. Godine in association with the Amon Carter Museum of Western Art, 1979), 21–22.

31. The Orvis company obtained copyright to Kilbourne's *Speckled Trout* image and distributed it, eventually using it as a sign provided to vendors to identify each as an "Authorized Orvis Dealer." An example in its original Orvis trademark mat appeared on the internet auction market; see e-Bay item number 1178263885, "Authorized Orvis Dealer Sign," copyright Orvis company, sold August 19, 2001.

32. William C. Harris, *The Fishes of North America that are Caught on Hook and Line* (New York: The Harris Publishing Co., [1891–1898]). Petrie's work appeared on occasion in *American Angler* and he seems to have been a favorite of Harris's, but he remains an obscure artist; I have found no record of him in other sources.

33. Harris, *The Fishes of North America,* iii.

34. Harris, *The Fishes of North America,* iv.

35. William C. Harris, "A Rare Gallery of Fish Portraits for Sale," *American Angler* 27, no. 3 (March 1897): 95–96.

36. A. C. Gould, ed., *Sport, or Fishing and Shooting . . . illustrated by the Fifteen Original Water Colors by A. B. Frost, Henry Sandham, F. H. Taylor, F. S. Cozzens, Frederic Remington, R. F. Zogbaum, and S. F. Denton* (Boston: Bradlee Whidden, 1889).

37. Gould, preface to *Sport,* n.p.

38. Gould, *Sport,* n.p.

39. Lloyd Goodrich explained that Homer's original title for the work, *Under the Lighthouse,* made clear that these geese had died when they flew into the structure and broke their necks, but John Wilmerding perceptively elaborated on the painting's subject, saying that the power of Homer's presentation comes from the ambiguity about the death of the birds, for a viewer might also assume that they were driven to their deaths when a hunter flushed them. See Goodrich, *Winslow Homer* (New York: The Macmillan Company for the Whitney Museum of American Art, 1945), 150; and Wilmerding, "The Payson Collection of Winslow Homers," *Winslow Homer: The Charles Shipman Payson Collection,* exh. cat. (New York: Coe Kerr Gallery, 1981), n.p.

40. Clarke purchased *An Unexpected Catch* (cat. 18), *Leaping Trout* (fig. 11), and *Rise to a Fly* (possibly cat. 16); Evans purchased *A Fisherman's Day* (Freer Gallery of Art, Washington, D.C.) and *A Good One* (cat. 11, ill. p. 56); information from object files, The Lloyd Goodrich and Edith Havens Goodrich/Whitney Museum of American Art Record of Works by Winslow Homer, Abigail Booth Gerdts, director. Clarke's interest in angling seems clear: he also owned Samuel A. Kilbourne's *Brook Trout;* see H. Barbara Weinberg, "Thomas B. Clarke: Foremost Patron of American Art from 1872 to 1889," *American Art Journal* 8, no. 1 (May 1976): 78.

41. There was no catalogue to the Reichard show and the exact number of works included has been reported differently. Goodrich states that there were thirty-two watercolors, and he may be accurate, for reviews indicate that there was included a proof print of Homer's etching *Fly Fishing, Saranac Lake* (cat. 19). Helen Cooper notes that of the thirty-two works, twenty-seven sold; see Helen A. Cooper, *Winslow Homer Watercolors,* exh. cat. (New Haven and London: Yale University Press for the National Gallery of Art, 1986), 193. "Only three of Mr. Homer's water-colors remained of thirty odd," reported *The Art Amateur* in its recap of the winter's exhibitions; see "Picture Exhibitions and Sales," *The Art Amateur,* April 22, 1890, 93. The *New York Sun* reported, "of the thirty-two watercolors only a small example or so still remains in the artist's possession." See *New York Sun,* March 3, 1890, 4.

42. "Aesthetics of Angling," *Forest and Stream* 18, no. 5 (March 2, 1882): 83.

43. *New York Sun,* March 3, 1890, 4.

44. See *Exhibition of Water-Colors, Oct. 28 to Nov. 16, 1895,* exh. cat. (Boston: St. Botolph Club, 1895), nos. 1–10. An annotated copy is in the St. Botolph Club Papers, microfilmed for the AAA, reel number 2241, no frame number; annotations to the catalogue show that three of the ten watercolors sold at $300 each.

45. See *Water Colors by Winslow Homer of Life and Scenes in the Province of Quebec (Canada), April, 1898,* exh. cat. (New York: M. Knoedler & Co., 1898); copy in Knoedler library and in AAA, microfilm reel number NY59-5, no frame number. The exhibition opened at the Carnegie Institute in mid-February; see "Sixteen Paintings sell for $20,819.70 . . . Magnificent Watercolors by Winslow Homer to Be Shown," *Pittsburgh Post,* January 29, 1898, 2.

46. Quoted in Goodrich, *Winslow Homer,* 149.

47. Quoted in Goodrich, *Winslow Homer,* 149.

48. Orson Lowell, "Water Colors by Winslow Homer. Of Life and Scenes in the Province of Quebec (Canada)," *Brush and Pencil* 2, no. 3 (June 1898): 131–134.

49. Homer's visits to the North Woods Club frequently overlapped with those of Yalden. Yalden was a young engineering student whom Homer would paint in *Paddling at Dusk,* a watercolor of 1892 (Memorial Art Gallery of the University of Rochester), which records Yalden's maiden voyage on Mink Pond in a canoe of his own making. Yalden's friendship with Homer has been well documented and described by David Tatham, in "Paddling at Dusk: Winslow Homer and Ernest Yalden," *Porticus* (Journal of the Memorial Art Gallery of the University of Rochester) 9 (1986): 16–19; and in Tatham, *Winslow Homer in the Adirondacks,* 124–127.

50. Winslow Homer, writing from the North Woods Club, Minerva, New York, to Martha (Mattie) Homer, June 21, 1900, 3 pp., The Homer Collection, Winslow Homer Papers and Family Memorabilia, Bowdoin College Museum of Art, 1964.69.87.

51. From object file, The Lloyd Goodrich and Edith Havens Goodrich/Whitney Museum of American Art Record of Works by Winslow Homer, Abigail Booth Gerdts, director.

52. I am grateful to Prosser M. Watts Jr., great-grandson of Richard Austin Watts, for sharing the story that has passed down through his family with Homer's painting; author's notes of telephone conversation with Prosser M. Watts Jr., January 2, 2001.

53. Homer's letter to Beatty is quoted in Goodrich, *Winslow Homer,* 149.

54. Homer, Prout's Neck, Maine, to M. Knoedler & Co., March 30, 1903; original in Knoedler library; copy AAA, microfilm reel number NY59-5, no frame number.

55. A chronology of Homer's documented visits to the Adirondacks is given in Appendix A, in Tatham, *Winslow Homer in the Adirondacks,* 137.

56. See Goodrich, *Winslow Homer,* 149.

57. Homer, Scarboro, Maine, to M. Knoedler & Co., April 15, 1901; original in Knoedler library; copy AAA, microfilm reel NY59-5, no frame number.

58. Homer, Scarboro, Maine, to M. Knoedler & Co., March 31, 1905; original in Knoedler library; copy AAA, microfilm reel number NY59-5, frames 566–568.

59. Homer, Scarboro, Maine, to M. Knoedler & Co., March 31, 1905; original in Knoedler library, copy AAA, microfilm reel number NY59-5, frames 566–568.

60. Homer, Scarboro, Maine, to M. Knoedler & Co., April 11, 1905; original in Knoedler library; copy AAA, microfilm reel number NY59-5, frames 571–573.

61. Lowell, "Water Colors by Winslow Homer," 132.

62. "Trout on the Full Jump," *Harper's Weekly* 34, no. 1738 (April 12, 1890): 279.

63. Lowell, "Water Colors by Winslow Homer," 132.

64. George Van Felson, "History of Winslow Homer's 'Study of a Trout,'" January 20, 1930, typescript, M. Knoedler & Co. Original in Knoedler library, copy AAA, microfilm reel number NY59-5, frames 609–614. For an outline of Van Felson's career, see David Tatham's essay in this catalogue.

65. *Forest and Stream* 75, no. 16 (October 15, 1910): 607.

The Fly-fishing Stories in Winslow Homer's Art

Paul Schullery

AMONG THEIR OTHER ATTAINMENTS, FLY FISHERS have at times been distinguished by the strength of their self-esteem. Their conviction that fly-fishing is the highest, noblest form of angling has been expressed countless times over the past few centuries. There may be nothing especially harmful in this conviction; many of us tend to regard our chosen pastimes with affection, if not passion. But it is central to any understanding of Winslow Homer's frequent use of fly-fishing themes in his art that he so often chose to portray what was so widely regarded as the most "aristocratic" of angling methods. And it is equally central to any understanding of fly-fishing's self-image as an act of considerable social refinement that so many historic figures—Homer is joined by Daniel Webster, Ernest Hemingway, Aldo Leopold, Andrew Carnegie, presidents and royalty beyond counting, and a diverse host of other famous people—were enthusiasts.[1]

But other things distinguish fly fishers and their sport, and to appreciate Homer's place in the sport, they must be considered briefly. The fundamentals of the sport of fly-fishing have not changed for several centuries, perhaps as long as a millennium.[2] Out of sympathy for the uninitiated, it is only fair to introduce those fundamentals, because fly-fishing is in fact a significantly different practice from all other types of fishing. The fly fisher's sense of being special, whether justifiable or not as proof of social superiority, is in fact based on something real.

The most important practical difference between fly-fishing and other forms of fishing is in the delivery of the fly. The lures (whether organic or artificial) used by other anglers are typically cast toward the fish or fishing area by their own weight. That is to say that the angler uses the rod to cast (or throw) the lure, which is heavy enough to pull the attached line along behind it. In fly-fishing, on the other hand, the angler casts *the weight of the line* (cat. 26). Modern fly lines, unlike other fishing lines, are not merely very long strings. They are much thicker and are usually tapered in diameter, just as were the buggy whips whose use required very similar motions.[3]

There is, in fact, a continuous taper from the angler's hand to the fly. The taper progresses, first, from the thick handle to the thin tip of the fly rod, then from the tip of the fly rod through the length of the ever-finer fly line, and then from the end of the line through the length of the likewise tapered monofilament "leader," to whose finest end the fly is attached. The tapering of all these elements is what allows for the smooth—even delicate, when need be—transfer of energy from the angler's hand along the length of the rod and line, so that when that hand is skilled, the line will go where it is needed. As it does, the fly goes along for the ride.

Fly casting is almost entirely an exercise in timing rather than in strength. The fly caster, rather than merely giving the rod a flip to toss a lure in a given direction, must get the line airborne, usually through a series of "false casts" that travel as far behind him (the "backcast") as in front of him. Once that is achieved—and competent casters can achieve it in one or two quick casts—then the angler must lay the line out across the water so that the fly is delivered to the desired spot. A well-cast line will seem to "unroll" across the water—just like Indiana Jones's whip unrolled itself into a perfectly straight line before snatching the revolver from the bad guy's hand. When cast by an expert, a fly line moves through the air with grace and precision. And, as any neophyte caster will complain, a badly cast line is a nightmare of tangles and exasperations.

Over the centuries, specialists have mastered dozens of obscure if not arcane casts, have refined casting equipment for all manner of special purposes, and have developed many passionate and conflicting opinions about how best all this should be done.[4] But setting aside the many styles and manners involved, all skilled casters will show you that same smooth back-and-forth motion of the fly line. The line must roll out straight behind the caster before it can be brought forward with an easy snap of the wrist, then to roll out straight ahead of the caster and land on target with improbable accuracy.

Once you've watched one or two masters at this, it is hard not to admit that there is something singularly graceful, even elegant, about it all. In that mood, it is easier to see why these people tend to think so well of themselves. And, more to the subject of this essay, it is easier to appreciate why Homer might have been attracted to celebrating this and other aspects of fly-fishing.

During the six centuries prior to the Industrial Revolution, a trout angler in England or France might have practiced the sport in essentially the same way, employing basically the same tackle and techniques—and adhering to the same sporting code of ethics—as his great-grandfather had a hundred years earlier. But toward the end of the seventeenth century, some elements of the sport, especially its

technology, began to change more rapidly, lurching forward periodically into new forms and broadened practices. These changes accelerated through most of the nineteenth century. Though some traditionalists might even yet harbor doubts that the changes constituted progress, they certainly had profound effects on sporting society. Among the many things revealed in Homer's portrayals of this sport are signs of the times.

THE ROD

Homer and his sporting companions were the beneficiaries of an authentic revolution in the manufacture of fishing tackle. Rods, reels, lines, and flies all underwent remarkable transformations in the nineteenth century.[5] Rods have perhaps received the most attention from historians who have considered nineteenth-century angling. Not only are rods (do not annoy their owners by calling them "poles") the largest and most obvious part of the angler's armament, they are the most collectible and are lavished with affection by their admirers.

Prior to 1800, virtually all fishing rods were solid wood sticks of varying quality. Many species of wood were used, sometimes in combination—a rod might feature sturdy butt and midsections of hickory and a fine, flexible tip of lancewood or other lighter wood (whalebone also worked). As global trade made more and more types of wood readily available, rodmakers experimented ceaselessly.

But the great breakthrough involved a few species of the huge grass known as bamboo. In the early 1800s a number of rodmakers discovered that the outer layers of certain species of Asian bamboo contained a density of fibers with almost miraculous strength and flexibility.[6] Whole bamboo canes had long been recognized as wonderfully strong and resilient "fishing poles" without any alteration, but these craftsmen were onto something more involved. By the time of the American Civil War, a

CAT. 26
Casting the Fly [Casting, Number Two], 1894. Watercolor over graphite on paper, 15 × 21 ⅜ in.
National Gallery of Art, Washington, D.C. Gift of Ruth K. Henschel in memory of her husband,
Charles R. Henschel (1975.92.2) Photograph © 2001 Board of Trustees, National Gallery of Art

FIG. 29
Winslow Homer's bamboo fly rod and case; three pieces with extra tip, length 11 feet.
Made by B. F. Nichols Co., Boston, Massachusetts. Photograph by Bruce Curtis.
The American Museum of Fly Fishing, Manchester, Vermont

few rodmakers had developed techniques for splitting the outer surface of the stalk, or culm, of bamboo into fine, long strips that contained the greatest strength. These strips were then glued together to produce a single stick that, as a casting tool, was as significant an advance in fly-fishing as repeating firearms were for hunters. One surviving fly rod known to have been owned and used by Homer (fig. 29) is a handsome eleven-footer produced by B. F. Nichols, a Boston tackle manufacturer of high-quality rods. It is a fairly typical late-1800s six-strip Calcutta cane rod of the quality that members of an exclusive trout-fishing club not only would be happy to own and use but would also pause for some congratulatory admiration when its owner first took it from its case.[7]

Though it is not possible to identify specifically the finer details of rod makeup in any of Homer's art, many of the pictures are still quite revealing of contemporary tackle. The wood engraving *The Fishing Party,* 1869, shows three young women on a rocky shore (fig. 30). One is fishing, one is working on her tackle, and one is holding a creel. One art historian has said of this picture that "Homer's women hold lightweight, hand-made sectioned rods of split bamboo, probably with cork grips and presumably fitted with a reel and machine-braided, oiled silk line."[8]

My interpretation of the picture is somewhat different. These young women appear to be using solid-wood rods. (In 1869 there were extremely few rodmakers working in split bamboo; their products were expensive and were not likely to be used for casual fishing outings of this sort.) They are almost certainly bait-fishing. The woman on the far right is actively fishing. She appears to be watching the end of her line, or perhaps a float or bobber, waiting for a bite. If she were fly-fishing or using any kind of outfit that included a reel, the line would be visible, running the length of the rod from her hand (the reel could conceivably be obscured behind her sleeve) to the end of the rod, passing through small metal guides along the length of the rod. No such line is visible. Instead, it seems that the line is probably attached only on the end of the rod tip. This was and is standard practice for bait-fishing for smaller fish.

Furthermore, if she were using a split-bamboo rod, as knowledgeable an angler as Homer would probably not have failed to indicate the "intermediate wraps"—the narrow bands of thread that were invariably wrapped at intervals of an inch or so the entire length of virtually all split-bamboo rods before about 1900 (these wraps were necessary because the animal glues used to hold the separate bamboo strips together were not wholly reliable). At our distance as viewers of this scene, such wraps would be prominent on both rods, and it is hard to imagine that Homer would have neglected to show them.

Another scenario becomes more likely when we study the second angler, the woman second from the right. She is also holding a rod and appears to be examining the end of her line. Again, if she were using an outfit that included a reel, the line would be visible passing along the length of the rod, through the guides, and would again be visible (and is) as it hangs suspended between the rod tip and her hand. It appears that just to the right of her right hand, visible against the dress of her companion, the somewhat twisted line is hanging from her left hand. At its end there seems to be a small, bare hook.

If this is a correct reading of the picture, then the actions of the third woman are explained. She is looking into one of the two creels in the picture and in her left hand holds a small tin, or cannister, which seems most likely to contain bait—worms, grubs, or some other organic material.

In this interpretation, then, the woman on the right is busy watching for a bite. Her nearest companion has just discovered that she has lost her bait. Perhaps she has just landed a fish, which the third woman has already creeled. In any case, the third woman may be in the process of getting another worm so that the woman in the middle can rebait her hook.

The historic Homer houses at Prout's Neck, Maine, still contain several fishing rods from the period of Homer's active fishing career, though there is no way of knowing now which if any of them he personally used.[9] None are fly rods, but they offer a representative cross-section of late-1800s solid-wood and split-bamboo construction styles. During most of the period represented in Homer's angling art, fishermen might own both solid-wood and split-bamboo rods. And though bamboo offered the angler advantages in its greater strength and lighter weight, it is almost impossible to determine which material a rod is made of solely from the generalized representations that Homer provided in his paintings.

FIG. 30

The Fishing Party, 1869. Wood engraving after Winslow Homer by John Filmer, 9 × 13¾ in. From *Appleton's Journal,* October 2, 1869. Bowdoin College Museum of Art, Brunswick, Maine. Museum Purchase, Elizabeth B.G. Hamlin Fund

THE CAST

In quite a few of Homer's fly-fishing scenes, there is not even a clear indication of where the rod ends and the line begins. In fact, if any additional proof is needed that Homer fully understood the dynamics of fly casting—that the arm, hand, rod, and line were all part of one continuously tapering tool—it must be in such paintings, where these disparate elements are melded into one long, undifferentiated expression of purposeful motion. Homer's portrayals of anglers in midcast—and of airborne fly lines—are among the most evocative and convincing such images ever produced. They have not been meaningfully improved on by a century of subsequent artists, though some of his successors have captured the motion and physics of a cast line superbly.

Homer's familiarity with the needs of fly casting is also evident in that he more often shows the backcast than the forward cast. Modern instructors relentlessly remind beginning casters that the backcast is as important as the forward cast—that what happens behind the angler is as important as what happens in front, out there where the fish wait. Two of Homer's paintings, *Casting,* 1897 (fig. 31), and *The Angler,* probably dating to 1874 (cat. 3, ill. p. 43), show the textbook form for making a backcast, though neither shows the line. In both, the fisherman has apparently stopped the rod's backward stroke just past the vertical—the rod is still pointed almost straight up, which was regarded as essential "good form" if you were to keep the line and fly elevated and thus prevent tangling the backcast in brush, trees, cows, and friends.

On the other hand, both pictures display Homer's independence from the sort of formality that later writers would ridicule as evidence of a Victorian prissiness in "old-time" fly casters. Just as the stereotypical debutante-in-training was counseled to cultivate correct walking posture by balancing a book on her head, so was the incipient fly caster advised to learn proper casting form by practicing with a book clamped firmly between the elbow of the casting arm and the body. This restriction was supposed to enforce on the caster certain disciplines, including keeping the backcast high. Though their postures do suggest a certain formality, Homer's two casters have adopted a less stiff approach, with their casting arms extended away from their bodies. The caster in *Casting* has both arms extended; the right holds the rod, and the left holds excess line with which to lengthen or shorten the cast as circumstance requires.

But most of the other backcasts Homer painted portray an even freer style. *Sunrise, Fishing in the Adirondacks,* 1889 (cat. 15, ill. p. 120), *Casting the Fly,* 1894 (cat. 26, ill. p. 73), *Fisherman in Quebec,* 1895 (fig. 32), *Two Men in a Canoe,* 1895 (cat. 36, ill. p. 143), and *The Rise,* 1900 (cat. 46, ill. p. 79), all show the rod having dropped much farther back toward the horizontal.[10] All are lake-fishing scenes, and on open water there is no obstacle behind the angler but the water itself, so anglers may safely drop their backcasts lower under these circumstances. In *Sunrise, Fishing in the Adirondacks, Fisherman in Quebec, Two Men in a Canoe,* and *The Rise,* the rod seems to have reached its full backward extension. The line's direction of motion is to the rear of the angler, and its loop will unroll until the line is straight out behind him. The line is not visible in *Casting the Fly,* but judging from the rod's straightness, it appears that the line is well back, and the angler is about to begin the forward cast. In *Sunrise, Fishing in the Adirondacks, Two Men in a Canoe, Casting the Fly,* and *The Rise,* the elongated, elliptical glow of a rise-form, where a fish has recently surfaced, appears to be the probable target of the imminent forward cast.

FIG. 31
Casting, 1897. Watercolor on paper, 13 15/16 × 20 15/16 in. The Addison Gallery of American Art, Phillips Academy, Andover, Massachusetts. Given anonymously (1928.22)

Homer's scenes of the forward cast are, if anything, even more exciting and revealing of his understanding of casting. *Trout Fishing, Lake St. John, Quebec,* 1895 (cat. 35, ill. p. 145), *Casting, "A Rise,"* 1889 (cat. 8), and *Fishing the Rapids, Saguenay River,* 1902 (cat. 48, ill. p. 152), capture various stages of the line being thrown forward. In all three cases, the rod has completed its forward stroke and the line is now responding, unrolling toward some hope-filled spot in the water. And in all three, the artist has left us with much to wonder about.

Modern fly-casting experts almost unanimously recommend what is known as a "tight loop" rather than a "wide loop."[11] The forward cast in *Trout Fishing, Lake St. John, Quebec* is a classic wide loop: the line is rolling forward with a generous gap between the lower and upper sides of the loop. By contrast, the forward loop in *Casting, "A Rise"* is tight: the gap between the top and bottom is much smaller. The cast in *Fishing the Rapids, Saguenay River* also has a reasonably tight loop, though because we see the cast at a foreshortened angle it is difficult to know the proportions of the loop.

The advantage of the tight loop is that it typically gives greater control and precision in placement of the fly, but it may have been considerably less practical a choice in Homer's day. Because of the limitations of photography at the time, we are virtually without photographs of actual airborne fly lines during Homer's life, but using period fly rods has taught us that the soft, slow action of most such rods, combined with their greater length, would have inclined more fishermen to cast the wide, open loops that dominate both the backcasts and forward casts in Homer's paintings. The tackle of Homer's day, though vastly improved over earlier equipment, still had certain other limitations. Leaders of silkworm gut broke considerably more easily than do modern monofilaments. The gentler changes of direction inherent in the slower, wide-open loop lessened the likelihood that the fly would be snapped off at the far extension of the backcast.

FIG. 32

Fisherman in Quebec, 1895. Watercolor over graphite on paper, 12 1/16 × 19 15/16 in. Cooper-Hewitt National Design Museum, Smithsonian Institution, New York. Gift of Charles Savage Homer, Jr. (1912-12-89)

There are some other wonderful puzzles in these paintings, especially in *Casting, "A Rise,"* which give us ample reason to wonder just how many levels there might have been to the story Homer told us in this picture. First, consider the line. The forward cast is well on its way, almost certainly aimed at the bright rise-form at the extreme right of the scene. But notice that there is still a great deal of undirected fly line above the head of the angler. Generally, this sort of "pile-up" of winding fly line is the result of not having allowed the backcast sufficient time to straighten out behind you before starting the forward cast. Even today, and certainly with the gut leaders of Homer's day, this was a good way to "crack the whip" of the line and snap off the fly. Was Homer simply exercising his artistic prerogatives to show us a gracefully flowing fly line, or was he having a little joke on his angler? Did all the extra line soaring around result because the angler was in midcast, aiming in another direction, when he suddenly noticed the rise and tried to send his fly line that way instead?

Even more curious is the obvious disproportion
of the cast and the scene. Take a visual measure of
the fly line, from the end of the rod through the
tight loop, and then back toward the angler and up
into the sinuous curves above his head. Straighten
all that line out and it will reach about twice the
distance necessary to reach the rise-form. Indeed,
the front end of the loop has already almost reached
the rise. Again, was Homer just enjoying the graceful flow of the line, or was he setting us up to
admire a picture so much that we wouldn't even
notice that it made very little sense as a casting

scene? What was this angler up to? As we ask these
questions, we are drawn further into the picture's
tale, and, I think, our admiration for the tackle-
savvy of the angler-artist is heightened.

Other intriguing complications emerge from
study of *Fishing the Rapids, Saguenay River*. It seems
straightforward enough at first glance. Two people
have made their way to a prominent rocky outcrop,
where one is now making a cast that, for its scale
and the water it covers, is little less than heroic.
Notice that in this case the unrolling loop is actually
rising slightly, rather than just being parallel to the

CAT. 46

The Rise, 1900. Watercolor over graphite on paper, 13 ¾ × 20 ¾ in. National Gallery of Art,
Washington, D.C. Gift of Ruth K. Henschel in memory of her husband, Charles R. Henschel (1975.92.14)
Photograph © 2001 Board of Trustees, National Gallery of Art

surface of the water. This seems to anticipate the advice of some modern long-distance casters, who suggest that to ensure that a long cast actually reaches its goal before succumbing to gravity and hitting the water, you should establish a mental target that is a few yards above the water where you wish the fly to land. This principle could not be better illustrated than it is in this painting.

But this picture has another quality, almost as if Homer intended an optical illusion. The angler is on a rock island, with the river roaring past on both sides. Stare at the man and his line for a few seconds and you may begin to wonder if he is casting toward you, into the wild golden rapids you see, or away from you, into some perhaps less frenetic and more promising reach of water out of our sight beyond the rock. Stare at it a little longer and you may also begin to wonder if what we see is in fact a backcast, either toward us or away from us, and if the angler will soon flex his wrist and bring the rod forward to shoot the line across the water we see or the water we can't. The picture is all the more absorbing for this ambivalence.

The Rise-Form— an Appreciation

It is worth noting another seemingly minor achievement of Homer's in his fly-fishing scenes. For the better part of a century, fly fishermen have been making a study of one of angling's most ephemeral elements, the rise. Homer knew and used the term, but after his time anglers grew ever more attentive to that slight, short-lived disturbance of the water's surface caused by the fish either taking a fly from the surface or turning to take some insect just underneath. It is the closest that fish come to leaving tracks. Twentieth-century scrutiny of this disturbance, and analysis of its meaning, would surprise those who think of fishing as a passive, uncritical enterprise. The British writers G.E.M. Skues,

in *The Way of a Trout with a Fly* (1924), and Eric Taverner, in *Trout Fishing from All Angles* (1930), categorized more than a dozen distinct types of "rise-form" caused by different types of feeding activity by trout.[12] Advances in photography have allowed more recent writers, such as Vincent Marinaro, in *In the Ring of the Rise* (1976), to dissect rise-forms even further,[13] and angling technicians continue to pursue this subject in a welter of considerations of the visual acuity of trout, the physics of refraction, and other marvelously absorbing obscurities.

But for all this study, nobody has more ably captured the spirit of the rise—what happens to the surface of a still water when a fish pushes up against the roof of its world—than Homer did in several of his angling scenes (see especially cat. 46). For devoted anglers, the scanning of any of his late-evening or early-morning lake scenes is a kind of treasure hunt in which the reward is the evidence of feeding fish. In the slanting light of dawn and dusk, when most of the water is still dark, the disruption caused by a fish swirling up to pull under an insect shows as a distinct, unmistakable little break in the darkness, followed by a quickly spreading circle of silver that dissipates even before your vision can satisfactorily resolve its form. The fish that caused it is probably cruising—steadily moving on in search of another insect—but if you cast quickly and drop the fly right into that fading ring, the fish may come again. Such is the irrepressible hope of the angler, anyway. (Homer's watercolor *Leaping Trout*, 1889 [cat. 13], shows an individual fish "rising" in that term's most extreme form—having left the water entirely to make an aerial grab at a vaguely represented flying insect, perhaps a mayfly. An identically titled work from the same year shows two fish airborne together [fig. 12, ill. p. 37]; a ghostly mayfly silhouette at the extreme top of the image offers a possible explanation for their leaps.)[14]

CAT. 13
Leaping Trout, 1889. Watercolor over graphite on paper, 14 1/16 × 20 1/16 in. Portland
Museum of Art, Portland, Maine. Bequest of Charles Shipman Payson (1988.55.7)

Once you are aware of rise-forms, you search Homer's water scenes (whether they involve fishing or not) just as you would search real water, because it is obvious that this man knew how integral a part of such places were the occasional rises of trout, bass, and other fish. Water without them is to the angler as sterile and unconvincing as a forest thicket without birdsong. Their understated presence in Homer's art is yet another reason to honor the authenticity of his work.

FIG. 33
Fly wallet with drawings and flies, 1883. Photograph by Bruce Curtis.
The American Museum of Fly Fishing, Manchester, Vermont

THE FLY

The fly itself, like the cast, is a primary distinguishing feature of the sport (fig. 33). Compared with other lures, flies are usually much smaller and practically weightless. This was especially true during the sport's first few centuries, when virtually all flies were made ("tied") to imitate small insects. In fact, parallel to the development of the sport of fishing with artificial flies was the ongoing use of real flies—especially certain larger species of mayflies that could readily be impaled on small hooks—by Old World anglers. The fragility of the actual insects must have been one of the primary incentives for developing artificial flies, which are much more durable. Modern anglers imitate a far greater range of life forms, everything from frogs to minnows to crustaceans. But the idea is the same—to trick fish into thinking these things are good to eat. And they are all still called flies.[15]

As with fly rods, Homer lived in an era of glorious new developments in flies. The same robust world trade that brought rodmakers exotic and beautiful woods brought fly tiers an incredible array of strangely hued feathers, furs, and fibers. Suddenly these craftspeople had at their disposal a wondrous diversity of natural colors and textures. Fly patterns proliferated as creative anglers applied personal sensibilities to this wonderful opportunity. The late nineteenth century was the heyday of colorful and often gaudy fly patterns for Atlantic salmon and various freshwater fish. For the American angler, this luxurious flow of vivid (almost lurid) new fly patterns may have received its finest celebration in Mary Orvis Marbury's monumental book *Favorite Flies and Their Histories*. First published in 1892, the book quickly went through several editions; anglers apparently couldn't resist the superb chromolithographs of hundreds of fly patterns. Most of the book was occupied by short letters to the

Orvis Company from American anglers reporting on the fishing and fly pattern preferences in their local neighborhoods.[16]

The Adirondacks, Homer's most frequent fishing destination, was and still is a stronghold of such regional favorites. It is home to one of American fly-fishing's unique local traditions. Though any individual angler in any region might be using almost any fly pattern from anywhere, angling historians and antiquarians have rightly come to identify different areas with different historical approaches to fly theory. Maine's brook trout and landlocked salmon waters are known for the development of many small minnow and "baitfish" imitations; the Catskills and Poconos are celebrated for giving rise to an imitationist school, in which fly fishers have become amateur entomologists so as to create more accurately successful fly patterns; steep-gradient Rocky Mountain streams were for many years associated with the creation of especially buoyant, durable rough-water flies. But more than any other region, the Adirondacks have been thought of as a sort of spiritual home for the tradition of the colorful Victorian wet fly—the style-conscious descendant of several centuries of experimentation with and evolution of the flies used in medieval Europe. Homer's art celebrates this tradition.

If Homer's personal preferences for flies are accurately represented by his paintings, he had fairly simple, orthodox tastes. Most of the flies are bright red, which could have been as much an artistic choice—a contained, vivid little splash of unlikely color among more subdued natural shades—as an angler's. The "favorite fly" paradigm represented by Marbury's book reflected both an aesthetic view and a fishing theory. Anglers chose and favored certain flies for highly subjective reasons of personal taste but simultaneously developed strongly expressed theories about why their favorite flies worked.

Much of this theorizing had little or nothing to do with the imitationist theories of other fly tiers, who attempted to imitate specific insect species in size, shade, and shape. Instead, it focused on prevailing and competing beliefs about what fish "liked" on some fundamental level. This was obviously great fun. Because no one knew how to ask the fish what they really preferred, it was possible

FIG. 34
"Trout Flies," made by C. F. Orvis company, Manchester, Vermont. Color lithograph by M. Bradley Company, from Mary Orvis Marbury (1856–1914), *Favorite Flies and Their Histories*, 1892. The Scarlet Ibis is shown as number 205. Princeton University Library, Princeton, New Jersey

to debate at great length over the relative merits of red or purple flies, or whether a white strip of winging might heighten the effectiveness of a yellow fly, or if a few turns of peacock herl around the butt end of the fly's body might have a salutary effect. Today, much of this dialogue sounds naive, even goofy, but it was seriously conducted and heartily enjoyed by countless anglers in Homer's day.

Homer's paintings suggest that he was a hard-core Scarlet Ibis man (fig. 34). Though it is not an exact match with the historic fly pattern, the fly shown in his painting *Spotted Weakfish (Sea Trout), Homosassa, Florida, for Mrs. R. A. Watts,* 1905 (cat. 53), is almost certainly intended to be a Scarlet Ibis.[17] This pattern has in a rather whimsical way become one of the leading symbols of the whole favorite-fly era.

Not only was the Scarlet Ibis a perfect statement of the notion that a fly need not look like anything in nature as long as it was spectacular in the eyes of anglers, but also its construction required the use of feathers from a bird species that could hardly stand the destructive pressure of such market demands. If changing fashions in fly tying had not caused the favorite-fly movement to go into eclipse, the rise of endangered species preservation would eventually have driven it there. But it remains one of the most intriguing aesthetic developments in the history of the sport in America, and it is fun to wonder what Homer, as an artist pioneering his own style, might have made, in purely aesthetic terms, of the stylings of commercial fly tiers. It is also fun to wonder if he was ever tempted to take up the craft himself.

CAT. 53
Spotted Weakfish (Sea Trout), Homosassa, Florida, for Mrs. R. A. Watts, 1905.
Watercolor over graphite on paper, 6 ⅜ × 15 ¹³⁄₁₆ in. Collection of Graham D. Williford

As with the rods Homer painted, it is not always possible to determine for certain which of the many popular red flies was being shown, if he was even showing us a specific known pattern; for all we know, Homer acquired his flies from local sources who tied their own bright-red killers without regard for the "official" prescription for the Scarlet Ibis. Indeed, one of the expressed reasons that Marbury said she was moved to publish her encyclopedic masterpiece in 1892 was to try to clean up the mess then existing in the commercial fly market, in which each fly maker interpreted each fly pattern differently. (It was also of inestimable value to the Orvis Company to stand up and become the arbiter in such a situation; their flies remained informal standards in the sport for much of the twentieth century.) So while we could safely say that Homer favored the Scarlet Ibis, most of his pictures in which the fly is shown suggest only a somewhat imprecise red shape, without the various details of the pattern being revealed. Of course that is a perfectly fair way to show a fly that is not only soaked but also being chewed on. Most of the flies shown are either Scarlet Ibises or nearly so, and we can readily believe the testimonials his paintings were offering— that these were good flies for at least half a dozen fresh- and saltwater fish.

A few of his pictures tell us more about fly use in his day. Both *Rising to the Fly*, 1861 (cat. 1, ill. p. 39), and *A Good Pool, Saguenay River*, 1895 (cat. 30, ill. p. 48), for example, show fish that are dealing with multiple-fly casts. In Homer's time, to a far greater extent than today, anglers routinely used "casts" of two or more flies. Some used a "ladder" of as many as twelve flies, though such rigs must have been an almighty nuisance to cast. But the rewards of offering the fish more than one fly at a time could be startling. *Under the Falls, the Grand Discharge, Lake St. John, P.Q.*, 1895 (cat. 37, ill. p. 146), seems to show an angler playing two large leaping fish at once.

Camping Out in the Adirondack Mountains, 1874, a woodcut published in *Harper's Weekly*, contains fly-fishing arcana applicable here (fig. 35). The bearded man in the middle of the picture is probably the guide. A landing net, a cased fly rod, and a crcel are carefully placed between him and the sportsman, whose hat is festooned with flies that may be complete "casts" (flies attached to a leader, all ready to be connected to the end of the line). The sportsman is holding a fly book. Prior to the 1890s, most flies were tied with short "snells" (made of silkworm gut in Homer's time) already attached. The snells ended in loops that could be quickly attached to the leader. Fly books, so called because of their felt or card "pages," often came with small springs or clips on which snelled flies could be safely stored in neat rows, ready for use. In these specifics, the angler was doing precisely what Homer must have done on many of his trips—fussing with his flies in anticipation of the next fishing outing.

FIG. 35
Camping Out in the Adirondack Mountains, 1874. Wood engraving after Homer by LaGarde, 9¼ × 13¾ in. From *Harper's Weekly*, November 7, 1894. Amon Carter Museum, Fort Worth, Texas

PLAYING THE FISH

Of course, all this tackle, theory, and hope are aimed at a single goal—actually hooking and landing fish. Homer's portrayals of the "fight" of the fish, like the other specifics of his art, are finely tuned to the realities of angling in his day. Naturally, these are scenes of the greatest drama, though even in Homer's day there was a reaction under way against overdramatization of what was at heart a wildly uneven contest between a two-hundred-pound human and a two-pound fish. In "A Fight with a Trout," Charles Dudley Warner's (1829–1900) hilarious spoof of William Henry Harrison Murray's (1840–1904) account of catching an Adirondack trout, angling writers and artists were served sufficient notice that they needed to calm their rhetorical excesses.[18] In *Adventures in the Wilderness; or, Camp-Life in the Adirondacks* (1869), Murray published an engraving that showed him standing in a small guide boat, fishing rod in hand, facing a sizable trout that has not only leaped head-high but also seems to be challenging, if not charging, Murray.[19] As Warner put it in his book *In the Wilderness* (1878), "No one who has studied the excellent pictures representing men in an open boat, exposed to the assaults of long, enraged trout flying at them through the open air with open mouth, ever ventures with his rod upon the lonely lakes of the forest without a certain terror. . . ."[20]

Homer's many pictures of anglers playing trout could only have been a corrective against such overstatement. But a sense of proportion and resistance to the temptation to overstatement were not the only special qualities Homer brought to this subject. His paintings of playing fish contain some curious surprises that, apparently, only anglers are likely to notice; neither the published reviews nor subsequent art historians seem to have noticed some of the subtleties and minidramas that Homer introduced into these scenes.

Before considering these, however, it is worth noting one way in which Homer chose not to portray the fishing life as it really was. Unlike almost all sporting artists since, Homer showed a strong tendency to disassociate his leaping fish from the water. The fish are cleanly airborne; there is no splash beneath them, and no water sheeting from their sides. This is not how fish really look. Apparently, once his fish were out of the water in their jump, Homer chose simply to ignore their native element, perhaps in favor of a more perfect and uncompromised rendering of the fish itself. Even when the fish were still partly in the water, Homer tended not to interfere with their image by showing the splashy disturbance of the water that usually attended such action. The stories told in *Life-size Black Bass,* 1904 (fig. 99, ill. p. 179), and *Black Bass, Florida,* 1904 (fig. 98, ill. p. 178), would have been treated much differently by almost any later outdoor artist. Bass are large, active fish whose explosive acrobatics invariably take place in wild, scattering showers of lake water. Homer's bass are emerging from perfectly still water, not at all like the disturbed water that would surround creatures in such violent motion.

Spotted Weakfish (Sea Trout), Homosassa, Florida, for Mrs. R. A. Watts, mentioned earlier, is a good example of the kinds of subtle storytelling Homer engaged in when showing the playing of fish. If this is, as it appears, a portrayal of a fish struggling to escape from the angler, it also depicts a minor embarrassment or disappointment for that angler. The fish is "foul-hooked," which is to say that it is not hooked conventionally in the mouth. It is instead snagged well back from the mouth, apparently on the right gill plate.

Foul-hooking often occurs when the fish has approached the fly but for some reason has chosen not to strike, but then has become snagged anyway; perhaps just as the fish turned away from the fly, the angler happened to give the line a tug to make the fly more attractive, and the fish was in the way

CAT. 50
Channel Bass, Florida, 1904. Watercolor over graphite on paper, 11 1/16 × 19 1/8 in. The Metropolitan Museum of Art,
George A. Hearn Fund, 1952 (52.155). Photograph © 1989 The Metropolitan Museum of Art

and became hooked. It also can occur entirely by accident, when the fly, moving through the water, simply hangs up on the fish's sides or fins regardless of the fish's interest; the fish was just in the wrong place at the wrong time. As the fly slides along the side of the fish, the angler, feeling resistance, may assume that a fish has taken the fly. At that point the angler sets the hook, which becomes randomly embedded in the fish's fin or body.

Of course to keep a fish caught by such means is considered poor sportsmanship, so after having successfully played and landed the fish, the angler discovers the problem and experiences a kind of retroactive embarrassment. The picture in this case gives us no clues as to why this particular saltwater fish has become foul-hooked, but the fact that it has adds a twist to the scene that angler-viewers will appreciate.

FIG. 36
Waterfall, Adirondacks, 1889. Watercolor over graphite on paper, 13 ⅝ × 19 ⅝ in. Freer Gallery of Art, Smithsonian Institution, Washington, D.C. Gift of Charles Lang Freer (F1912.78)

A similar complication has occurred in *Channel Bass, Florida,* 1904 (cat. 50). In this picture the fish may not be hooked at all. For whatever reason, this fish has managed to entangle its mouth in the leader, though the hook of the fly is actually extending below its jaw. What Homer achieves in these pictures is the stimulation of the angler-viewer's curiosity—what do *we* think is happening here? Perhaps the fish grabbed the fly at first, then in its struggle rolled completely over, entangling its jaw hinge in the leader. Meanwhile, the hook came loose, leaving the fish precariously connected only to the line. In a situation like this, whether or not the angler finally does land the fish will depend partly on keeping a good tension on the line. But it will probably depend even more on dumb luck.

Other stories are told by larger fishing scenes in which the angler and the fish are both shown. It is useful in this context to again respectfully disagree with an art historian. In her beautiful book *Winslow Homer Watercolors* (1986), Helen Cooper made the following statement about *A Good Pool, Saguenay River,* 1895 (cat. 30, ill. p. 48):

The three tiny men in the canoe are in dramatic juxtaposition—at left, a French-Canadian guide; in the middle, the fisherman in his deerstalker cap; and, at right, an Indian wearing a feather headdress and a red sash. The precarious position of the fishermen in the turbulent water adds to the tension of their struggle to land the fish. The elegant sweep of the casting line declares the experience and discipline of the angler, while the vigorous, rapid watercolor technique— scraped paper at the right to suggest foam, and bold sweeps of orange and bright blue washes for the waves—underscores the movement, challenge, and unpredictability of the contest.[21]

The descriptions of the artistic elements and techniques may well be perfectly accurate, but the fisherman is showing neither experience nor discipline. Under these circumstances, in fact, it is hard to imagine how the angler could be behaving more badly.

CAT. 27
Playing Him [The North Woods], 1894. Watercolor over graphite on paper,
15 ⅛ × 21 ½ in. The Currier Gallery of Art, Manchester, New Hampshire.
Gift of Mr. and Mrs. Frederic Haines Curtiss (1960.13)

Most important, the picture reveals why generations of anglers have been fond of the parting phrase, "Tight lines!" It is a nearly ancient axiom of the sport that under almost all circumstances there must be no slack between the end of the rod and the fish; slack line greatly increases the likelihood that the hook will come loose. Look at the fish, then follow the leader from its mouth. The leader swirls around in easy curves off to the right, where the second fly (the "dropper") is bright against the dark water. From there it is impossible to determine quite where the leader and line go, but eventually they make their way back to the angler, who has his own additional problems. Rather than having the rod aimed forward, more or less at the fish, he has hauled it back well behind him, thus further increasing the amount of loose line between himself and the fish. With the rod in this position, the angler has the least possible chance of applying greater pressure on the fish, which is, for all practical purposes, as out of control as a hooked fish can be. Things are not going well here, and elegance, discipline, and experience seem to be in short supply.

If a generalization may be hazarded about Homer's pictures of fish being played, it is that he seems to have dearly loved showing the strain and arc of a long, flexible fly rod under the weight of a strong fish—even if he had to make the fisherman look a little clumsy to do so. As already mentioned, the rods of his day were both long and limber, and he rarely even gave us a clear indication of where the rod ended and the line began. In picture after picture, including *The Painter Eliphalet Terry Fishing from a Boat,* 1874 (fig. 15, ill. p. 41), *Waterfall, Adirondacks,* 1889 (fig. 36), *St. John's River, Florida,* 1890 (cat. 21, ill. p. 170), *Boy Fishing,* 1892 (cat. 24, ill. p. 115), *Playing Him,* 1894 (cat. 27), and *Homosassa Jungle in Florida,* 1904 (cat. 51, ill. p. 176), Homer gave us a short course in the dynamics of a hard-working fishing rod. In most of these pictures,

the rod appears capable of flexing clear back to its handle, which it certainly was. Modern anglers, unfamiliar with the extreme flexibility of the rods of Homer's time, may be surprised or even skeptical at the sight of rods bent as much as three quarters of a circle, but such was the reality of the day; fish were played somewhat more cautiously back then, just as lines and flies were cast more gently, but the job still got done.[22]

THE FISH

Homer's fish are, of course, magnificent. If we accept the one condition with which Homer seems to present us—that we suspend concern over the lack of water on them when they fly through the air—we find little or nothing else to mind about them. The sharkish dorsal fin on the landlocked salmon in *A Good Pool, Saguenay River* (cat. 30, ill. p. 48) is perhaps a little unconvincing, but even there Homer somehow gets away with it.

The great safety net under all wildlife artists is that nature is so full of variation that almost any reasonably accurate portrayal of a given species of animal is defensible. Add to that natural variability the infinite additional possibilities provided by perspective and natural light, and our eye is really quite forgiving, even if the artist isn't as masterful as Homer clearly was. In nature, the brook trout, apparently Homer's favorite fish subject (cat. 23), appears in countless variants, depending on local environment and its own genetic makeup. All of Homer's brook trout, though they may look very little like each other, do in fact look like real brook trout.

This does not mean that they are portrayed doing typical things. Presumably for reasons of clarity of presentation, Homer's airborne fish are virtually always seen broadside, in the middle of perfectly even, tastefully arcing jumps. Many jumps by fish (perhaps most among hooked fish) are not

CAT. 23
A Brook Trout, 1892. Watercolor over graphite on paper, 13 ¾ × 19 ¾ in. Private collection

this symmetrical, nor are they this conveniently photogenic. Once in the air, hooked fish operate in three planes, with their bodies angled, rolled, and torqued in endless contortions of panic and flight. But this is not necessarily a valid criticism, because nothing Homer shows us is impossible, or even improbable, in nature. Though the modern eye might be more receptive to a fish that isn't so flatly presented, it was not necessarily Homer's obligation

to show us all those variations. He was certainly within his rights to show us the more conventional, even photographically convenient, positions of fish that he did.

Moreover, it is clear he knew that fish did not always jump as if posing for tackle-company brochures. Homer's jumping fish that were shown at a greater distance were usually presented in less diagnostic poses than the close-ups. When jumping fish were part of a larger scene (rather than a device to facilitate a more or less formal fish portrait), they flexed and twisted with remarkable verisimilitude. The two airborne fish in *Under the Falls, the Grand Discharge, Lake St. John, P.Q.* (cat. 37, ill. p. 146) are convincingly active individuals in this regard. The two bass pictures that were mentioned earlier for their lack of accompanying splashes are in fact terrifically accurate otherwise; countless later artists and photographers captured largemouth bass in precisely these attitudes—twisting and climbing up into the air, rattling their gills (the vivid red in the gills in Homer's pictures has been verified in countless high-speed photographs), and shaking their gaping mouth in a desperate effort to dislodge the fly.

CONCLUSIONS

To a far greater extent than has been generally recognized, Winslow Homer truly was an angler-artist and, even more important, an angler's artist. His lovely, bucolic scenes of anglers and angling action are satisfactory not only as enjoyable vignettes of outdoor recreation in his day but also as animated episodes in the lives of real anglers facing real angling situations.

The fishermen who choose to can look deeply into these scenes. When they do, and when they overcome their awe at the perfection and the beauty, they will find curiosities, mysteries, and maybe even a few jokes. Most of all they will see that stories are being told beyond the simple portrayal of some person trying to catch a fish. Some of the stories are fairly dramatic, while others just reveal the odd little misadventures that all anglers encounter if they spend enough time on the water. But all of them send us a trustworthy message—that we are being engaged, entertained, and even inspired by a fellow angler who has "been there" and knows as well as we do what makes this sport so special.

Winslow Homer's fly-fishing art sends us more important messages than that, of course. It sends us glorious messages about the physical, aesthetic, and spiritual rewards of a life so closely connected to the wonders of the aquatic world. For those who love the life of rivers and lakes, there is a special truth in Homer's famous prediction, "You will see, in the future I will live by my watercolors."[23] As long as there are fly fishers, and as long as they are the least bit reflective about the beauty of their sport and its environs, Homer will most assuredly live among them.

NOTES

1. The premier institution collecting historical artifacts relating to fly-fishing is The American Museum of Fly Fishing, Manchester, Vermont, which houses the fishing tackle of many of these historically famous anglers, including that of Winslow Homer.

2. Important books on the history of fly-fishing or sport angling include William Radcliffe, *Fishing from Earliest Times* (London: Murray, 1921); John Waller Hills, *A History of Fly Fishing for Trout* (London: Allan, 1921); Charles Waterman, *A History of Angling* (New York: Winchester Press, 1981); Paul Schullery, *American Fly Fishing: A History* (New York: Lyons & Burford Publishers, 1987); and Andrew Herd, *The Fly* (Shropshire: The Medlar Press, 2002). The foremost source of historical information on fly-fishing is the quarterly journal of The American Museum of Fly Fishing, *The American Fly Fisher,* which has been published since 1974.

3. Homer's illustration *The Straw Ride,* which originally appeared in *Harper's Weekly,* September 25, 1869, 620, shows a buggy whip at work. Homer has compressed its backward stroke with a pair of curves, perhaps to keep the whole whip within the available space of the scene. But the image is similar to the curving fly line of *Casting, "A Rise."* See Barbara Gelman, *The Wood Engravings of Winslow Homer* (New York: Bounty Books, 1969), 131.

4. A surprisingly large number of people have been exposed to an example of these conflicting opinions and approaches. Norman Maclean's book *A River Runs through It, and Other Stories* (Chicago: University of Chicago Press, 1976) and Robert Redford's 1992 film based on the book portray a key period in the evolution of casting theory. The Maclean boys, Paul and Norman, are taught by their father the traditional, high-backcast conventions of fly casting, but as Paul's fishing skills grow, he develops his own approaches, which are vividly portrayed in a scene in the film, and which reach far beyond the formality of his father's method and ability. For more on the history of casting, with special emphasis on competition casting, see Cliff Netherton, *History of the Sport of Casting: People, Events, Records, Tackle and Literature, Early Times* (Lakeland, Fla.: American Casting Education Foundation, 1981).

5. Two standard references on the history of fly rods are Martin J. Keane, *Classic Rods and Rodmakers* (New York: Winchester Press, 1976); and A. J. Campbell, *Classic and Antique Fly-Fishing Tackle* (New York: Lyons & Burford Publishers, 1997).

6. Besides Keane and Campbell, in n. 5 above, see Luis Marden, *The Angler's Bamboo* (New York: Lyons & Burford Publishers, 1997).

7. G. Dick Finlay, "Museum Research and Technological Studies, Part I," in *The American Museum of Fly Fishing, Acquisitions Catalogue 1969–1973,* unpaginated, describes the Winslow Homer rod as follows:

The Winslow Homer Rod

Winslow Homer's brother stated Winslow was a good fisherman, always taking the most and largest fish. Homer painted his first series of fly fishing watercolors while at Mink Pond in the Adirondacks, vacationing with his longtime friends and former employers, the Bakers of Boston. Later he travelled to New Brunswick bringing back to his Prout's Neck studio his birch canoe. Although there is no published record of his fly fishing, his enthusiastic paintings of fly fishers and a water color in the Currier Museum at Manchester, N.H., a self portrait depicting him casting from his birch [bark canoe] entitled "The Fly Fisher," give good evidence of his participation. His fly rod bears his name.

B. F. Nichols Co., Boston, Mass. Calcutta bamboo; 3 pcs; extra tip; Nickel silver drawn ferrules and reel seat, butt cap and reel bands; Snake guides. Length 11 ft.; inscribed wood rod holder.

Curiously, when the museum journal illustrated the fly rod two years later (*The American Fly Fisher* 2, no. 2 [spring 1975]: 22), the caption read as follows: "Winslow Homer's fly rod in the Museum's exhibit. It is in such pristine condition that is seems doubtful if it was ever used."

This description of the condition of the rod was surprisingly inaccurate. I became director of the museum in 1977 and was able to examine the rod closely, and reexamined it on April 24, 2000, as it was being prepared for transport as part of the museum's traveling exhibit. It was obviously a well-used rod: both guides are missing from the butt section, at least one guide has been rewrapped, and there is a small amount of accumulated grime under some of the guides, as would be expected of a rod that had received at least light usage. Homer identified himself as the owner in three places. "W. HOMER____ Scarboro,____" is written on the rod-form "case"; "HOMER" is scratched on the reel seat just up from the reel slot; and "WHOMER" is scratched in a semicircle on the end of the butt cap. The most logical explanation for the error in the 1975 journal caption is that the editor, Austin Hogan, lived in Cambridge, Massachusetts, and visited the museum in Vermont only occasionally. He edited the journal by mail and telephone, and probably forgot the condition of the rod and could not examine it again before writing the brief caption.

8. David Tatham, *Winslow Homer in the Adirondacks* (Syracuse, N.Y.: Syracuse University Press, 1996), 58.

9. Paul Schullery, "Report on Fishing Tackle Examined at the Winslow Homer Studio, Prout's Neck, Maine, April 17, 2000," 6 pp., copies filed with Amon Carter Museum, Fort Worth, Texas; The Adirondack Museum, Blue Mountain Lake, New York; and The American Museum of Fly Fishing, Manchester, Vermont.

10. Bernard "Lefty" Kreh, in his modern classic *Fly Fishing in Salt Water* (New York: Crown, 1974) and other books, has been the foremost champion of an alternative low-backcast style of casting, which has become extremely popular in open-water situations such as are found in saltwater fly-fishing.

11. An extended discussion of the issue of loop width in a modern fly-fishing book appeared in Douglas Swisher and Carl Richards, *Fly Fishing Strategy* (New York: Crown, 1975), 46–56. Many others have followed, in a variety of excellent books on fly casting.

12. G.E.M. Skues, *The Way of a Trout with a Fly* (London: Adam & Charles Black, 1924; 4th ed., 1949). The fourth edition was the last revision by Skues. Its discussion of rise-forms is found on 48–68. Eric Taverner, *Trout Fishing from all Angles* (London: Seeley, Service, 1930), 262–276.

13. Vincent Marinaro, *In the Ring of the Rise* (New York: Crown, 1976).

14. The beautiful Homer painting *Trout Breaking*, 1889 (cat. 16, ill. p. 119), which shows a trout perhaps trying to grab one of two butterflies that are also shown, and *Fish and Butterflies*, 1900 (cat. 45, ill. p. 55), are other examples of these high-flying fish aerobatics.

15. Some excellent recent sources on the earliest known period of European fly-fishing, fisheries management, and fish culture are by the medievalist Richard Hoffmann, "A New Treatise on the Treatyse," *The American Fly Fisher* 9, no. 3 (1982): 2–6; "Fishing for Sport in Medieval Europe: New Evidence," *Speculum* 60, no. 4 (1985): 877–902; *Fisher's Craft and Lettered Art: Tracts on Fishing from the End of the Middle Ages* (Toronto: University of Toronto Press, 1997); "The Craft of Fishing Alpine Lakes, ca. 1500," *Offa* 15 (1994): 308–312; and "The Evidence for Early European Angling III: Conrad Gesner's Artificial Flies, 1558," *The American Fly Fisher* 2, no. 11 (1995): 2–11. See also Herd, *The Fly,* for additional new interpretations of this earliest known period of fly-fishing history.

16. Mary Orvis Marbury, *Favorite Flies and Their Histories* (Boston and New York: Houghton Mifflin, 1892). For the early publishing history of the Mary Orvis Marbury book, see Paul Schullery, "The Mary Orvis Marbury Fly Plates," *The American Fly Fisher* 6, no. 3 (summer 1979): 15–18.

17. At least it most closely seems to resemble that fly as it is presented in Marbury's book; the fly in the weakfish portrait appears to have darkly barred feather in the wing along with the red feather. The barred feather, perhaps mallard flank, does not appear in the "authentic" Scarlet Ibis, either as it is shown by Marbury or as it is described in other authoritative books, such as J. Edson Leonard, *Flies* (New York: A. S. Barnes and Company, 1950), 232, 284.

18. Charles Dudley Warner, *In the Wilderness* (Boston: Houghton Mifflin and Company, 1878).

19. William Henry Harrison Murray, *Adventures in the Wilderness; or, Camp-Life in the Adirondacks* (Boston: Fields, Osgood, & Co., 1869), 136A.

20. Warner, *In the Wilderness,* 41.

21. Helen A. Cooper, *Winslow Homer Watercolors,* exh. cat. (New Haven and London: Yale University Press for the National Gallery of Art, 1986), 204.

22. In *Adventures in the Wilderness,* Murray's illustration of a man in a boat playing a trout, in which the man's rod has formed a complete 360-degree circle, still raises eyebrows among skeptics, but Murray, writing of a favorite fly rod, maintained that "Many a time have I seen that rod doubled up until the quivering tip lay over the reel" (31). On the other hand, in Homer's painting *Ouananiche, Lake St. John,* 1897 (cat. 42, ill. p. 149), the rod is unaccountably short for a fly rod, though it appears the reel is mounted correctly for it to be a fly reel. More to the point of rod action, the action of this sort of rod is more like a modern graphite rod, with most of the bend in the tip, or like a heavier and stiffer trolling rod of Homer's day.

23. Homer to an unidentified friend, quoted in Cooper, *Winslow Homer Watercolors,* 239.

Winslow Homer
Time in the Adirondacks

Theodore E. Stebbins Jr.

WINSLOW HOMER'S ADIRONDACK WATERCOLORS OF 1889–1894 have been much admired since they were executed, and in recent years the details of when and where they were made, and of what they portray, have been thoroughly studied. However, relatively little attention has been paid to the meaning of these works in the context of their period, what Homer might have intended by them, or how they can be read in terms of the history of the Adirondacks and of American attitudes toward the wilderness. Nor have the development of this series or Homer's changing interests within the series been considered. These questions will be the subject of this paper.

It is now well known, largely through the research of David Tatham, that Homer first visited the Adirondacks in the 1870s, traveling both to Keene Valley, a small town in the High Peaks region that was already becoming popular as a summer resort and artists' colony in those years, and the more isolated Baker's farm situated near Minerva, New York, some thirty miles southwest of Keene Valley (fig. 37).[1] Here he would have found more privacy and serenity than in Keene Valley, and probably better fishing as well. In the handful of paintings, watercolors, and designs for wood engravings of the area that he made in this decade, Homer established his iconography of the region, depicting scenes of both deer hunting and lumbering, painting two well-known local guides—one old, one young —and finally, on two occasions making watercolors of men fishing alone from small boats on Adirondack lakes (see fig. 38, and fig. 15, ill. p. 41).[2]

There was nothing original in Homer's choice of subjects, for since the Adirondacks had first come to public attention in the 1840s and 1850s, the region was known as a wilderness good for little else besides fishing, hunting, and logging, and as a place where visitors needed guides. Charles Fenno Hoffman's (1806–1884) *Wild Scenes in the Forest and Prairie* of 1839 describes the author's adventures in hiking to "the sources of the Hudson" and his reliance on two legendary guides of the period, John Cheney and Harvey Holt.[3] In *The Adirondack; or, Life in the Woods* (1849), Joel Tyler Headley (1813–1897), establishing the view of the region that still reigns, said that he went to "seek mental repose and physical strength in the woods." He traveled throughout the area, favoring Raquette Lake in the center of the region, and most of his text was devoted to his adventures while trout fishing and hunting for deer, wolves, bear, and moose. Headley loved to fish, and he describes using a pole "cut from the forest," as he had purposefully left at home his "light and delicate rod."[4]

In 1869, the year before Homer's initial foray, William Henry Harrison ("Adirondack") Murray (1840–1904), a Yale graduate and for a time a popular Boston preacher, published his *Adventures in the Wilderness; or, Camp-Life in the Adirondacks.*[5] This

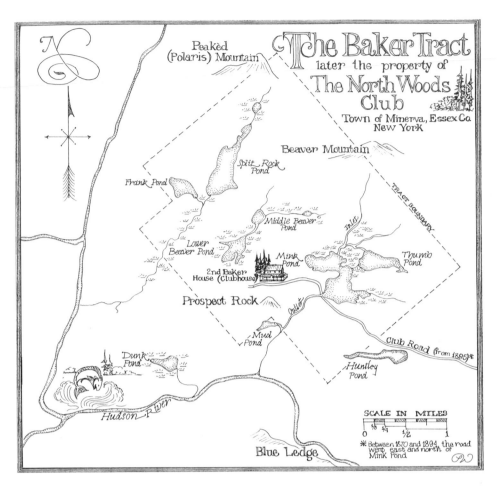

FIG. 37
Map of the Adirondack Region showing the Baker tract, later the property of the North Woods Club. Drawn by Lucie Wellner. The original version of this map was first published by David Tatham in *Winslow Homer in the Adirondacks* (Syracuse, N.Y.: Syracuse University Press, 1996).

[page 94]
DETAIL: CAT. 15
Sunrise, Fishing in the Adirondacks, 1889.
Watercolor over graphite on paper, 14 × 21 in.
Fine Arts Museums of San Francisco, Achenbach Foundation for Graphic Arts. Mildred Anna Williams Collection (1966.2)

volume was part guidebook—with matter-of-fact advice about where to go, where to stay, and what to take in the way of fishing and other gear—part tall tale—with its outlandish fishing escapades and ghost stories—and part medical advice—with the author swearing by the pure air of the Adirondacks for the cure of dyspepsia, consumption, or almost any other illness. Unaccountably, the book became immensely successful, going through eleven printings in a few months, and causing a flood of visitors to the region. As Paul Schneider writes in his excellent recent study of the area, in 1850 there were only a handful of places a visitor could stay, whereas by 1875 the Adirondacks boasted more than two hundred hotels—many of them built directly as a result of Murray's book.[6]

After 1877 Homer did not visit the region again until 1889, when he returned to Baker's clearing. It had recently been purchased by a group of sport- and conservation-minded business- and professional men from New York, Boston, and Albany, and its lodging house, lakes, and five thousand acres had in 1887 become the property of the Adirondack Preserve Association, which was later renamed the North Woods Club.[7] As such it was one of the more modest of the sixty or so private clubs that by the 1890s "together controlled hundreds of thousands of woodland acres."[8]

The club's register confirms that Homer went for two long stays during 1889, one of nine weeks from early May to mid-July, another of seven weeks from October 1 to late November.[9] During the nine-month period beginning with his arrival in May and extending through January 1890, Homer executed an extraordinary group of some thirty-seven watercolors devoted to Adirondack subjects.[10] He sent about thirty-two or thirty-three of them, along with two earlier oils, to his New York dealer Gustave Reichard for an exhibition—the only one of his life devoted wholly to Adirondack subjects—that ran from February 14 to March 1, 1890.[11]

Homer's watercolors received a warm reception. Almost all found buyers, and numerous contemporary critics recognized the painter's achievement. One writer admired "those effects of color, extreme breadth and facility of treatment and that science of abstraction on which the artist had based his powerful style."[12] Another saw in these works "a directness and simplicity, an individuality and character . . . that is inexpressibly refreshing," while a third lamented that Homer "rates himself below his proper worth," adding that he "ought to have asked more for these admirable water colors than $125 apiece."[13] Fishing scenes made up about two-thirds of the exhibition. They depicted men fishing from boats or, occasionally, beside streams or waterfalls; fish being netted; trout jumping from the dark waters or hanging from tree branches after having been caught. The show included other Adirondack subjects: guides in their boats, hunters and dogs in autumn, deer swimming for their lives, as well as a view of the forest and one of a log jam on the Hudson River, just a mile away.[14] But as the *New York Times* reported, "it is his trout-fishing pieces . . . that are richest in color and done with the greatest pleasure."[15]

After his successful exhibition, Homer took a year off before returning to the club for two visits in 1891. Following the pattern he had established in 1889, he went first in the early summer, for most of June and July—for the fishing, one would guess—and then returned in October for the hunting season. He did much the same in 1892, with two monthlong stays at the club, and he went back for a month in the early summer of 1894. During these four years (1891–1894), he produced another forty-nine watercolors devoted to Adirondack subjects (cat. 24, ill. p. 115).[16] These he sent to his dealers in New York and Boston; Doll & Richards in the latter city sold many of them for him, at new prices beginning at $175. Though they were exhibited with depictions of other locales, they continued to be

FIG. 38
Trapping in the Adirondacks, 1870. Wood engraving after Homer by J. P. Davis, 8 ¾ × 11 ½ in. From *Every Saturday,* December 24, 1870. Bowdoin College Museum of Art, Brunswick, Maine. Gift of Howard S. Reid

FIG. 39
Guide Carrying a Deer, 1891. Watercolor over graphite on paper, 14 × 20 in.
Portland Museum of Art, Portland, Maine. Bequest of Charles Shipman Payson (1988.55.10)

singled out for critical acclaim. Thus a writer for the *Boston Evening Transcript* commented in December 1892, "we have looked over a portfolio of his water-color sketches of the Adirondacks, where he has lately been hunting, . . . and we are more than ever impressed by the superb breadth and mastery."[17]

In this second Adirondack series, Homer's earlier concentration on fish and fishing was replaced by a heightened interest in deer hunting and in the Adirondack guides (fig. 39).[18] The earlier series had spoken eloquently to the beauty of the trout them-selves, especially their magical grace and color, and to the skill of the fisherman guiding his boat across the still, dark waters, making long, lyrical casts with rod and line, and in bringing the fish to the net. Homer showed that he knew and loved the sport, which in the end has far more to do with the inexpressible beauty of being alone on a still lake at

twilight, with the love of the quiet and the antici-pation involved, and a devotion to purposeful solitude, than to whatever one might catch. The new watercolors were quite different. Hunting, unlike fishing, is a communal sport, undertaken in pairs or groups of people. The game is stalked or hounded by men and dogs, and the enterprise is punctuated with the noise of barking hounds, hunters calling out, and guns being discharged. Unlike a day of fishing, a hunt without a kill is a failure. It requires as much ability to track and kill a deer as to catch a trout, but the sports themselves and the skills required are dissimilar.

Homer's watercolor technique, already honed to a high pitch in 1889–1890 (Judith Walsh found in these works "an almost perfect exploitation of the transparency, fluidity, and apparent spontaneity of watercolor"[19]), somehow grew even richer as

Homer's mastery of the medium climaxed between 1892 and 1894. His brushstrokes in *Deer Drinking*, 1892 (fig. 40), its dark palette enlivened with brilliant touches of yellow in the water, become more calligraphic than before even while continuing to serve his illustrative ends. It is no wonder that works like this have been called both "realistic" and "abstract," for they are indeed both. While Homer's watercolors of fish and fishing are studies of a hushed, twilight world, his depictions of the hunt show it occurring at all hours of the day, the intrinsic excitement of the chase often enlivened with brilliant autumn colors. Homer recorded every phase of the hunt as he had the fishing expedition, demonstrating as much interest in the beauty of the deer at the edge of a lake as he had in the jumping trout. He showed the deer both during the chase and after being killed, just as he had shown the trout. But because people are likely to feel more kinship with the large, warm-blooded victim of the chase than the small, cold-blooded ones, Homer's contemporaries and some modern observers have found his hunters "low and brutal in the extreme" and the hunt itself an "intense natural tragedy."[20] Homer himself was both a hunter and fisherman; Tathum's researches demonstrate that he participated in one hunt in the fall of 1892, and there is every reason to believe—given the watercolors—that he went on many.[21]

On the reverse of his watercolor *Fallen Deer*, 1892 (fig. 41), which depicts a beautiful, freshly killed doe, he wrote, "Just shot—a miserable [illegible] pot hunter," perhaps showing his anger at a trespasser who had hunted on club property (as Tatham suggests). There is little evidence as to what position Homer took in the ongoing debate in the 1880s and 1890s caused by the decline in the number of deer, which shortly thereafter led to a prohibition of "hounding" of deer with dogs and guide boats (1901) and later to limiting hunters to one doe per season (1919).[22] There seem few grounds

FIG. 40
Deer Drinking, 1892. Watercolor over graphite on paper, 14 1/16 × 20 1/16 in. Yale University Art Gallery, New Haven, Connecticut. The Robert W. Carle, B.A. 1897, Fund

FIG. 41.
Fallen Deer, 1892. Watercolor over graphite on paper, 13 3/4 × 19 3/4 in. Museum of Fine Arts, Boston. Charles Henry Hayden Fund. © Museum of Fine Arts, Boston

CAT. 14
A Quiet Pool on a Sunny Day, 1889. Watercolor over graphite on paper, 13 × 20 in.
Kevin Kennedy Collection, Courtesy of the James Graham & Sons Gallery, New York

CAT. 10
Fishing in the Adirondacks, 1889. Watercolor over
graphite on paper, 14 × 20 in. Private collection

FIG. 42
Alvah Dunning, Adirondack Guide and Hunter, 1891. Photograph by Seneca
Ray Stoddard (1844–1917), Glens Falls, New York. The Adirondack Museum,
Blue Mountain Lake, New York

for Nicolai Cikovsky's position that Homer "often depicted [the guides'] uncaring cruelty to life and nature with an intensity of feeling," and that in these works the artist indicted "their inhumane savagery."[23] Given the values of Homer's period, as one sees from contemporary hunting and fishing literature, the hunts he recorded were both common-place and completely acceptable. However, in his work Homer does seem to suggest that hunting is a sport for unthinking young men, just as fishing is an activity for thoughtful, older ones.

All of Homer's hunters, and most of his fisher-men as well, are—importantly—locals. He does not record the daily events he would have seen at the club or much of the fishing and hunting carried on by the men and women members, or "sports," as they were called. Rather, his subjects are natives, the men who off-season worked as loggers, caretakers, or builders, but who in season became Adirondack guides. By Homer's time, the great guides of the past had already become legendary, and people looked with longing to the "golden years" of the Adirondacks (the thirty years before Murray's book appeared), when such giants as Bill Nye, Alvah Dunning (fig. 42), and Orson ("Old Mountain") Phelps had formed their reputations.[24] The great guide by definition was prodigiously strong, for he had to be able to carry heavy provisions, the wooden guide boat, and sometimes an injured "sport" as well. Skill with an axe was taken for granted, for the guide could build a passable lean-to in a few hours, and a cabin in days. He could set a roaring fire with the wettest wood. He tracked deer, bear, and other game in all seasons; handled the dogs; knew the mountains and the trails; and he rowed the guide boat swiftly and tirelessly. He was an expert fisherman, who knew every method for bringing even the most wary trout to the net. He cooked mouthwatering meals, though his repertoire was limited (flapjacks and venison being his staples). He was coolheaded in times of crisis, and he was well mannered and sober, at least on the job. And, if he aspired to fame, he became a great storyteller as well, one who built his own legend and added to the pleasure of those under his care with tales of harrowing escapes, great adventures, and triumphal fishing and hunting expeditions. The painter-photographer William James Stillman (1828–1901), who ventured to the Adirondacks in 1858 with such companions as Ralph Waldo Emerson (1803–1882) and Louis Agassiz (1807–1873), described the guides as "rude men of the woods, rough and illiterate, but with all their physical faculties at a maximum acuteness, senses on the alert and keen as no townsman could comprehend them."[25] Above all, the guide was "true as steel," as Joel Tyler Headley wrote of the legendary Mitchell Sabattis.[26] The guides were indispensable figures; without them, the "sport" had little chance of enjoying the wilderness experience, and there were times when his life depended on them.

The guides themselves, whether fishing, hunting, or simply observing the woods, became increasingly important subjects for Homer. He characterizes these men as indigenous figures as completely at home in the woods as the deer, the trout, and the ancient trees of the forest. Homer would surely have agreed with Thoreau when he said, "Fishermen, hunters, woodchoppers, and others, spending their lives in the fields and woods, in a peculiar sense a part of Nature themselves, are often in a more favorable mood for observing her . . . than philosophers or poets even, who approach her with expectation."[27] In the watercolors of 1889–1890, the painter clearly distinguishes between the visitors, with their store-bought outfits

FIG. 43
The Guide, 1889. Watercolor over graphite on paper, 14 × 20 in. Portland Museum of Art, Portland, Maine. Bequest of Charles Shipman Payson (1988.55.8)

FIG. 44
Adirondack Guide, 1894. Watercolor over graphite on paper, 15 ⅛ × 21 ½ in. Museum of Fine Arts, Boston. Bequest of Mrs. Alma H. Wadleigh. © Museum of Fine Arts, Boston

Sketch for "Hound and Hunter," 1892. Watercolor over graphite on paper, 13 15/16 × 20 7/8 in. National Gallery of Art, Washington, D.C. Gift of Ruth K. Henschel in memory of her husband, Charles R. Henschel. Photograph © 2002 Board of Trustees, National Gallery of Art

The Blue Boat, 1892. Watercolor over graphite on paper, 15 1/8 × 21 1/2 in. Museum of Fine Arts, Boston. Bequest of William Sturgis Bigelow. © Museum of Fine Arts, Boston

(as in *An Unexpected Catch,* cat. 18, ill. p. 112, or *Netting the Fish,* cat. 20, ill. p. 44), and the guides, with their old clothes and their hats pulled down around their ears (see *A Quiet Pool on a Sunny Day,* cat. 14, ill. p. 100, and *Fishing in the Adirondacks,* cat. 10, ill. p. 101).

The older guide who appears in many of Homer's watercolors is a bearded, ageless figure apparently based on one of the men who worked at Baker's Farm/North Woods Club, Rufus Wallace.[28] He appears with his dog in *Adirondack Woods, Guide and Dog* (Montgomery [Alabama] Museum of Fine Arts), among charred stumps in *A Guide and Woodsman* (Museum of Fine Arts, Boston), and skillfully paddling his guide boat through heavily wooded waters in *The Guide* (fig. 43), all of 1889.

In the later series, dating from 1891–1894, Homer gives up depicting the "sports" altogether and concentrates on the guides themselves. The same older guide is included in numerous compositions, not fishing now but rather contemplating an ancient tree, and perhaps his own mortality, in *Old Friends,* 1894 (Worcester [Massachusetts] Art Museum), or going hunting by himself. He is pictured in a simple rowboat, with his back to us, turning as if to listen to a sound in the brilliant nearly fauve-colored *Adirondack Guide,* 1894 (fig. 44). Increasingly he is found in the company of a much younger guide, a figure Homer based on the nineteen-year-old Michael Francis Flynn, who apparently worked at the club for only two years, 1891 and 1892.[29] Flynn appears in Homer's work almost always as a hunter, posing as the central figure in both of the painter's major Adirondack oils of these years, *Huntsman and Dogs,* 1891 (Philadelphia Museum of Art), and *Hound and Hunter,* 1892 (National Gallery of Art), in the watercolor versions of both pictures (see fig. 45), and in a number of other compositions as well. For Homer, he must have been the perfect young local, with his stolid, even loutish

CAT. 25
Canoeing in the Adirondacks, 1892. Watercolor over graphite
on paper, 15 ½ × 20 in. James and Frances McGlothlin

FIG. 47
Log Jam at Luzerne Falls, ca. 1880s–1890s. Photograph by Seneca Ray Stoddard (1844–1917),
Glens Falls, New York. The Adirondack Museum, Blue Mountain Lake, New York

FIG. 48
Log Jam, Hudson River at Blue Ledge, Essex County [The Log Jam], 1889. Watercolor over graphite on paper,
14½ × 21 in. Norton Museum of Art, West Palm Beach, Florida. Bequest of R. H. Norton (53.83)

appearance, his obvious physical strength, and his unthinking gaze. One is not surprised to see him carrying a recently killed deer on his shoulder or holding another by the antlers after having drowned it in the lake.

In a half dozen works of 1892, the two guides hunt together as a team, the older man—one senses —bringing his wisdom and experience to the venture, the younger one his strength and his willingness to learn (cat. 25). In some of the watercolors, such as *The End of the Hunt* (fig. 53, ill. p. 110), the men's purpose is made clear by the presence of dogs or the deer carcass in their boat. In others, there are only subtle indications of what they are doing. The justifiably admired *The Blue Boat* (fig. 46), for example, shows the older guide in his usual stern position in the boat, paddling it on a narrow inlet while his companion turns to face forward, staring intently into the distance. One surmises that they have heard or seen some hint of game; that they are hunting is confirmed only by the butt of a rifle glinting in the sun. A contemporary of Homer's described a similar scene: "Frank, the guide, neither smiles nor speaks; he has resumed his paddle, and, with that quiet, slow movement of his head peculiar to guides, and which we cannot imitate, he is scanning the shore, dimly lit by the twilight."[30]

Homer painted the Adirondacks, not as they were, but as they were said to have been. He portrayed them as the home of plentiful three-pound trout and endless game, as a place inhabited from time immemorial only by woodsmen, an unspoiled wilderness where railroads, steamships, millionaires' camps, and luxury hotels were unknown. As Helen Cooper, among other historians, has recognized, Homer was far from being "a flaming realist—a burning devotee of the actual," as Kenyon Cox had described him and as critics continued to think of him until recently.[31] Rather, as Cooper points out, the artist's Adirondack watercolors "present a purified ideal of the angling life."[32] In fact, the

CAT. 28

The Rapids, Hudson River, Adirondacks, 1894. Watercolor over graphite on paper, 15 ⅛ × 21 ½ in.
The Art Institute of Chicago. Mr. and Mrs. Martin Ryerson Collection (1933.1250)

FIG. 49
Prospect House, Blue Mountain Lake, New York, built by Frederick Durant, beginning in 1879.
Photograph by Edward Bierstadt (1824–1906). The Adirondack Museum, Blue Mountain Lake, New York

FIG. 50
Brush Cottage, on the grounds of the North Woods Club, built by member Charles Brush, 1894–1895.
Photographer unknown. The Adirondack Museum, Blue Mountain Lake, New York

Adirondacks that the painter depicted had largely vanished by 1890, or were widely perceived to have vanished, under pressure from loggers on the one hand and tourists on the other. One traveler on the Saranac River commented in 1885, "We all look with disquiet at the frequent barren hillsides, either covered with blackened stumps or else so denuded of timber"; another reported in 1891, "the havoc of lumbermen is seen on every hand and is constantly increasing."[33] As a matter of record, Paul Schneider tells us, "by 1885 some two-thirds of the forest in the Adirondacks had been cut over for spruce at least once." And by then the loggers were being sent back for a second and third cutting, now going for trees down to five inches in diameter.[34]

Everyone seemed to have the old days in mind. Article after article in the sporting journals described the pristine wilds, with huge fish and plentiful game, of a half century before. The lead article in *Forest and Stream* for August 27, 1891, for example, spoke of those who had "known the region in its primitive condition, when the sportsman might go wheresoever his own sweet will prompted, fish in any and all waters unmolested, follow deer without let or hindrance, and camp where fancy dictated." The halcyon early days were contrasted with the present: "The Adirondacks of today stand largely for a district of vast private parks and preserves, posted with trespass notices and guarded by primitive police; of lakes plowed by steamboats and dominated by huge summer hotels; of sickening woodland wastes devastated by the ax and by fire."[35]

The newspapers and magazines of the day were full of such material. While these dire views sound hyperbolic today, they were genuinely and widely felt, and they were based on considerable evidence. The Adirondacks had seen dramatic change, even in the years since Homer's first visit in 1870. One reason he had left Keene Valley, which was situated far more picturesquely among the mountains than was the North Woods Club, may have been the plethora of artists already at work there, not to mention the hotels and the many summer visitors. At Blue Mountain Lake, just fifteen miles west of Baker's clearing, Frederick Durant in 1879 began building Prospect House, which boasted three hundred rooms, along with bowling alleys, a wax museum, and daily water sports and concerts (fig. 49).[36] Paul Smiths at Lower St. Regis Lake was even larger, with five hundred rooms. Moreover, many guides went to work for the hotels, with the result that their profession was diluted and diminished. A sign of the changing times was the formation in 1891 of the Adirondack Guides Association, something that surely would have been unthinkable for the stalwart, independent characters who had pioneered the profession fifty years earlier.[37]

By the 1870s a million logs a year were being floated out of the Adirondacks, and almost every river of any size was reserved for this use, as one sees in Homer's several watercolors of logs in the Hudson River, which lies only a mile from Baker's (figs. 47, 48). The logging companies had built a number of railroads to facilitate removal of the timber, and in 1892 "William Seward Webb, a son-in-law of Cornelius Vanderbilt Whitney, completed the first railroad to cross the heart of the park."[38] Webb himself in 1892 built his magnificent Forest Lodge in Nehasane Park (which in Indian meant "beaver-crossing-river-on-a-log"), his 34,000-acre property on the western side of the Adirondacks (figs. 51A, 51B). Finally, there were the Adirondack "camps" that were constructed by the rich, largely in the Raquette Lake region. First, in 1878, came William West Durant's Camp Pine Knot, which combined the Adirondack log cabin with "the long low lines of the graceful Swiss chalet," from which blend came the architectural style found in all of the Great Camps to follow.[39] In the same year, he established his Blue Mountain and Raquette Lake Steamboat Line. Numerous camps followed, each

FIG. 51A
Forest Lodge, Nehasane Park, the Adirondacks, built by William Seward Webb, 1892. Photograph by T. E. Marr, Boston. The Adirondack Museum, Blue Mountain Lake, New York

FIG. 51B
Living Room of Forest Lodge, Nehasane Park, the Adirondacks, built by William Seward Webb, 1892. Photograph by T. E. Marr, Boston. The Adirondack Museum, Blue Mountain Lake, New York

FIG. 52
Guides and dogs in a guide boat on an Adirondack lake, 1880s–1890s. Photograph by Seneca Ray
Stoddard (1844–1917), Glens Falls, New York. The Adirondack Museum, Blue Mountain Lake,
New York. The guide at right has been identified as Charles Oblenis, Stoddard's brother-in-law.

FIG. 53
The End of the Hunt, 1892. Watercolor over graphite on paper, 15 ⅛ × 21 ⅜ in. Bowdoin
College Museum of Art, Brunswick, Maine. Gift of Misses Harriet and Sophie Walker

larger and more extravagant than the last. The Stokes family took eleven servants to their camp on Upper St. Regis Lake beginning in 1883, and some of their neighbors (including the Whitneys, Carnegies, Vanderbilts, Morgans, and Huntingtons) required more.[40] Between 1890 and 1892, Durant himself hired a crew of two hundred men to build Uncas—named, in all likelihood without irony, for the Native American character in James Fenimore Cooper's (1789–1851) *Last of the Mohicans.* With its huge central lodge and numerous out-buildings including a blacksmith shop and farm, it was luxurious enough to satisfy J. P. Morgan, who acquired it in 1895.[41] Even the North Woods Club was not immune: the main building there was a simple, three-story log structure of 1863 that served as clubhouse, but in 1894–1895 member Charles Brush built for himself an elegant "camp" with three levels of decorative porch-railings in the Swiss style (fig. 50).

It may be instructive to compare Homer's watercolors of the Adirondacks with the photographs of the same region by his contemporary Seneca Ray Stoddard.[42] While Homer was an upper-middle-class club-member, who visited the area on vacations, Stoddard was a native who lived and worked for his entire career in Glens Falls, which lies a few miles from the boundary of the future Adirondack Park. And where Homer made about one hundred twenty Adirondack works in all media between 1870 and 1908, all devoted to the limited number of subjects we have discussed, Stoddard moved indefatigably over the area during the same period making thousands of different images of a far greater range of subjects. These photographs "furnish evidence," as Susan Sontag puts it, of a very different Adirondacks than Homer suggests.[43] At times, Homer and Stoddard are remarkably close, as when the photographer captures on film two hunters in a guide boat with their dogs and a dead buck (fig. 52). The photograph tells us that

Homer's mythic renderings of the same subject (fig. 53) are grounded in fact, as we suspected. We notice also how democratic the camera's eye is, how every facet of foreground and background are given equal attention, while the watercolorist by contrast blurs out the background to draw our attention to the figures in the boat.

Stoddard's patrons were the visitors who flooded the Adirondacks in the years after Murray's book, the very people Homer assiduously avoided both in his art and in his life. These weekend adventurers did not know or care much about the Adirondack wilderness of yesteryear; instead, they enjoyed its old lakes and trails, and its new hotels and steamships, as they found them. Like the rich, they returned with souvenirs that attested to their wilderness experience: but instead of bearskins and stuffed heads of moose and deer, they bought Stoddard's photographs of mountains and lakes, boating parties, hunters and guides, trains and steamboats, logging on the Hudson, and of the grand new camps of the wealthy and the magnificent hotels in which visitors stayed (figs. 54, 55). Stoddard photographed everything he thought the tourist might want to preserve as memories of his trip, allowing the buyer to do his own editing of the Adirondack experience. For his more sophisticated audience, Homer on the other hand created timeless Adirondack images, editing out all references to the tourist boom and to the attendant "improvements" it brought in terms of travel and accommodation.

Interestingly, Homer's favorite Adirondack subject, trout fishing, rarely figures in Stoddard's work. One knows from the guidebooks (including Stoddard's own) and from other sources that fishing remained a popular recreation in these years, so one wonders why this quintessential Adirondack activity, so privileged by Homer, was largely edited out by Stoddard. The reason may lie in the two media. Homer, working in watercolor, could make the tiny fish (which rarely weigh more than a pound and

FIG. 54
The steamer *Killoquah* at the bottom of Raquette Lake, the Adirondacks, 1880s.
Photograph by Seneca Ray Stoddard (1844–1917), Glens Falls, New York.
The Adirondack Museum, Blue Mountain Lake, New York

FIG. 55
On the piazza, Prospect House, Blue Mountain Lake, New York, 1880s.
Photograph by Seneca Ray Stoddard (1844–1917), Glens Falls, New York.
The Adirondack Museum, Blue Mountain Lake, New York

CAT. 18
An Unexpected Catch [A Disappointing Catch], 1889–1890. Watercolor over graphite on paper, 10 × 20 in.
Portland Museum of Art, Portland, Maine. Bequest of Charles Shipman Payson (1988.55.9)

FIG. 56
Mink Pond, 1891. Watercolor over graphite on paper, 13 ⅞ × 20 in. Harvard University Art Museum (Fogg Art Museum),
Cambridge, Massachusetts. Bequest of Granville L. Winthrop. © President and Fellows of Harvard College

FIG. 57
Pickerel Fishing, 1892. Watercolor over graphite on paper, 10 ¾ × 19 ½ in. Portland Museum of Art, Portland, Maine. Bequest of Charles Shipman Payson (1988.55.11)

average ten inches in length) as big as he wanted. When Stoddard did include the fish in his work, as in *Camp Life at Lake George, Aug. 7, 1876,*[44] the fish look so tiny as to be almost unnoticed. Moreover, the watercolorist could do things that the camera could not: he could render visible the invisible (such as line and leader), and he could stop action to portray the cast line stretching out over the water or the fish at the highest point on its leap.

The need to preserve what remained of the Adirondack forest, to protect the watershed, and to save the region from gross overdevelopment was widely felt, and beginning in the 1870s legislative efforts were made toward these ends. During exactly the years in which Homer was painting his great

watercolors, from 1889 to 1894, the debate about the future of the region and the need for its protection reached a climax. One can follow the ebb and flow of public opinion and of the changing political climate for preservation almost weekly in the pages of the magazine *Forest and Stream.* A first step in a long, complex process was taken when the state founded the New York Forest Preserve in 1885. In 1892 Adirondack Park, consisting of 2.8 million acres (of which the State of New York owned about one-fifth) was established, and finally and most important, toward the end of a long drought— caused in part, many thought, by the massive logging—the New York State Constitution was amended in the fall of 1894 to provide that the lands of the park "shall be forever kept as wild forest lands" and could never be sold or timbered.[45]

Finally, what about the big fish and plentiful deer, the great hunting and fishing, that had long been the hallmarks of the Adirondacks and that served as central themes in Homer's work there? Certainly no one would guess from his watercolors and paintings that any changes had occurred. Nor do the records of the North Woods Club suggest otherwise (at least at first glance), for the club's historian reports that "in 1890 seventy members (the high point for all time) took 500 trout and incidentally killed just five deer. . . ." But Leila Wilson goes on to say: "In 1890 and 1891 the New York State Commission provided 100,000 brook-trout fry for stocking Huntley, Beaver, Mink and Frank [Ponds], and then, in 1892, provided 20,000 brown-trout fry and 5,000 landlocked salmon plus some black bass for Beaver Pond."[46] Fish are "stocked" only when the native trout have been fished out, as a last resort. That the fishing was poor can be confirmed from the club's register in those years. Homer himself, avid and expert as he was, reported catching only six trout during his seven-week stay in June and July 1891 (though the waters had been stocked in May of that year).[47]

CAT. 24

Boy Fishing, 1892. Watercolor over graphite on paper, 15 ⅛ × 21 ½ in. San Antonio Museum of Art, Texas. Purchased with funds provided by the Robert J. and Helen Kleberg Foundation and Friends of the San Antonio Museum of Art (86.130)

This is not to say that stocking cannot produce exciting fishing. Troutlings bred in hatcheries and introduced to natural waters such as Beaver or Mink Ponds adapt quickly to their new environment, and fishing for them can be very like fishing for native fish. But there are two major differences. First, stocked fish are generally smaller than native ones; they are likely to be stocked, fished out, and stocked again, so the legendary big ones of yesteryear become only memories. Second, the fisherman (or -woman) knows when the waters contain stocked fish, and simply feels different than when angling for a native species. Fishing for stocked fish, within what was now a park, was far from a wilderness experience.

Homer's watercolors speak to the issue of fished-out waters. One of the most celebrated of the Adirondack works, *Mink Pond,* 1891 (fig. 56, ill. p. 113), portrays a magical corner of one of Homer's favorite fishing sites, but rather than portraying trout or anglers, it illustrates a standoff between a sunfish and a frog. *An Unexpected Catch* (cat. 18, ill. p. 112) shows a sport who is dressed to kill trying to pull his fly away from another sunfish, an inedible "junk" species abhorred by the fisherman. A third work, *Pickerel Fishing,* 1892 (fig. 57), pictures the tough young guide having caught a big pickerel, another species likely to replace trout and thus also a sign that the trout fishing was declining. As one contemporary of Homer's wrote, "Big Trout Lake contains no brook-trout; the savage pickerel or equally relentless bass have driven poor salmo fintinalis from these lovely waters."[48] Interestingly, Homer himself in 1894 reported in the Club House Register that his only catches for that season were two large pickerel.

The least remarked of Homer's Adirondack watercolors are the dozen or so compositions that have nothing to do with hunting, fishing, or the guides, but which are landscapes very much in the Hudson River School tradition. One group of these compositions (for example, *Log Jam, Hudson River at Blue Ledge, Essex County,* 1889, fig. 48, ill. p. 106) depicts the Hudson itself, the archetypal subject of John Frederick Kensett (1816–1878), Frederic Edwin Church (1826–1900), and their contemporaries. When Homer painted the Hudson, however, he showed it, not as it was in the old days—a pure stream flowing through an American paradise—but as it had become, an industrial conduit for the massive flow of twelve- and sixteen-inch logs to market.

The larger number of these works—about eight in all, dating between 1889 and 1894—are panoramic landscapes of the forest and hills near the North Woods Club and of mountains in the distance. Some are bleak indeed. *Valley and Hillside* (fig. 58) includes a foreground of fresh stumps, the result of recent cutting, in a composition that recalls works by Thomas Cole (1801–1848) and George Inness (1825–1894). *Hilly Landscape,* 1894 (private collection), depicts a ragged hawk presiding over a fresh, green landscape from the branches of a dead pine tree; the careful viewer will notice a road being cut into the wilderness. Other works from this series are more romantic, as Homer apparently looked to precedents from Chinese painting as he made of the Adirondacks an atmospheric or poetic dream. *Landscape in Morning Haze [Deer at Fence]* (Cooper-Hewitt, National Design Museum), with its spare, calligraphic touches, and *The Interrupted Tête-à-Tête, Adirondacks* (The Art Institute of Chicago), both from 1892, mark an atypical retreat into elegance for this rugged observer of nature. In a sense, Homer can be regarded as the last of the Hudson River School painters. Like Cole and Church and the others, he painted nature, not as backdrop, not as decoration, but as elemental, as lying at the very heart of American culture.

Homer largely ceased painting Adirondack subjects after 1894. He went back to the subject briefly in 1900, with a group of four watercolors, including one reprise of his trout fishing series

(*The Rise,* cat. 46, ill. p. 79) and one depiction of a woodchopper going out to take down the last large trees in the area (*The Pioneer,* fig. 59). In 1902 he took a last look at the mountains in the unremarkable *Burnt Mountain* (Addison Gallery of American Art, Andover Academy, Andover, Massachusetts).[49] Yet though the Adirondack subject matter, like the fishing there, was played out for Homer, he continued to go to the North Woods Club for the rest of his life, after 1894 making early summer visits of several weeks' duration in eleven of his remaining sixteen years.[50] Apparently, he never lost his affection for this American forest, but he stopped painting it when its iconography lost meaning for him, just when it was permanently established as a "forever wild" park, and at exactly the time—perhaps not coincidentally—when Frederick Jackson Turner (1861–1932) announced that America's western frontier no longer existed either.

The painter left behind no reminiscences that might shed light on his thinking, so we can only surmise that once he had completed painting the dream of the Adirondack past—the great guides and the unlimited trout and other game, all set in an unsullied wilderness—from the vantage of a much compromised present, he needed the inspiration of new, unspoiled fishing grounds to reenergize his art. In Quebec he found what he needed, in the form of larger, faster rivers; more powerful, wilder fish; and unspoiled nature. His Canadian watercolors of 1895, 1897, and 1902 have a freshness and vitality that reflect Homer's new environment. They are brilliant, but different; their paler tones and more limited palette, along with their reportorial quality and their concern for energy and motion, all distinguish them from the profound, introspective work done at the North Woods Club.

Critics have suggested that Homer was a "painter of modern life," a kind of American equivalent to Edouard Manet (1832–1883).[51] This view seems defensible for the Homer of the 1860s

CAT. 12
Jumping Trout, 1889. Watercolor over graphite on paper, 13 15/16 × 19 15/16 in.
Brooklyn Museum of Art, New York, in memory of Dick S. Ramsay (41.220)

CAT. 16
Trout Breaking [Rise to a Fly], 1889. Watercolor over graphite on
paper, 13 ⅞ × 19 ⅞ in. Museum of Fine Arts, Boston. Bequest of
John T. Spaulding (48.729). © Museum of Fine Arts, Boston

CAT. 15
Sunrise, Fishing in the Adirondacks, 1889. Watercolor over graphite on paper, 14 × 21 in.
Fine Arts Museums of San Francisco, Achenbach Foundation for Graphic Arts.
Mildred Anna Williams Collection (1966.2)

and 1870s. After all, he had been an illustrator of current fashions and current events for *Harper's* before and during the Civil War. But his paintings of the 1870s of boys on the farm or at the Gloucester shore are highly nostalgic, and by the time he got to England in 1881 he seems to have been in full retreat from the modern world. Many of his contemporaries, from Thomas Wilmer Dewing (1851–1938) and William Merritt Chase (1849–1916) to John La Farge (1835–1910) and Edmund Tarbell (1862–1938), working in differing styles in various locales, shared Homer's mind-set and like him sought meaning in the places and people untouched by the modern world. Like his fellow painters, Homer was responding in his own way to growing anxiety about a world increasingly ruled by timetables and standardized clocks, by the needs of the telegraph and the railroad.[52] When Homer recorded the life of the women at Cullercoats on the North Sea as they repaired fishnets and baskets, when he depicted the stalwart fishermen at the Grand Banks, and when he painted the last of the old-time Adirondack guides, he expressed his admiration both for the now outdated skills of these people and for his longing for simpler times.

In the Adirondacks, Homer explored time on a variety of levels. As we have seen, he employed present-day models, the local men, along with fish and deer and the landscape itself to evoke the mythic identity of that wilderness region. Like his contemporary Thomas Eakins (1844–1916), he painted people whom he admired, especially those with special skills and moral stature. Eakins painted the rowers, musicians, surgeons, and teachers of Philadelphia; Homer depicted the woodchopper, the guide, and the fisherman—figures from the wilderness, as skilled in their own ways, and as admirable, he tells us, as their urban counterparts. And like Eakins, though less scientifically, Homer was a student of stopped time. He did not require the photographic experiments of an Eadweard Muybridge (1830–1904)

to help him depict the white wake a boat leaves behind when steered across a still pond, the arched back of a leaping trout (cats. 12, 16, ill. pp. 118, 119), or the long, complex curve of a fisherman's line being cast (cat. 28, ill. p. 107). Homer was also a student of the time of day (cat. 15) and of the seasons, as he was of man's time on earth. The contrast between the young guide and the older one tells us of the hubris and energy of youth, of the knowledge and fatigue of age. Homer tells us also how days end, how the hunter's day, whatever the chronological hour, closes with a bloody death and the dead weight of a carcass, and how the fisherman's day seems to last and last until the onset of twilight first blends all natural forms into a common darkness, then finally, imperceptibly, becomes night.

NOTES

This article is dedicated with admiration to Beatrice Stewart ("Bobbie") Smith (1914–2001), who loved the Adirondacks with a contagious joy.

I owe special thanks in the preparation of this essay to Abigail Booth Gerdts, director of The Lloyd Goodrich and Edith Havens Goodrich/Whitney Museum of American Art Record of Works by Winslow Homer, in granting access to the Goodrich files. I am deeply grateful for the generosity of Patricia Junker at the Amon Carter Museum, and for the help of Theodore S. Wickersham of the North Woods Club; and I greatly appreciate the assistance of Kimberly Orcutt and Stephanie Mayer at the Fogg Art Museum. Caroline Welch and Jim Meehan at the Adirondack Museum provided generous assistance with the illustrations.

1. Homer went again in 1874, visiting both Keene Valley and the Baker Farm, and in 1877 he returned to Keene Valley. See David Tatham, *Winslow Homer in the Adirondacks* (Syracuse, N.Y.: Syracuse University Press, 1996); and Tatham, "Winslow Homer at the North Woods Club," in *Winslow Homer: A Symposium,* ed. Nicolai Cikovsky Jr. (Washington, D.C.: National Gallery of Art, 1990), 114–30.

2. See also the following works by Homer: *Deer-stalking in the Adirondacks in Winter,* wood engraving, *Every Saturday,* January 21, 1871; *Lumbering in Winter,* wood engraving, *Every Saturday,* January 28, 1871; and *Man in a Punt, Fishing,* watercolor (private collection), as listed by Tatham in *Winslow Homer in the Adirondacks,* 138–139.

3. Charles Fenno Hoffman, *Wild Scenes in the Forest and Prairie: With Sketches of Adirondack Life* (2 vols., London: Richard Bentley, 1839–1840; first American ed., 1 vol., New York: Colyer and Co., 1843).

4. Joel Tyler Headley, *The Adirondack; or Life in the Woods* (New York: Baker and Scribner, 1849), vol. 1, 25ff. Headley alternated between fishing with wet flies (he recommended red and black hackles for all seasons) and with bait.

5. William H.H. Murray, *Adventures in the Wilderness; or, Camp-Life in the Adirondacks* (Boston: Fields, Osgood, & Co., 1869).

6. Paul Schneider, *The Adirondacks: A History of America's First Wilderness* (New York: Henry Holt and Co., 1997), 181.

7. Leila Fosburgh Wilson, *The North Woods Club: 1886–1986* (Minerva, N.Y.: privately printed, 1986). According to Wilson, a number of prominent figures from Pittsburgh, including Andrew Mellon, Henry Clay Frick, and Alfred R. Whitney, joined in 1889 or after. According to Tatham, Homer was elected a member of this club in January 1888; see "Winslow Homer at the North Woods Club."

8. Schneider, *The Adirondacks,* 268–269. Largest of the clubs was the Adirondack League Club in the southwest corner of the region, which by 1893 controlled some 200,000 acres; the Tahawus Club in the center of the region leased 96,000 acres; while the Adirondack Mountain Reserve (the Ausable Club) near Keene Valley owned about 40,000 acres including much of the High Peaks region. See Edith Pilcher, *Up the Lake Road: The First Hundred Years of the Adirondack Mountain Reserve* (Keene Valley, N.Y.: Centennial Committee for the Trustees of the Adirondack Mountain Reserve, 1987).

9. "Club House Register of the Adirondack Forest Preserve (North Woods Club)," April 1887–April 1968 (courtesy of the North Woods Club and the Adirondack Museum).

10. Tatham in *Winslow Homer in the Adirondacks* lists all of Homer's Adirondack works, basing his compilation on the list presented by Lloyd Goodrich and Edith Havens Goodrich in their *Winslow Homer in the Adirondacks* (Blue Mountain Lake, N.Y.: The Adirondack Museum, 1959). I have followed Tatham's list of the 1889 and early 1890 watercolors with the following caveats: 1) the work he calls *The Adirondack Guide,* 1889 (Museum of Fine Arts, Boston), is properly titled *Guide and Woodsmen;* and 2) I have not included in my calculations the small vertical work entitled *Trout,* as I have not had the opportunity of examining the original. I am deeply grateful to Abigail Booth Gerdts for sharing the Goodrich files with me.

11. Lloyd Goodrich, *Winslow Homer* (New York: Macmillan Co., 1944), 117–118. *The New-York Commercial Advertiser* reviewed the exhibition on February 15, 1890, 9, so the show was open by February 14. The two oils included were *The Two Guides,* 1877 (Sterling and Francine Clark Art Institute, Williamstown, Massachusetts) and *Camp Fire,* 1880 (The Metropolitan Museum of Art, New York).

12. Unknown critic, quoted in Goodrich, *Winslow Homer,* 117.

13. *New York Evening Post,* February 19, 1890; unknown critic cited in Goodrich, *Winslow Homer,* 119.

14. Of the 37 known watercolors from the 1889–1890 series, 22 portray fish or fishing (13 being devoted to fishermen, and 9 to the fish themselves either jumping or dead); 8 of the watercolors deal with the hunt (4 showing deer near lakes, 4 being of the dogs or hunters); 4 other works illustrate the guides in their boats or in the woods, while 3 have to do with logging and the forest.

15. *New York Times,* February 18, 1890, 4.

16. Again I rely on the Tatham-Goodrich list in Tatham, *Winslow Homer in the Adirondacks.* Regarding the approximately fifty-three Adirondack watercolors of 1891–1902, it should be noted that *Man and Boy in Boat (On the Lookout),* 1892, is owned by the Fogg Art Museum (not a private collection); and that both *Casting the Fly,* now titled *Casting,* 1894, and *The Rise,* 1900, are in the National Gallery of Art rather than the Portland (Maine) Museum of Art.

17. "The Fine Arts," *Boston Daily Evening Transcript,* December 23, 1892.

18. The subjects of the 49 works of 1891–1894 can be divided by subject as follows: deer hunting, 16; fish and fishing, 9; guides, in their boats or in the woods, 8; panoramic landscapes, 8; logging, 3; the woods, 3; boating, 2.

19. Judith Walsh, "Innovation in Homer's Late Watercolors," in Nicolai Cikovsky Jr. and Franklin Kelly, *Winslow Homer,* exh. cat. (New Haven and London: Yale University Press for the National Gallery of Art, 1995), 284.

20. Alfred Trumble, as quoted in Goodrich, *Winslow Homer,* 123, referring to *Hound and Hunter,* 1892 (National Gallery of Art); Cikovsky and Kelly, *Winslow Homer,* 270–271. But see Tatham, *Winslow Homer in the Adirondacks,* for a more balanced view.

21. Tatham, *Winslow Homer in the Adirondacks,* 119.

22. Anne La Bastille, "Doctors of the Wilderness," *Natural History,* May 1992, 42–45.

23. Cikovsky and Kelly, *Winslow Homer,* 251.

24. Charles Brumley, *Guides of the Adirondacks: A History* (Utica, N.Y.: North Country Books, 1994), 1. Homer knew Phelps, who lived in Keene Valley, and painted him as the bearded, older man in *Two Guides,* 1877 (Clark Art Institute).

25. William James Stillman, "Philosopher's Camp," in Paul J. Jamieson, ed., *The Adirondack Reader* (New York: MacMillan Co., 1964), 78.

26. As quoted by Schneider, *The Adirondacks,* 169. See also Schneider, 188, and Fannie P. Hardy's obituary of the young guide Wilber R. Webster in *Forest and Stream* 38, no. 4 (January 28, 1892): 76. Russell M.L. Carson in "Great Adirondack Guides, No. 5: Harvey Holt," *High Spots* 11, no. 1 (1934): 5, speaks of the guides' "almost unbelievable skill in the woods, and their modest bravery and intelligent philosophy of life."

27. Henry David Thoreau, "Walden," in Carol Bode, ed., *The Portable Thoreau* (New York: The Viking Press, 1964), 457.

28. David Tatham, "Trapper, Hunter, and Woodsman: Winslow Homer's Adirondack Figures," *American Art Journal* 22, no. 4 (1990): 40.

29. Tatham, "Trapper, Hunter, and Woodsman," 40.

30. Martin Burke, "In the Adirondacks with Rod and Rifle," *Catholic World* 42 (October 1885): 19.

31. Kenyon Cox, "The Art of Winslow Homer," *Scribner's* 56 (September 1914): 378.

32. Helen A. Cooper, *Winslow Homer Watercolors,* exh. cat. (New Haven and London: Yale University Press for the National Gallery of Art, 1986), 170.

33. Cooper, *Winslow Homer Watercolors,* 11; *Forest and Stream* 37, no. 6 (August 27, 1891): 103.

34. Schneider, *The Adirondacks,* 216–217. As Schneider says, Barbara McMartin, *The Great Forest of the Adirondacks* (Utica, N.Y.: North Country Books, 1994) makes a good case that the logging was not as extensive or as harmful as was thought at the time, but the important thing for Homer is what he and his contemporaries believed.

35. "The Wane of the Adirondacks," *Forest and Stream* 37 no. 6 (August 27, 1891): 101.

36. Schneider, *The Adirondacks,* 184.

37. Brumley, *Guides,* 28.

38. This was the Mohawk and Malone Railroad. See Schneider, *The Adirondacks*, 229. See also Harold K. Hochschild, *Adirondack Railroads: Real and Phantom* (Blue Mountain Lake, N.Y.: The Adirondack Museum, 1962). On Webb's Nehasane, see Craig Gilborn, *Adirondack Camps: Homes Away from Home, 1850–1950* (Blue Mountain Lake, N.Y.: The Adirondack Museum, 2000), 225–227.

39. Alfred L. Donaldson, *A History of the Adirondacks*, 2 vols. (1921; reprint, Port Washington, N.Y.: Ira J. Friedman, 1963), vol. 2, 92.

40. Schneider, *The Adirondacks*, 241.

41. Schneider, *The Adirondacks*, 246. See also Harvey Kaiser, *Great Camps of the Adirondacks* (Boston: D. R. Godine, 1982).

42. On Stoddard, see Jeanne Winston Adler, *Early Days in the Adirondacks: The Photographs of Seneca Ray Stoddard.* (New York: Harry N. Abrams, 1997); Maitland C. De Sormo, *Seneca Ray Stoddard: Versatile Camera-Artist* (Saranac Lake, N.Y.: Adirondack Yesteryears, 1972); Jeffrey L. Horrell, *Seneca Ray Stoddard: Transforming the Adirondack Wilderness in Text and Image* (Syracuse, N.Y.: Syracuse University Press, 1999).

43. Susan Sontag. "On Photography," *New York Review of Books,* October 18, 1973.

44. Collection of Chapman Historical Museum, Glens Falls, New York. The two major collections of Stoddard's work, comprising some twelve thousand prints altogether, are held by this museum and by the Adirondack Museum, Blue Mountain Lake, New York.

45. Frank Graham Jr., *The Adirondack Park: A Political History* (New York: Alfred A. Knopf, 1978), 119–132.

46. Wilson, *The North Woods Club,* 17. Notes in the "Club House Register" confirm the stocking, May 11–15, May 30, and July 20, 1890.

47. See "Club House Register" entries for May–June 1891. Homer reported catching no fish during his October 1891 visit. During June–July 1892 he caught seven, with none on his September trip. In 1894, when he was there only once, in June, he caught two good-size pickerel, but no trout. Members who came in earlier, in May, typically reported catching ten fish a week, but the fishing declined in June and July for everyone—some people reporting no catches at all—before picking up significantly in August and September.

48. Burke, "In the Adirondacks," 13.

49. Combining the 37 watercolors of 1889–1890, the 49 made between 1891 and 1894, and the 5 dating 1900 and 1902, one can summarize Homer's subjects in the Adirondack watercolors roughly as follows: fish and fishing, 34 works (37%); hunting, 24 works (26%); guides, 12 works (13%); landscape subjects including logging, the forest, panoramic landscapes, and miscellaneous boating scenes, 21 works (23%).

50. See "Club House Register"; Tatham, *Winslow Homer in the Adirondacks,* 137.

51. Cikovsky and Kelly, *Winslow Homer,* 61ff.

52. See Stephen Kern, *The Culture of Time and Space, 1880–1918* (Cambridge, Mass.: Harvard University Press, 1983), and T. J. Jackson Lears, *No Place of Grace: Antimodernism and the Transformation of American Culture, 1880–1920* (Chicago: University of Chicago Press, 1994).

Winslow Homer in Quebec

David Tatham

ON JUNE 19, 1892, WINSLOW HOMER WROTE TO his older brother, Charles, from the Adirondacks: "I shall be all through with my work by July [date illegible] and shall loaf about in different places, *Canada preferred.*"[1] By Canada, he meant the Province of Quebec. Whether he actually went to Canada in 1892 is uncertain, but by no later than the end of the next summer Quebec had become a new locus of his attention as a sport fisherman. He fished in the province in 1893, and when he returned in 1895, he brought along his watercolor kit as well as his fishing tackle. He did so again in 1897 and 1902.[2] Charles accompanied him on most if not all of these visits to Quebec. From Homer's time in French Canada came some fifty watercolors and two oil paintings, a body of work even more confident and adventurous than that which he had produced a few years earlier in the Adirondacks. His Quebec paintings stand with his great marine subjects of the same period as culminating works in the career of an artist whose powers grew steadily as years passed.

In journeying to Quebec to fish, the brothers joined a wave of sportsmen from the United States who had been drawn to the interior of the province beginning in the late 1880s. Two decades earlier, the salmon rivers that flowed into the St. Lawrence had attracted anglers from the United States, but not until the 1880s did American fishermen in significant numbers head into the great wilderness north and northwest of Quebec City. Within this wild region the Homer brothers returned repeatedly to two locations (fig. 60). One was in the Laurentides, a mountainous realm of unbroken forest, fast-running streams, and countless lakes and ponds. The mountains extended for more than a hundred miles north of the city before reaching the Saguenay River and its vast source, Lake St. John. The brothers' second fishing site was at Lake St. John's outlet, the Grand Discharge. The lake had long been accessible to sportsmen willing to endure an arduous journey up the Saguenay, but until the late 1880s the Laurentides had remained largely an unknown territory. It had been a domain for local hunters and trappers rather than gentlemen anglers. By the time the Homer brothers ventured to Quebec, however, both the Laurentides and Lake St. John had been opened to sportsmen by a newly built railway that carried thousands of anglers from the United States into the region each year.

The two locations at which Homer fished and painted were about a hundred miles apart. They were also of distinctly different character. In the southern Laurentides he went to the Tourilli Fish and Game Club at a quiet location on a mountain-hemmed river within the deep forest. The brothers were members of the club. The place pleased them so much that they arranged to have their own cabin built facing a lake on the club's preserve.[3] Their second fishing site was at Lake St. John's tumultuous outlet, the Grand Discharge. The Discharge consisted of nearly twenty miles of rapids coursing

FIG. 60
Map: Winslow Homer's Quebec. Drawn by Lucie Wellner

[page 124]
DETAIL: CAT. 48
*Fishing the Rapids,
Saguenay River*, 1902.
Watercolor over graphite
on paper, 13½ × 20 in.
Private collection

through rock-filled gorges, interrupted now and again by a waterfall or a deep-running stretch of unbroken water. The Discharge marked the beginning of the Saguenay River's majestic journey to the St. Lawrence.

The social setting of the two locations was equally dissimilar. Fishing at the Tourilli Club's wilderness preserve was limited to members and guests, of whom relatively few were present at any given time. By comparison, the Discharge was a busy place. There fishing was open to the guests of a hundred-room summer hotel, the Island House, and campers at a campground operated by the hotel. In his Tourilli watercolors, the only sportsman Homer depicted seems to have been Charles. At the Discharge, he portrayed other anglers as well, identities now unknown.

The brothers had traveled to Quebec in search of fishing sites wilder and more abundant than those they had known in New York and New England. But they went also to find at the Grand Discharge a fish unknown in the United States. While the trout they netted at the Tourilli Club were of a familiar sort, at the Discharge they cast for a variety of land-locked salmon (fig. 61) distinctive to Lake St. John and its outlet: the "fighting" ouananiche (*salmo salar*).[4] This was a fish whose description called for superlatives. In 1922 the outdoorsman-author T. Morris Longstreth described it through a character in his *The Laurentians* as "the most high-minded fish, the cleanest feeder, the merriest liver, the loftiest leaper, and the bravest warrior of all creatures that swim. . . . Flesh vitalized by spirit, he feeds on flies and his food is transformed into an aerial passion for flight."[5]

On Homer's visits to Quebec in 1895, 1897, and 1902 he painted not only landscapes and fishing scenes but also bits of Quebec City and its environs, an Indian settlement near Lake St. John, guides at work, woodsmen dancing, and a marauding bear. Despite the variety of his subjects, all his Quebec

CAT. 34
Montagnais Indians [Indians Making Canoes], 1895. Watercolor over graphite on paper,
14 × 20 in. Henry E. Huntington Library and Art Gallery, San Marino, California.
Gift of the Virginia Steele Scott Foundation

paintings in one way or another reflected his devotion to the art of fishing. His views of places around Quebec City acknowledged it as the gathering point for the sportsmen from throughout the United States who in the 1890s flocked to the province by rail. Many stayed for a night or two at the Hotel Victoria, as Homer did.[6] His depictions of woodsmen at ease and Montagnais Indians in their summer encampment at Lake St. John (cat. 34) were subjects he encountered and recorded on his travels to and around his fishing sites. His painting of a bear tearing apart a birch-bark canoe depicts an incident outside his cabin at the Tourilli Club.

His Quebec paintings have left an impression that he and Charles "roughed it" in the wilds. The few snapshots Homer took on these trips, especially one of their cabin (fig. 8, ill. p. 23), reinforce this conception of sportsmen living in relatively primitive conditions, attended only by guides. But their spacious cabin (cat. 33, ill. p. 131) was undoubtedly comfortable in its rustic way and much warmer and freer of mosquitoes, black flies, gnats, and no-see-ums than the tents in which their guides camped. The brothers were almost certainly well-provisioned, if not perhaps with quite so elaborate a larder as that recommended for Canadian angling a few years earlier in a sporting journal. It advised, "Put up champagne baskets covered with canvas, a fair allowance of dry sherry, Pale India ale, sound claret, add a magnum of *eau de vie pale et vieille* for medicinal purposes."[7] When they were not at the Tourilli Club's lodge, their cabin, or a hotel, the brothers traveled through the forests of Quebec on trains equipped with sleeping and parlor cars. They moved along the Saguenay and St. Lawrence on steamships offering first-class accommodations. Homer's paintings are silent concerning the comforts of modern tourist life that he and Charles enjoyed in Canada, for this was not a subject that interested him as an artist, nor was there much of an audience for such images. Neither did he paint anything illustrative of the brothers' hearty companionship with other sportsmen. Yet, few days passed without the two men being in the agreeable company of gentlemen anglers like themselves—socially respectable, well-to-do, professional men of the middle class.

These anglers had been drawn to the Laurentides and Lake St. John in good part by fishing reports that appeared regularly in the American sporting press.[8] The numbers of anglers had swelled in the mid-1880s as an outgrowth of two closely related developments that established the Laurentides and Lake St. John as complementary realms within a single sport-fisherman's paradise. The historical context of Homer's Quebec paintings rests on these developments of the 1880s. They determined where he went, how he traveled, and, to some extent, what he painted.

First came the Canadian government's decision to lease fishing rights on huge tracts of crown lands for ten-year renewable periods. By 1883 nearly all the fishable waters in the Laurentides and around Lake St. John had become available for leasing to individuals, organizations, and business interests. Next came the American entrepreneur Horace J. Beemer (ca. 1845–1906), who in the mid-1880s pressed ahead with construction of the Quebec and

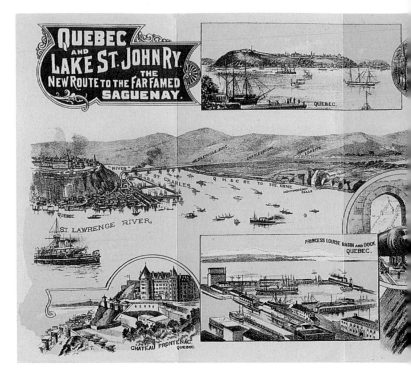

FIG. 62
Fold-out map: *Quebec and Lake St. John Railway, the New Route to the Far Famed Saguenay,* 1890s. Lithograph by Toronto Lithographing Company, Canada. Private collection

Lake St. John Railway (Q&LStJ). It ran from Quebec City across the southern edge of the mountains before turning north near Rivière-à-Pierre to wend its way through high land to Roberval on Lake St. John (fig. 62). Much of the route was cut through wilderness. Borrowing a phrase from Henry Wadsworth Longfellow's well-known poem *Evangeline,* one writer in 1888 spoke of the line's locomotive moving through "the forest primeval."[9]

By 1886 ninety of the railway's one hundred thirty-five miles were open.[10] When the line reached Roberval two years later, Beemer had already instituted steamboat service from that large town to the Grand Discharge, twenty-five miles distant. A journey by railway and steamboat from Quebec City to the lake's outlet was much faster and easier than the only alternative. This was travel by steamship or rail via the St. Lawrence and the

Saguenay Rivers to the town of Chicoutimi and then overland more than forty miles to the lake. But once a sportsman had completed fishing at the Discharge, a return to Quebec down the Saguenay from Chicoutimi by boat offered a leisurely and highly scenic trip. As we will see, Homer returned this way at least once, and perhaps every time that he fished at the Grand Discharge.

A prime function of the Q&LStJ was to transport freight and raw materials to and from Roberval, but Beemer also cultivated a passenger trade among sportsmen and tourists, and he did so with great success. Having leased the fishing rights along most of the line, he threw them open to the public. While it was true that few persons could take advantage of this largesse without also being a passenger on the railway—there was no other practical mode of transportation along most of the

FIG. 61
"The Celebrated Ouananiche," as depicted on the cover of a promotional brochure for the Quebec and Lake St. John Railway, 1890s. Lithograph by Toronto Lithographing Company, Canada. Private collection

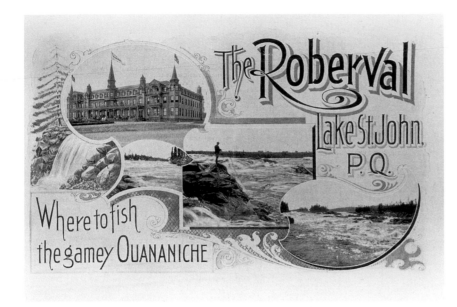

FIG. 63
The Roberval, Lake St. John, P.Q., from Horace J. Beemer's promotional brochure, 1890s.
Photographs by Jules-Ernest Livernois (1851–1933), Quebec City. Private collection

FIG. 64
Views of the Island House and surroundings, the Grand Discharge, Quebec, from
Horace J. Beemer's promotional brochure, 1890s. Photographs by Jules-Ernest Livernois
(1851–1933), Quebec City. Private collection

route—the policy nonetheless was met with praise.[11] More important, the line's passage through the foothills south and west of the mountains opened access to vast tracts of previously unbroken Laurentide forest. The fishing rights for watersheds on these government-owned lands extended far into the mountains. For the most part, private sporting clubs secured these leases. Indeed, they had organized themselves for this purpose. The leases allowed the clubs to construct lodges, cabins, and other facilities on a few acres of a preserve. By the time the Homer brothers made their first visit to the Tourilli Club, that organization controlled the fishing rights to more than 1,100 acres containing some 125 ponds and 250 miles of rivers and streams.[12]

The situation at Lake St. John was different. While building his railway Beemer had erected three tourist hotels. One was on Lake Edward, west of the mountains. Two were at Lake St. John. One of these was at Roberval (fig. 63), and the other, the Island House (fig. 64), was on Alma Island at the Grand Discharge. This was the sole hotel of any size at the Discharge. The railway controlled the fishing rights for nearly all the hundred-mile circumference of Lake St. John, its major tributaries for certain distances upstream, and, crucially, the Grand Discharge itself.[13] The Q&LStJ's liberal extension of rights to anglers along its line and at the lake stopped at the Discharge. To fish at this prime location, one needed to be a registered guest at the Island House or its campgrounds, or pay a daily fishing fee. One needed also to rent the hotel's canoes, hire its guides, and use its buckboards and drivers to move about the large island, all at premium prices. One aim of this policy, beyond profits to Beemer, was to prevent overfishing by restricting the number of anglers who cast for ouananiche.

The railway constructed an enticing public image for a part of Canada previously little known to most American sportsmen. Its advertisements in sporting publications merged the Laurentides and

Log Cabin, Tourilli Club, 1895. Watercolor over graphite on paper, 14 × 20 in.
Private collection. Photograph courtesy Kennedy Galleries, Inc.

Lake St. John into a single entity. In 1891, in a display ad in the New York sporting magazine *Forest and Stream,* the railway boomed itself as the "only rail route to the delightful summer resorts north of Quebec through the Canadian Adirondacks . . . Magnificent scenery. Beautiful climate."[14] Yet the Adirondacks and the Laurentides differed in many respects. Among the distinctions glossed over in the railway's ads was the fact that the Adirondacks were full of summer hotels and boardinghouses, while the Laurentides had precious few rooms for tourists, except, of course, at the railway's hotel at Lake Edward.

The Q&LStJ published and freely distributed Beemer's handbook for fishermen in the region.[15] At its terminals it presumably sold Eugene McCarthy's (1857–1903) treatise on the ouananiche published by *Forest and Stream* in 1894; Homer owned a copy of this fifty-two-page booklet.[16] The railway itself produced an edition of *The Doom of the Mamelons: A Legend of Lake St. John and the Saguenay* by William Henry Harrison Murray (1840–1904).[17] In 1869 Murray's bestselling *Adventures in the Wilderness; or, Camp-Life in the Adirondacks* had been instrumental in establishing the Adirondacks of northern New York in the public mind as a pristine natural world offering great rewards to discerning sportsmen and tourists.[18] Two decades later crowded hotels, widespread logging, and declining populations of fish and game had tarnished the region's reputation. Murray and others then began to tout the interior of Quebec as a successor region.[19] In 1870 Homer had been part of "Murray's Rush" to the Adirondacks. In 1893 he again joined a flood of sportsmen heading for what they hoped would be true wilderness teeming with fish and game.

Forest and Stream's Canadian correspondent, the Quebec City journalist Edward Thomas Davies Chambers (1852–1931), boosted the railway and its hotels by mentioning them frequently in his engaging reports on Canadian fishing. He told his American readers of tantalizingly large catches, individual fish of impressive weight, and the "fighting" instincts of the denizens of Quebec's lakes and streams. In 1890 he noted that two members of the Tourilli Club who had fished in unpromising weather nonetheless "secured an average of one and one half pounds of the gamiest trout on this continent. . . ." The next day the two men caught "six fine fish [ranging from four and a half to two and a half pounds] . . . all with the fly. . . ." In the same report he relayed the information that, in the case of one Tourilli Club member, "eighty yards of line were spun out in less than ten seconds. It took thirty-five minutes to play the four and a half pound fish."[20] In 1891 he reported that one Canadian fisherman had recently "killed no less than twenty six ouananiche on Tuesday last at the Grand Discharge. . . . An American gentleman killed twenty three on the previous day."[21] A steady stream of such accounts stirred the interest of fishermen south of the border.

Chambers's use of "killed" rather than "caught" was not unusual in reports from Canadian waters throughout the 1880s and 1890s. It presumably arose from distinctions made between catching fish and returning some to the water alive, and killing

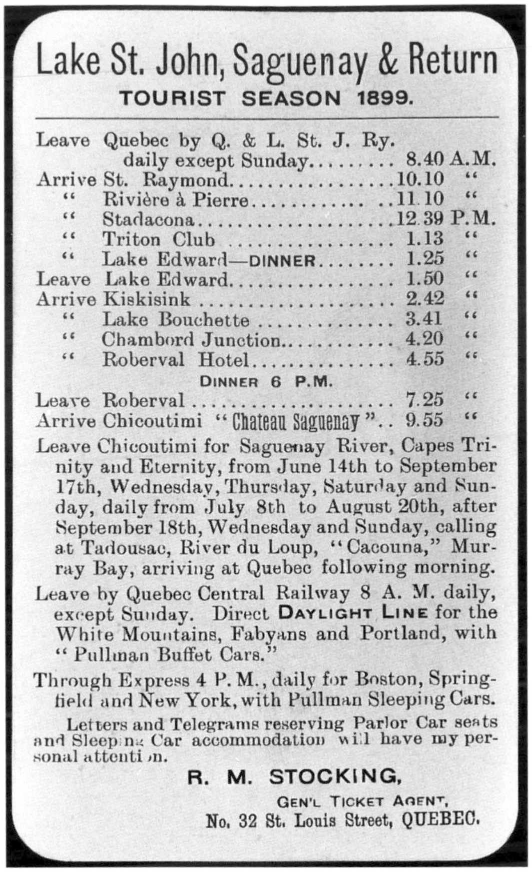

Lake St. John, Saguenay & Return
TOURIST SEASON 1899.

Leave Quebec by Q. & L. St. J. Ry.
        daily except Sunday. . . . . 8.40 A.M.
Arrive St. Raymond. . . . . .10.10 "
    " Rivière à Pierre. . . . .11.10 "
    " Stadacona. . . . . .12.39 P.M.
    " Triton Club . . . . 1.13 "
    " Lake Edward—DINNER. . . . . . . 1.25 "
Leave Lake Edward. . . . . 1.50 "
Arrive Kiskisink . . . . 2.42 "
    " Lake Bouchette . . . . 3.41 "
    " Chambord Junction. . . . . 4.20 "
    " Roberval Hotel . . . . 4.55 "
                DINNER 6 P.M.
Leave Roberval . . . . 7.25 "
Arrive Chicoutimi " Chateau Saguenay ". . 9.55 "

Leave Chicoutimi for Saguenay River, Capes Trinity and Eternity, from June 14th to September 17th, Wednesday, Thursday, Saturday and Sunday, daily from July 8th to August 20th, after September 18th, Wednesday and Sunday, calling at Tadousac, River du Loup, "Cacouna," Murray Bay, arriving at Quebec following morning.
Leave by Quebec Central Railway 8 A. M. daily, except Sunday. Direct DAYLIGHT LINE for the White Mountains, Fabyans and Portland, with " Pullman Buffet Cars."
Through Express 4 P. M., daily for Boston, Springfield and New York, with Pullman Sleeping Cars.
    Letters and Telegrams reserving Parlor Car seats and Sleeping Car accommodation will have my personal attention.
        R. M. STOCKING,
            GEN'L TICKET AGENT,
        No. 32 St. Louis Street, QUEBEC.

FIG. 65
Schedule, Quebec and Lake St. John Railway, Tourist Season, 1899. The schedule notes daily service to Portland, Maine, featuring "Pullman Buffet Cars," and through service to Boston, Springfield (Massachusetts), and New York with Pullman sleeping cars. Private collection

or keeping them. This distinction was, however, too fine for most readers. In 1901 it occasioned an objection in *Forest and Stream* from a sportsman who must have represented a growing uneasiness about the term, for the use of "killing" gradually declined thereafter. In his letter he noted: "The word 'catch' implies skill and strategy. The word 'kill' implies murder."[22]

Nearly every week from spring to fall Chambers listed a few of the members and guests of sporting clubs who had arrived or departed by train. His column at times took on aspects of a social register as he mentioned industrialists, diplomats, physicians, attorneys, architects, military men, political figures, and occasionally a woman. He regularly mentioned clubs, some of which were American in origin and membership. Among these were the Springfield, the Triton, and the Laurentian. Little appeared in Chambers's columns to cast doubt on the region's attractiveness. It was left to others to report that in dry seasons cinders from the Q&LStJ locomotive set fires in the woodlands along its route and that by the mid-1890s there were signs of overfishing in some lakes and streams.[23]

In 1891 a woman who during the previous season had accompanied her husband by rail from Quebec to Roberval and then on to the Grand Discharge found everything disappointing until she reached the ouananiche:

Lured by the highly colored pictures and glowing advertisements of the large trout of Lake Edward and the ouananiche of Lake St. John and the Grand Discharge . . . we took the train for Lake Edward. [We passed] . . . on the way a region extending for twenty or thirty miles formed of a network of streams that were said to be alive with trout and ouananiche, but every part of it is controlled by some club.

After being disappointed by service at the hotel at Lake Edward and catching no fish in its waters, the couple traveled on to Roberval and took the steamer to the Grand Discharge. "The passage . . . was $1. When we got there the steamboat anchored in the middle of the rushing stream and 25 cents each was charged to take us ashore, which could be done only in a canoe. . . ."[24]

Their camp cost two dollars a day per person and each of their guides cost two dollars a day. But now their investment reaped rewards. "The ouananiche seemed abundant. Their fins could be seen as they rolled over porpoise-fashion wherever the foam gathered in patches. . . . The average catch is six a day to each rod, and the largest caught last summer, according to the record of the camp,

was five and a half pounds. The average is one to two pounds." When their fishing was done, the couple with their guides descended the whole of the Grand Discharge to Chicoutimi by canoe, a distance of forty-two miles, in five and a half hours. They then took the steamer down the Saguenay and up the St. Lawrence to Quebec City.[25] (By the mid–twentieth century, the Discharge had changed almost beyond recognition following the damming of the upper rapids, the diversion of water to a hydroelectric station, and the construction near Alma Island of paper mills, an aluminum plant, and other industrial facilities.)

The occasional sense of disappointment reported by some anglers seems never to have touched the Homer brothers. From all evidence, and from Winslow's paintings above all, they found in Quebec everything that Chambers and correspondents for other journals had promised. The best way to comprehend the nature of Homer's response as an artist to what he saw and did in Quebec is to follow his movements and examine representative paintings from each site. The record of his visits is by no means complete, but enough remains to establish in a general way why he found these parts of Canada so rewarding.

When Homer departed for Quebec in 1893, he had been resident for a decade in his studio-home at Prout's Neck on the coast of Maine. Charles and his wife, Martha (Mattie), who resided in New York City, spent part of each summer at the Ark, their seafront house close to Homer's studio (fig. 6, ill. p. 21). There seems to be no way of knowing how long the two brothers had contemplated an expedition to the Laurentides and Lake St. John, but they undoubtedly knew about these places from the accounts of angler friends returned from Canada as well as from sporting magazines. Getting to Quebec from Prout's Neck was an easy matter. The Grand

FIG. 66
The Tourilli Fish and Game Club, 1890–1900. Photograph by
Jules-Ernest Livernois (1851–1933), Quebec City. From an album
compiled for the Canadian Department of Mines and Resources.
National Archives of Canada, Ottawa

FIG. 67
Interior view, clubhouse of the Tourilli Fish and Game Club, 1890–1900.
Photograph by Jules-Ernest Livernois (1851–1933), Quebec City. From an
album compiled for the Canadian Department of Mines and Resources.
National Archives of Canada, Ottawa

Trunk Railway left its great shedlike terminal at
India Wharf Station in Portland and ran directly to
Montreal and then along the St. Lawrence to Quebec
City. The journey to Montreal could take ten hours
with another five to Quebec, though in 1895 express
trains carried Homer all the way from Portland to
Quebec City in twelve and a half (fig. 65).[26]

Three hours out of Portland, when the train
reached Gorham, New Hampshire, the stop may
well have aroused in Homer a retrospective thought
or two. At that point the line ran close by the
northeast edge of the Presidential Range of the
White Mountains, where he had painted and probably fished in the summers of 1868 and 1869. Later,

approaching Montreal, he would have appreciated
that he was less than a hundred miles due north of
the places in the Adirondacks where he had painted
and fished now and again in the 1870s and 1880s—
indeed, as recently as 1892. He and Charles doubtless spent the evening at a Montreal hotel and left
by rail the next morning for Quebec City. They
would have spent the night there and set out the
next morning on the Q&LStJ for the village of St.
Raymond, some thirty miles due west. Along the
way scratchy farmland spread to the south while the
spruce-covered mountains of the Laurentides rose
immediately to the north. Met at the St. Raymond
station, probably by one of the club's guides, they

traveled north by buckboard for fifteen miles along a road that followed the St. Anne River to the point where the Tourilli flowed into it. Not far up this tributary, the road ended at the lodge of the Tourilli Fish and Game Club.[27]

The building, and several nearby members' cabins, overlooked a large pool in the Tourilli River. The Quebec City photographer Jules-Ernest Livernois left a valuable record of the club's setting and buildings in a series of photographs he took in the 1890s. It includes a landscape (fig. 66) in which mountains crowd against the spruce-lined river. In a cabin interior (fig. 67) a Q&LStJ Railway poster, emblazoned with a leaping ouananiche (see fig. 61), rests on the mantelpiece. Another photograph shows a handful of Tourilli Club members on the steps of the lodge (fig. 68). Landscape photography was among Livernois's many specialties. A fisherman himself, he recorded many of the places Homer visited in Quebec, including the Grand Discharge.[28]

The Tourilli Fish and Game Club had been founded in Quebec City in 1886. The name Tourilli came from a Native American phrase meaning "rushing waters."[29] Membership was limited to seventy sportsmen from Canada and the United States.[30] Though all the members were men, spouses and other women visited and fished. The organization's founders and moving spirits were its genial president, Commodore John Uriah Gregory, the Quebec City agent of the province's Marine and Fisheries Department, and his hearty nephew, George Van Felson, both from a long-established, socially prominent Quebec City family. A third founder, Edward A. Panet, was the member of the Provincial Parliament for St. Raymond. He had been instrumental in gaining legislative support for Beemer's railway project. Indeed, the provincial government, the railway, the clubs, and the sporting press seem to have worked hand in glove to develop Quebec as a premier destination for fishermen.

FIG. 68
Tourilli Fish and Game Club, members gathered on the clubhouse porch, 1890–1900. Photograph by Jules-Ernest Livernois (1851–1933), Quebec City. National Archives of Canada, Ottawa

Van Felson was a lively presence. Some of his humor survives in his *Report of the St. Anne and Tourilli Exploring Expedition.* This forty-one-page pamphlet, privately printed for members of the club in 1890, is an account of a two-week trip into the club's leased wilds. The exploring party consisted of Van Felson, two fellow club members (one of whom was his brother-in-law), and four guides. The report offers itself as a mock natural-history treatise in the form of a military expeditionary report. The reader learns among other amusingly recounted exploits that the explorers with great ceremony bestowed names on most of the twenty-five lakes and ponds they came across as they bushwhacked through the wilderness that lay between the headwaters of the St. Anne and Tourilli Rivers. Honored in this way were Van Felson's sister Georgiana, his sister-in-law Emelie, each of the three explorers, and all four of their guides, as well as other persons no less distinguished.[31] (Some of the lakes' names survive on mid-twentieth-century maps of the area.) The narrative of discovery pauses now and again to report such things as recipes for field-improvised culinary delicacies.[32] Van Felson's prowess as a fly fisherman led him to write to sporting journals on fine points of nomenclature for tied flies.[33]

Homer knew him well. In a letter to Charles, he referred to "Von Fitson," perhaps alluding to his friend's animated manner.[34] Lloyd Goodrich, in preparing his biography of Homer (1944), corresponded with Van Felson, who in recalling the brothers said, "We were more than friends. . . . They treated me with the affection of a father."[35] Homer presented Van Felson with a watercolor of a leaping trout.[36] When their fishing days were done, the brothers gave Van Felson their cabin.

In early September 1893 Chambers noted in *Forest and Stream* that Homer was visiting the club. "Winslow Homer, the well-known American artist whose picture of 'Fox and Crows' [i.e., *The Fox Hunt;* Pennsylvania Academy of the Fine Arts, Philadelphia] appears in the August *Century Magazine,* has been fishing the waters of the Tourilli Club with marked success, accompanied by Com. J. U. Gregory of Quebec."[37] In the same column, Chambers mentioned the presence of the older Boston artist Walter Brackett (1823–1919) at his own fishing lodge on the St. Marguerite River, a tributary of the Saguenay, "where he has spent the greater part of the summer for the last eighteen years."[38] Brackett, a portrait artist, also painted fish. Two years later the same journal reported that Frederic Remington (1861–1909) was with a party of sportsmen headed to Montreal and thence to Lakes Edward and St. John for fishing.[39] The architect C. Grant La Farge was a member of the Laurentian Fish and Game Club, but his father, Homer's friend the painter John La Farge (1835–1910), was not a sportsman and did not journey to Canada with his son. No artist of note other than Homer seems to have been a member of the Tourilli Club.

During their stays at the club in 1893 and later, the Homer brothers traveled mostly by canoe, each brother attended by two guides, paddling fore and aft. The guides carried the canoes and the brothers' gear on portages around rapids, prepared meals, set up camp, and otherwise made it possible for these two middle-aged sportsmen, aged fifty-seven and fifty-nine, to reach lakes, streams, and pools well away from the Tourilli River itself. Charles seems to have felt his age. Van Felson recalled the older brother's request on one of his later visits: "I want two guides in the boat and one on the road [i.e., trail], so that in traversing the portages one man will be with me to repair damages, as my bones are getting brittle with age."[40]

Guides appear in many of Homer's Canadian paintings, often independent of other figures. In *End of the Portage* of 1897 (cat. 39), two guides carry a birch-bark canoe on their shoulders. Sunlight reflected from the canoe, the foliage, a fallen log, and the ground give buoyancy to a scene composed of heavy objects. *Guide Hiding a Canoe* (cat. 41) is a scene that seems to follow in sequence. In *The Portage* of the same year (cat. 43), Homer depicts a lone guide who shows a greater sense of effort as he carries a canoe on his back uphill while bypassing a rapid on the St. Anne River.[41] In all three works Homer's respect for skilled labor shines through.

Two years earlier, in 1895, Homer had also painted guides at the Tourilli Club, but these were small-scale figures (cat. 29, ill. p. 144) who appear chiefly as distant details in a few of the dozen monochromatic watercolors he painted that year. The monochromes of 1895 are distinct as a group within the Homer canon in both consistency of tone and variety of subject. The topics include scenes at Quebec City, the Laurentides, Lake St. John, the Grand Discharge, and the Saguenay.

CAT. 39
End of the Portage, 1897. Watercolor over graphite on paper, 14 × 21 in.
Brooklyn Museum of Art, New York. Bequest of Helen B. Sanders (78.151.1)

CAT. 41
Guide Hiding a Canoe, [1897]. Watercolor over graphite on paper, 14 × 21 in. Private collection

CAT. 43
The Portage [The Return up the River], 1897. Watercolor over graphite on paper, 13 ¾ × 20 ½ in.
Yale University Art Gallery, New Haven, Connecticut. Bequest of Doris M. Brixey (1984.32.17)

FIG. 69
View from Cape Diamond, Levis, Quebec, 1895. Watercolor over graphite on colored paper, 13 ¾ × 18 ⅞ in.
Norton Museum of Art, West Palm Beach, Florida. Gift of Mr. Channing Hare (71.12)

FIG. 70
Cape Diamond, Quebec, 1895. Watercolor over graphite on colored paper, 13 ⅞ × 20 ⅛ in.
National Gallery of Canada, Ottawa. Purchased 1994 with the assistance of a grant from
the Government of Canada under the terms of the Cultural Property Export and Import
Act. Photograph © National Gallery of Canada

Geographically they encompass the entirety of Homer's sporting travels in the province. He painted most of them in tightly controlled modulations of browns and grays, sometimes with hints of other colors, and occasionally touched with Chinese white. He tended to eschew the vigorous brushwork so compelling in his color-filled watercolors of the same year. A few of the monochromes, such as *View from Cape Diamond, Levis, Quebec* (fig. 69), are quick sketches in wash. In others, he manipulated and controlled washes in ways that make it clear that they are products of his studio as much as of the field. He may have limited his palette in the monochromes to be able to work rapidly in new environments (though most of these watercolors are in fact meticulously executed and show little sign of hurry).

The monochromes' tonal unity and quiet mood suggest another possibility: that Homer made them with the thought that at least some of them might reach publication. They would have served the photomechanical processes of the day better than would any of his work in full color. Since their subjects constitute an itinerary of sorts for a sportsman in Quebec, he may have hoped to offer a selection of them to *Century* or another magazine.[42] If this was his hope, nothing came of it.

One of the monochromes related to Quebec City, *Cape Diamond, Quebec* (fig. 70), depicts a headland on the St. Lawrence. The Citadel of Quebec lies just out of sight beyond its top. Not far along the river was another of Homer's subjects, *Wolfe's Cove, Quebec* (fig. 71). The hint of urban feeling in these works contrasts with the wilderness settings and fishing subjects that dominate the series. *Two Men in a Canoe* (cat. 36, ill. p. 143), a product from Homer's time at the Tourilli Club, is a masterful example of the use of tone to create light, air, distance, and mood. Another in the series, *Three Men in a Canoe* (fig. 72), with its view of the passage of the smooth-flowing St. Anne or Tourilli

River through the crowding mountains, is equally remarkable in this respect and includes Charles as the passenger in a canoe. The washes of *Trout Fishing, Lake St. John, Quebec* (cat. 35, ill. p. 145) give a sense of a livelier atmosphere. Though Homer finished these dozen monochromes in his studio at Prout's Neck, he took care to preserve their sense of place as well as their tonal integrity. They reflect a remarkable intensity of feeling for the subjects.

The most brilliantly hued and vigorously executed of Homer's subjects in 1895 came from the Discharge. *Under the Falls, the Grand Discharge, Lake St. John, P.Q.* (cat. 37, ill. p. 146) depicts a pool in the fast-running river. Two guides steady a canoe while the fisherman they attend casts. (He is surely Charles.) The ouananiche leap; one has taken a fly. Homer captured this activity with panache. The thundering white water, racing current, paddling guides, bounding fish, and straining line all contribute to a sense of excitement more vivid than in any of his Adirondack watercolors. It counterbalances the near-serene mood of the Tourilli monochromes. The contrast echoes the dualities of action and repose ever present in the sport of fishing.

He sometimes borrowed compositional devices from the past. In boldly placing a hooked ouananiche in midair at the picture plane in *A Good Pool, Saguenay River* (cat. 30, ill. p. 48), he repeated what he had done on a few occasions in his Adirondack work. Now, however, the setting is wilder, the fisherman and guides more active, the fish bolder, and the watercolor technique freer to a breathtaking degree. Homer was not alone in placing a hooked fish at the picture plane with a line leading to a small-scale fisherman in the background, for such images had appeared from time to time in sporting magazines. But no one else managed to draw this subject with such skill or to invest it with such convincing freshness and energy. His depiction preserves the rich, wet colors of a living fish, hues

that disappear soon after its death. Using freshly netted fish as models, he rendered a wholly believable account of a fish in the wild as it moved through air at a virtually imperceptible speed. Not even the cameras of his day could have effectively stopped motion in this way.

In Quebec as elsewhere, Homer succeeded in capturing the varied moods of the art of fishing with extraordinary success, but he knew also that no single representation, however robustly or delicately executed, could ever amount to an adequate report on the sport's many-faceted sensations. Most of those sensations involved perceived motion. His Canadian watercolors convey with stunning success the momentary sensual experience of being on a lake or a stream surrounded by some combination of swaying trees, moving water, and changing light. Most sporting artists failed in their attempts to suggest

FIG. 71
Wolfe's Cove, Quebec, 1895. Watercolor over graphite on paper, 13 ⅞ × 20 in. Bowdoin College Museum of Art, Brunswick, Maine. Museum purchase, with donations from Neal W. Allen, Class of 1907, John F. Dana, Class of 1898, and Benjamin R. Shute, Class of 1931

FIG. 72
Three Men in a Canoe, 1895. Watercolor over graphite on paper,
13 ¾ × 19 ⅜ in. Private collection

these transitory sensations; many never made the attempt. Homer succeeded as fully as any painter of his time in capturing the effects of color, light, and motion that accompany the act of fishing. Anglers and non-anglers alike invariably recognize in his watercolors something of their own physical experiences in the out-of-doors. But for anglers these qualities of the natural environment constitute the backdrop for a more vivid sensation, the sharp tug of a fish that has taken the hook and the rush of adrenaline that accompanies the playing, reeling in, and netting of the catch.

Homer's Canadian work offers key examples of the largeness of concept—the "bigness"—that characterizes his style. He structured his compositions with large forms, eliminated much detail, gave heft and weight to the objects he rendered, used

colors and values that amplified each other, and executed boldly. In many of his Quebec watercolors the fishing sites themselves contributed to this quality of "bigness." The vast Laurentide forest did so in some of the monochromes. The cyclopean scale of the gorges and the prodigious torrents in the Grand Discharge reinforced the richer palette of the watercolors he set there.

The Discharge was so extensive and varied a passage of water through rock—so tremendous in so many ways—that it was impossible in a single painted or photographic image to achieve anything approaching an adequate sense of its place. Even a photographer as skillful as Livernois, who knew the Discharge well, could offer no more than small samplings of its appearances (fig. 73, ill. p. 147). His most interesting images record the sporting life of the place (figs. 74, 75, ill. p. 148), rather than any of its physical details. Writers were able to suggest more. In 1895 Henry Van Dyke, the clergyman-teacher-statesman who also wrote engaging essays about gentlemanly sporting life, described the Discharge in *Scribner's Magazine*:

It is a wonderful place, this outlet of Lake St. John. All the floods of twenty rivers are gathered here and break forth through a net of islands, in a double stream, divided by the broad Île d'Alma *into the* Grande Décharge *and the* Petite Décharge. *The southern [Petite] outlet is small, and flows somewhat more quietly at first. But the northern outlet is a huge confluence and tumult of waters. You see the set of the tide far out in the lake, sliding, driving, crowding, hurrying in with smooth currents and swirling eddies, toward the corner of escape. By the rocky corner where the Island House peers out through the fir-trees the current already has a perceptible slope. It begins to boil over hidden stones in the middle, and gurgles at projecting points of rock. A mile farther down there is an islet where the stream quickens, chaffs, and breaks into a rapid. Behind the islet it drops down in three or four foaming steps. On the outside it makes one long,*

CAT. 36
Two Men in a Canoe, 1895. Watercolor over graphite on paper, 13 ⅛ × 19 ⅜ in. Portland
Museum of Art, Portland, Maine. Bequest of Charles Shipman Payson (1988.55.12)

CAT. 29
Canoe on a Canadian Lake, 1895. Watercolor over graphite on paper, 11 ¾ × 20 in. Private collection

CAT. 35

Trout Fishing, Lake St. John, Quebec, 1895. Watercolor over graphite on paper, 11 × 20 in. Museum of Fine Arts, Boston. Warren Collection. William Wilkins Warren Fund (99.29). © Museum of Fine Arts, Boston

CAT. 37
Under the Falls, the Grand Discharge, Lake St. John, P.Q., 1895. Watercolor over graphite on paper,
13 ⅞ × 19 ¹⁵⁄₁₆ in. Brooklyn Museum of Art, New York. Bequest of Helen B. Sanders (78.151.2)

straight rush into a line of white-crested standing waves. . . . Half a mile below we could see the river disappear between two points of rock. There was a roar of conflict, and a golden mist hanging in the air like the smoke of battle. All along the place where the river sank from sight dazzling heads of foam were flashing up and falling back. . . . It was the top of the first chute, *a wild succession of falls and pools. . . . [A few miles farther along appears* Île Maligne.*] The scattered waters of the Discharge are drawn together here into one deep, narrow, powerful stream, flowing between gloomy shores of granite. In mid channel the wicked island shows its scarred and bristling head, like a giant ready to dispute passage. The river rushes straight at the rocky brow, splits into two currents, and raves away on both sides of the island in a double chain of furious falls and rapids.*[43]

This intensity of conflict between water and rock approached that of the breakers pounding the shore at Prout's Neck. The drama of the setting, coupled with the rewards of hooking and playing the spirited ouananiche, suited Homer as an artist, as much as an angler, for he set most of his Quebec watercolors of 1897 and 1902 in the Discharge. His guides transported him through navigable rapids and carried his gear on portages, making it possible for him to move with relative ease from one location to another on shore and on islands. In his *Casting* (fig. 31, ill. p. 76), a solitary angler stands against a background charged by roaring water and sloping ridgelines. The absence of green foliage places this work early in the season, probably late May or early June. Secure and confident, this finely equipped sportsman goes about his business with a concentration that speaks of experience and a knowledge of the behavior of the fish he seeks. Homer depicts a choice specimen of this large-tailed salmon in *Ouananiche, Lake St. John* (cat. 42, ill. p. 149), where a different fisherman stands alone, bracing a leg against a rock as he reels in his catch. The sun here is higher, brighter, and warmer.

These fishermen were doubtless aware that Homer had painted them and were presumably pleased to pose. Still, he would have been reluctant to intrude on the attention of any gentleman angler for more than a short while. Guides were different, for he paid them to pose. They probably found this to be a novel diversion and perhaps even a compliment of sorts. In *Entering the First Rapid, Grand Discharge* (cat. 40, ill. p. 28), Homer may have sketched the two guides while their canoe was at dockside and later added both the foreground's roiling stream and the silvery, smooth-surfaced, faster-running current beyond it. In the distance is Lake St. John's low horizon and open sky.

FIG. 73
The Grand Discharge, Lake St. John, Quebec, 1890–1900. Photograph by Jules-Ernest Livernois (1851–1933), Quebec City. From Horace J. Beemer's promotional brochure, 1890s. Private collection

In *Canoe in the Rapids* (cat. 38, ill. p. 150) two guides propel their vessel through the fast-moving water—blue and white but also touched with gold, tan, black, and green. Here, too, Homer may first have sketched the guides in still water, but their kinetic postures suggest that he drew them as he followed in a second canoe. In either case, he completed the work with its exquisitely balanced composition in his studio. When he returned to Quebec five years later, in 1902, he undertook another variation on the theme of guides in rapids. He heightened the subject's drama by setting *Shooting the Rapids* (cat. 49, ill. p. 151) in rougher waters. The prow of the canoe noses into the space through which it will drop in the next moment. The guides pull with great force to keep the canoe moving faster than its surrounding waters, for otherwise they will lose control of it.

The work that in many ways marked the culmination of Homer's treatment of the Discharge was his *Fishing the Rapids, Saguenay River* (cat. 48, ill. p. 152). Here he depicted in watercolor the elemental power of moving water with a success approaching that of his oil paintings of breakers pounding the coast at Prout's Neck. The work is at once naturalistic and abstract. From the scene he observed, Homer extracted forms and colors, simplified them, and returned them to the composition with heightened strength. The angular band of blue-violet water that drives across the lower quarter of the composition acts as a barrier, distancing the viewer from the casting angler and his guide and making their isolation on the rock more dramatic. (His canoe and another guide will be waiting for him on the farther side of this island.) Incised against the washes of the abstracted background, the fisherman's cast line sweeps through the air. Mist rises behind him as evidence of the torrents that perpetually strike the rock. The gold and white of the main current, set against the serrated edge of dark water, become a passage of great strength and painterly splendor.

CAT. 42
Ouananiche, Lake St. John, 1897. Watercolor over graphite on paper, 13 ½ × 20 ½ in. Private collection

CAT. 38

Canoe in the Rapids, 1897. Watercolor over graphite on paper, 13 ⅝ × 20 ½ in. Harvard
University Art Museums (Fogg Art Museum), Cambridge, Massachusetts. Purchase,
Louise E. Betten Fund (1924.30). © President and Fellows of Harvard College

CAT. 49
Shooting the Rapids, 1902. Watercolor over graphite on paper, 13 ⅞ × 21 ¾ in. Brooklyn
Museum of Art, New York. Museum Collection Fund and Special Subscription (11.537)

CAT. 48
Fishing the Rapids, Saguenay River, 1902. Watercolor over
graphite on paper, 13 ½ × 20 in. Private collection

The drama is at a scale beyond anything that Homer had previously attempted in Quebec, and it is a drama wholly of the natural world. The distant angler is at once a nearly insignificant element within the context of his wild surroundings and a detail of great importance as someone who has conquered the dangers of the place for no reason more compelling than his sport.

Perhaps the rawness of the natural world in so many of these Canadian works was one reason why Homer's Quebec watercolors at first met with disappointing sales. Still, the works received much critical praise.[44] This was especially the case when the Carnegie Institute in Pittsburgh, M. Knoedler & Company in New York, and Doll & Richards in Boston exhibited twenty-seven of them in 1898 and 1899. The published reviews were among the warmest and most perceptive that Homer had ever received. The critic for the *New York Evening Post* wrote,
It will not do at all to merely see one or two of the number. . . . But someday, when the hurry and din of the town are a burden, go and sit quietly in the presence of this breezy, spirited, and often dramatic transcription of nature. From an aesthetic point of view, and yet more frequently from a technical one, these powerful if hasty studies are no doubt often open to criticism, but for what they purport to be, they are a joy. It is . . . in the many glimpses of the rapids, with their smooth oily surface agitated here and there into foam of dashing white, that . . . Mr. Homer finds free expression.[45]

The *New York Sun*'s critic observed that *in all of the pictures the artist's various qualities of excellence appear in more or less striking evidence, and the collection is one of great artistic interest. The fresh air of the locality, the wild character of the scenery, the typical signs of the men who fish and navigate these picturesque and ever-changing waters are all given with freshness of touch and convincing directness. . . . Mr. Homer is surpassed by no living*

FIG. 76
Shooting the Rapids, Saguenay River, 1904–1910. Oil on canvas, with chalk, 30 × 48 ½ in. The Metropolitan Museum of Art, New York. Gift of Charles Savage Homer, Jr., 1911 (11.57). Photograph © The Metropolitan Museum of Art

artist in originality of method and satisfying results in interpreting such phases of life and nature as appear in these admirable pictures.[46]

In 1899 the *Boston Evening Transcript* said, *We watch Winslow Homer's work from season to season without being able to observe in it any trace or reflection of what other painters have done or thought. His peculiarity extends to his style, which is full of personal idiosyncrasies. . . . There is genius in the way he touches off the unbridled rush and fury of a Northern cascade; there is power and breadth in his suggestion of the swift gliding of the black river and the headlong plunge of the foaming rapids; there is rude and convincing eloquence in his masterly drawing of the birch bark canoe and the skillful hunters and fishermen who guide their frail bark so wonderfully between the threatening jagged rocks that protrude from the boiling chaos of water.*[47]

In 1895 the same critic had observed of Homer's first group of Quebec watercolors,

It is a little rough, but so strong, so true, so genuine, that we would not dare to wish for any modification. . . . And it is so deliciously, largely, and spontaneously American, so of the soil. . . . There is nothing worldly, nothing modish, nothing sophisticated about him; he is a full-chested, out-of-door, big-hearted American.[48]

The *New-York Daily Tribune* in reviewing the watercolors said,

They celebrate the excitements and joys of fishing. . . . Mr. Homer paints the rapids as if he had breasted them and got their strength into his brush. He is rapid, broad, and yet wonderfully concise. Each watercolor is a sketch, but it is as eloquent of the wild beauty of the rocks and rapids as though it had been pondered for weeks and then produced with the utmost deliberation. The color is brilliant, sometimes it is gorgeous, but it is always true and pure. . . .[49]

When Homer placed several of his Canadian subjects in the annual exhibition of the New York Watercolor Club in 1902, the praise was no less enthusiastic. The critic for the *Sun* wrote,

What a master he is! Even before one approaches near enough to study the individual pictures, their aggregate effect communicates an exhilaration, for bigness of feeling, directness of expression, and spontaneous force carry their message even from a distance. And the nearer view sustains the impression.[50]

•

In 1902, when Homer returned from Canada to his studio at Prout's Neck, he may have wondered whether at age sixty-six he had seen the last of Quebec. Still, he maintained his membership in the Tourilli Club and as late as 1904 spoke of a return to the Grand Discharge. In 1902 he began one of two oils based on his times in Canada.[51] He adapted *Shooting the Rapids* (fig. 76) from his watercolor of the same title, altering the figures of the two guides and adding a passenger between them. There can be little doubt that the passenger is Charles. The work is unfinished: one paddle is missing, another is incomplete, and the face of the rear guide remains undeveloped. Other passages lack final articulation. Homer's chalk marks remain as evidence of what he planned to do next. Yet, as was remarked at its first exhibition in 1911, the painting is complete in its essentials, though details are unfinished.[52]

During the last five years of his life Homer kept this work on an easel in his studio, where it stood prominently as a memoir of the dramatic wildness he had found so satisfying. It was as well a token of his affection for his brother. When Charles visited the studio the painting may well have evoked recollections not only of canoes in the Discharge but also of their larger Quebec experience: Van Felson and Gregory, the guides, the cabin, the railway, the all-encompassing forest, and waters full of hungry fish.

Begun in 1904, Homer's second Canadian oil, *Cape Trinity, Saguenay River* (fig. 81, ill. p. 157), moved intermittently to completion. It amounted to a memoir of Homer's return to Quebec City from Lake St. John by descending the Saguenay on a steamboat from Chicoutimi. As the river flowed to the St. Lawrence, quieted after its birth in the Discharge, it took the form of a long fjord. Peat-laden tributaries darkened its waters as the broad stream moved along its course. Granite hills rose sharply on each side with low mountains just beyond, all creating a passage of beguiling scenic grandeur. For many travelers, the trip's most dramatic and memorable moments arrived when the boat approached the towering forms of Cape Trinity and Cape Eternity on the south bank.

These colossal headlands had been much photographed, including by Livernois (figs. 77, 78). More widely known was the oil painting of 1880 by the distinguished Canadian artist Lucius O'Brien (1832–1899), *Sunrise on the Saguenay*. This striking view has been described by J. Russell Harper in his history of Canadian painting as one that "may

FIG. 79
After Lucius O'Brien (1832–1899), *Cape Trinity [or Sunrise on the Saguenay]*, 1880. Wood engraving from *Picturesque Canada* (Toronto: Belden Bros.), 1882. Courtesy The New York Public Library, Astor, Lenox and Tilden Foundations

be construed as an echo of the grandiose light effects Albert Bierstadt (1830–1902) and others developed south of the border, or as a glow of divine approval shining on the British Empire."[53] It is an impressive work. Homer may have seen it on one of his visits to Montreal. He probably knew O'Brien's black-and-white reproduction of the painting in *Picturesque Canada* (1882; fig. 79). The two quarto volumes of this popular book, profusely illustrated, very likely graced the lounges of most Laurentide sporting clubs.[54]

On his passage down the Saguenay in 1902, Homer had made and kept a small sketch of Capes Trinity and Eternity (fig. 80). When he set to work on his oil of this subject in 1904, he made a nocturne of the scene, possibly meaning to complement O'Brien's resplendent morning view. After much delay, *Cape Trinity, Saguenay River,* reached completion

FIG. 80
Sketch for "Cape Trinity, Saguenay River," 1902. Graphite on paper, 4 ⅞ × 7 ⅛ in.
Cooper-Hewitt, National Design Museum, Smithsonian Institution, New York.
Gift of Charles Savage Homer, Jr., 1912 (1912-12-196)

in 1909. In mood and subject alike, the moonlit view of the massive headlands differs from all Homer's other Canadian works. It conveys a feeling of mystery, of things intimated rather than defined. In his drawn image of 1902 the landforms recede from the river, but in the painting the dark rocks billow out more assertively as though coming to life in darkness. The meanings of this remarkable landscape are ineffable, as in a symbolist painting, but they are surely in some sense valedictory. While Homer's image of the capes says nothing directly about fishing, it nonetheless preserves a moment of visual memory shared by many anglers as the river carried them away from their favored fishing grounds.

By the time Homer first saw these landforms, they were already well-established wonders of Canadian scenery. Since the 1860s shiploads of summer excursionists had plied up the Saguenay on a day's outing from Tadoussac on the St. Lawrence

to marvel at the great forms before turning back. One such tourist was the poet Walt Whitman (1819–1892). On August 20, 1880, accompanied by his Canadian friend the physician Richard Maurice Bucke, Whitman traveled by steamer up the Saguenay to see the capes.[55] The self-described "half-paralytic" (strokes had impaired his motor abilities) published his account two years later in his *Specimen Days*. His description has a few coincidental correspondences with Homer's painted image. In his account, Whitman was at his most painterly, just as Homer was at his most poetic in painting the scene. Whitman wrote,

Up these black waters, over a hundred miles—always strong, deep (hundreds of feet, sometimes thousands), ever with high rocky hills for banks, green and gray, at times a little like some parts of the Hudson, but much more pronounced and defiant. The hills rise higher, keep their banks more unbroken. The river is straighter and of more resolute flow, and its hue, though dark as ink, exquisitely polished and sheeny under the August sun. Different, indeed, is this Saguenay, from all other rivers—different effects— a bolder, more vehement play of lights and shades. . . . But the great, haughty, silent capes themselves; I doubt if any crack points, or hills, or historic places of note, or anything of the kind elsewhere in the world, outvies these objects (I write while I am before them, face to face). They are very simple; they do not startle—at least they did not me—but they linger in one's memory forever. . . . Cape Eternity is bare, rising . . . sheer out of water, rugged and grim (yet with an indescribable beauty) nearly two thousand feet high. Trinity Rock, even a little higher, also rising flush, round topped like a great head with close-cut verdure of hair. I consider myself well repaid for coming my thousand miles to get the sight and memory of the unrivalled duo. . . . No, indeed—life and travel and memory will preserve to me no deeper-cut incidents, panorama, or sights to cheer my soul than . . . my days and nights up and down this fascinating savage river—the rounded

FIG. 81
Cape Trinity, Saguenay River, 1904–1909. Oil on canvas, 28 ¼ × 48 ¼ in.
Curtis Galleries, Minneapolis, Minnesota

mountains, some bare and gray, some dull red, some draped all over with matted green verdure or vines— the ample calm eternal rocks everywhere—the long streaks of motley foam, a milk-white curd on the glistening breast of the stream. . . .[56]

The twin capes drew from poet and painter alike images rooted in powerful visual experience. Whitman wrote about them as a tourist—an outsider to the region—excited by his single encounter with these wonders of nature. Homer painted them as a frequenter to the region—an insider. His moonlit depiction of the rocks came from memory at least as much as from his sketch. To him the capes stood as a portal to a world of wild nature

that he had known intimately for a decade as a fisherman and an artist. Whitman, by contrast, saw the capes as sentinels standing at the entrance to a world into which he was unable to go. Homer and other sportsmen heading home down the Saguenay found in the capes a concluding statement of the grand scale of the wilderness they had left. At this point their season's adventures became memory.

Homer seems not to have returned to Quebec City after 1902, but he visited Montreal from time to time in his last years, usually on his way to or from the Adirondacks. He was there for a few days at least as late as the summer of 1908.[57] Then in 1909, as an ill man, he put the finishing touches to his dark, brooding, richly painted *Cape Trinity, Saguenay River*. In doing this he effectively closed the book on his relationship with Quebec. Because he was then in declining health, the painting has sometimes been interpreted as a conscious or unconscious expression of his anticipation of death. There may be some validity to this reading of the work, but it does not find much support on the painting's vitally brushed surface. Everything on the canvas—indeed, everything about the painting from its conception through its crafting—speaks of a still-burgeoning creative impulse more than of feelings of despair or failing powers. Within his increasingly frail body, Homer strove in *Cape Trinity* to say new and deeper things about Quebec. He transcended the documentary nature of his sporting watercolors to capture in the dark capes an essence of the bigness and rawness of the Quebec wilderness. With *Cape Trinity* he made his final bow to the wild lands and waters that had served him so well for so many years as artist and angler.

NOTES

The author thanks the Bowdoin College Museum of Art, Brunswick, Maine, for permission to publish the text of Winslow Homer's letters; Jim Burant of the National Archives of Canada for guidance in Livernois matters; Barbara T. Johnson for her assistance in research; and Lucie Wellner for her design of the map of Homer's Quebec.

1. Winslow Homer to Charles Homer, June 19, 1892, The Homer Collection, Winslow Homer Papers and Family Memorabilia, Bowdoin College Museum of Art, 1964.47. The emphasis *"Canada preferred"* is Homer's. The letter has been cited in several publications since 1944 as having been written in 1895, but it is in fact dated three years earlier. Homer's "work" presumably involved the painting of Adirondack watercolors. The North Woods Club register records his presence in 1892 from June 18 through July 28 and again from September 17 through October 10. From the Adirondacks he had relatively easy access by rail to Montreal and Quebec City. If he in fact went to Canada in August and early September 1892, he would have been there at a prime period for fishing.

2. One of Homer's letters suggests that he also made a late winter visit to Quebec. Winslow Homer to Charles Homer, February 23 [no year], Homer Collection, Bowdoin College Museum of Art, 1964.69.66/1d. But as Patricia Junker shows in her essay in the present volume, despite Homer's mention of a Canadian hotel, he wrote the letter from and about Florida. The documentation of Homer's visits to Quebec is by no means complete. He may have gone to Quebec to fish before 1893, but he seems to have painted there, always in watercolor, only in 1895, 1897, and 1902.

3. Much of the Homer literature locates the club's lodge (clubhouse) at Lake Tourilli, but that lake was at the headwaters of the river, more than twenty miles north of its junction with the St. Anne River and would have been accessible only by extensive portages through rough terrain. The lodge was in fact located not far from the point where the Tourilli met the St. Anne. The building appears on the 1:50,000 topographical map *Rivière Tourilli Sheet* 21 M/4 (East Half) published in 1953 by the Department of Mines and Technical Surveys, Canada. The location of the Homer brothers' cabin may have been on the remote Lake Tourilli.

4. The name is from the Montagnais (Native American) meaning "little salmon." Typically pronounced wahn-a-nish, the name also appears in sporting publications of the 1880s and 1890s spelled "wa-na-nish," "winninish," and "winanish."

5. T. Morris Longstreth, *The Laurentians: The Hills of the Habitant* (New York: Century, 1922), 285.

6. Homer notes his presence at the Hotel Victoria in a letter to his brother. Charles Homer, Sunday [no date], 1895, Homer Collection, Bowdoin College Museum of Art, 1964.69.58d.

7. *Forest and Stream* 1, no. 4 (September 4, 1873): 53.

8. For an early column promoting the Saguenay and ouananiche fishing, see *Forest and Stream* 1, no. 4 (September 4, 1873): 53.

9. James M. Scovel, "Speaker Boyd's Winninish," *Forest and Stream* 32, no. 26 (July 18, 1888): 533.

10. *American Angler* 9, no. 9 (February 27, 1886): 13.

11. "Club Leases," *Forest and Stream* 33, no. 13 (October 17, 1889): 247.

12. George Van Felson, *Report of the St. Anne and Tourilli Exploring Expedition* (Quebec: Printed by L. Turcot for the Tourilli Fish and Game Club, 1890).

13. E.T.D. Chambers, "Angling in Canada," *Forest and Stream* 36, no. 19 (May 28, 1891): 376.

14. *Forest and Stream* 36, no. 19 (May 28, 1891): 387.

15. Horace J. Beemer, *A Guide to the Lake St. John and Its Tributary Waters* (Montreal: Lovell, n.d. [ca. 1890]).

16. Eugene McCarthy, *The Leaping Ouananiche: What It Is, Where, When, and How to Catch It* (New York: Forest and Stream, 1894). See David Tatham, "Winslow Homer's Library," *American Art Journal* 9, no. 1 (May 1977): 92–98.

17. William Henry Harrison Murray, *The Doom of the Mamelons: A Legend of the Saguenay and Lake St. John* (Philadelphia: Hubbard Brothers, 1888). The railway published its edition in the same year. That edition's continuing popularity is noted in "Angling Notes," *Forest and Stream*, February 27, 1890, 107.

18. William Henry Harrison Murray, *Adventures in the Wilderness; or, Camp-Life in the Adirondacks* (Boston: Fields, Osgood, & Co., 1869).

19. For Quebec as a successor to the Adirondacks, see Charles Hallock, "Club Preserves," *Forest and Stream* 33, no. 11 (October 3, 1889): 203.

20. "Canadian Clubs and Waters," *Forest and Stream* 34, no. 26 (July 17, 1890): 314.

21. E.T.D. Chambers, "American Anglers in Canada," *Forest and Stream* 37, no. 2 (July 30, 1891): 28.

22. Terry Smith, "Killing Fish," *Forest and Stream* 56, no. 22 (June 1, 1901): 429.

23. "Angling Notes," *Forest and Stream* 36, no. 22 (June 18, 1891): 436.

24. C.S.W., "A Three Weeks' Outing," *Forest and Stream* 36, no. 20 (June 4, 1891): 394.

25. C.S.W., "A Three Weeks' Outing," 394.

26. Winslow Homer to Charles Homer, Sunday [no date], 1895, Homer Collection, Bowdoin College Museum of Art, 1964.69.58d. For an account of the Grand Trunk line with its routes and timetables, see Jeff Holt, *The Grand Trunk in New England* (Toronto: Railfare Enterprises, 1986).

27. For accounts of other persons' travels from St. Raymond to the clubhouse in these years, see Fontinalis [pseud.], "Angling in Canada," *Forest and Stream* 34, no. 17 (May 15, 1890): 333; R. Bayinston, "Fishing à la Tourilli," *Outing: The Gentleman's Magazine of Sport, Travel, and Outdoor Life* 20 (September 1892): 488–492. These accounts confirm that the club's lodge was near the junction of the Tourilli and St. Anne Rivers, and not on Lake Tourilli.

28. The National Archives of Canada holds more than 1,500 of Livernois's photographs. Some of his work appeared in American sporting magazines. See E.T.D. Chambers, "Angling in Canadian Wilds," *Shooting and Fishing* 15, no. 9 (December 21, 1893): 174–177. For Livernois as a fisherman, see *Forest and Stream* 46, no. 18 (May 23, 1896): 419.

29. Fontinalis [pseud.], "Angling in Canada," *Forest and Stream* 32, no. 17 (May 16, 1889): 333.

30. *Tourilli Fish and Game Club, 18th Annual Report* (Quebec, 1907), 3. The report, for the 1906 season, was written by George Van Felson, who had served as the club's secretary since 1888.

31. Van Felson, *Report of the St. Anne and Tourilli Exploring Expedition*. The occasional misspellings and instances of odd punctuation are probably a result of a Francophone typesetter's struggles with Van Felson's handwriting.

32. Van Felson, *Report of the . . . Exploring Expedition*, 24: "Biscuits à la Gregory. Take for each two persons one and a half sailor biscuits (hard tack), let it soak over night. Having collected the grease of our morning's bacon, let this be in the frying pan over the fire, but only enough to cover the bottom. Lay in the biscuit halves and brown on both sides, season well. This being done, lay on a thin coating of marmalade, and serve hot. Whoo!!! Exclaims my Lieutenants when such a dish comes across their hungry gaze."

33. For example, his "Flies for the Ouananiche," in the Boston journal *Shooting and Fishing* 13, no. 25 (April 13, 1893): 7.

34. Winslow Homer to Charles Homer, Sunday [no date], 1895, Homer Collection, Bowdoin College Museum of Art, 1964.69.58d. Homer reports his arrival in Quebec from Portland and says that he planned to stay in the city for a day and would try to look up "Von Firson" (Van Felson). In the club's annual report for 1906 (see n. 30), which appears to list members in the order of their election, Homer is number 5 of 70. Charles is number 34, which suggests that he had joined the club at a later date than his brother. The report records a transfer of membership from N. F. Pulsifer to N. W. Atterbury. Pulsifer was the son-in-law of Charles Homer's late business associate, Lawson Valentine. By 1906 a heavy majority of the members were from the United States.

35. Lloyd Goodrich, *Winslow Homer* (New York: Macmillan, 1944), 147.

36. Goodrich, *Winslow Homer*, 147.

37. *Forest and Stream* 41, no. 9 (September 9, 1893): 212. The reproduction of the painting, engraved in wood by Henry Wolf, appears in *Century* 46, no. 4 (August 1893): 519.

38. *Forest and Stream* 41, no. 9 (September 9, 1893): 212.

39. A. N. Cheney, "Angling Notes," *Forest and Stream,* June 1, 1895, 444.

40. Goodrich, *Winslow Homer,* 147.

41. Van Felson later specified the site of *The Portage* and the identity of the guide. Goodrich, *Winslow Homer,* 147.

42. He had made drawings for publication in *Century* in the 1880s, some of which were then included in Robert Underwood Johnson and Clarence Clough Buel, eds., *Battles and Leaders of the Civil War*, 4 vols. (New York: Century, 1887–1889).

43. Henry Van Dyke, "Au Large," *Scribner's Magazine* 18, no. 3 (September 1895): 293–296.

44. Goodrich, *Winslow Homer,* 149–150.

45. *New York Evening Post*, April 6, 1898, 4.

46. *New York Sun*, April 3, 1898, 6.

47. *Boston Evening Transcript*, March 17, 1889, 5.

48. *Boston Evening Transcript*, October 30, 1895, 6.

49. *New-York Daily Tribune*, April 10, 1898, 6.

50. *New York Sun*, November 27, 1902, 6.

51. For the painting's genesis and reception, see Natalie Spassky et al., *American Paintings in the Metropolitan Museum of Art*, vol. 2, *A Catalogue of Works by Artists Born between 1816 and 1845* (Princeton, N.J.: Princeton University Press in association with the Metropolitan Museum of Art, 1985), 496–499.

52. Spassky et al., *American Paintings,* 496–499.

53. J. Russell Harper, *Painting in Canada: A History,* 2d ed. (Toronto: University of Toronto Press, 1977), 185.

54. George Munro Grant, ed., *Picturesque Canada: The Country as It Was and Is,* 2 vols. (Toronto: Belden, 1882), 2:716.

55. For a summary of Whitman's tour of eastern Canada, see David S. Reynolds, *Walt Whitman's America* (New York: Knopf, 1995), 529–530, 533.

56. Walt Whitman, *Specimen Days* (Philadelphia: Rees Welch, 1882). I have used the text from the modern edition compiled, edited, researched, and designed by Lance Hidy (Boston: David Godine, 1971), 101.

57. Winslow Homer to Charles Homer, July 18, 1908, Homer Collection, Bowdoin College Museum of Art, 1964.69.135a.

Fishing on the St. John's and Homosassa Rivers

Winslow Homer's Florida

Patricia Junker

Instead of wading icy-cold and over-fished brookes, tearing clothes and flesh in creeping through briers and brush, and being subjected to the sanguinary attention of mosquitoes and black flies in bringing to creel a few fingerlings, in Florida the angler can cast his fly from a sandy beach or boat, inhale the invigorating atmosphere, bask in the sunshine, and capture specimens of the finny tribe, the weight of which can be determined by pounds instead of ounces.

Dr. J. C. Kenworthy, a.k.a. Al Fresco,
Florida correspondent to *Forest and Stream*, 1883[1]

IT IS PROBABLY NOT JUST A COINCIDENCE THAT Winslow Homer's first trip to Florida overlapped with his fiftieth birthday, on February 24, 1886. Florida surely represented to him a special place, a place to mark such a major milestone in life— the ultimate place to indulge a growing passion for fly-fishing.

In the mid-1880s Florida was already regarded as an angler's heaven. The Standard Oil man Henry Morrison Flagler (1830–1913) had not yet developed the railways and luxurious resort hotels that would attract tourists to Florida's ocean beaches and transform the sunshine state into the northerner's winter playground. But northern sportsmen had already led the tourist advance into the tropical paradise. They had been discovering and touting the surpassing pleasures of hunting and fishing in Florida during the 1870s. Readers of *Forest and Stream* had been treated to sketches of adventure in Florida "almost from the first number," so the paper's publisher, Charles Hallock (1834–1917), declared in 1890. And, as a result, "Multitudes of visitors to the State have been prompted to seek its game resorts and fishing waters because the FOREST AND STREAM has made them known," he noted.[2] As that paper's correspondents penetrated the Everglades and charted the fishing waters of Florida's west coast during the 1870s, northern sportsmen enthusiastically read of their progress and followed not far behind, taking advantage of the sporting resorts already established in the accessible regions of the state. Some fishermen of the 1880s went to the gulf coast of Florida for the ocean fishing, for the great tarpon, the Silver King. But for Homer, as for most fly fishermen of his time, the attraction of Florida proved to be the fishing on inland waters, home to a great variety of tropical game fish: sea trout, channel bass, mangrove snapper, cavalli, and largemouth black bass, the last a fabled fighter, which grows to enormous size in southern waters. These Florida fish could provide fly fishermen with some of the most challenging and rewarding sport to be found anywhere. And anglers could enjoy their activity on Florida's beautiful, lazy, palmetto-fringed rivers amid comfortable surroundings at hostels perfectly suited to the needs of the northern sportsman.

Homer was not simply a tourist in Florida, he was an angling tourist, and his travels there were dictated by the fishing. He did in Florida

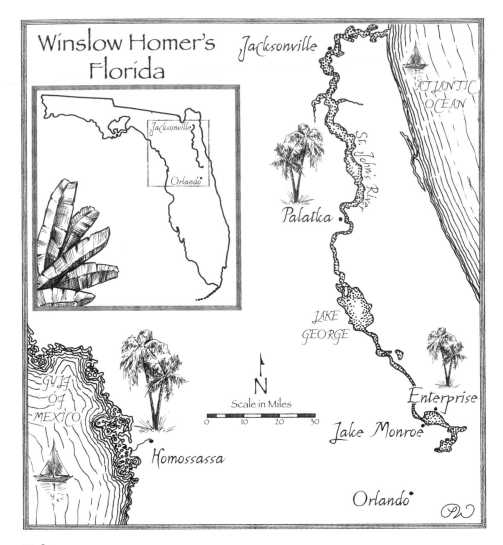

FIG. 82
Map showing Enterprise and Homosassa, Florida. Drawn by Lucie Wellner

[page 160]
DETAIL: FIG. 98
Black Bass, Florida, 1904.
Watercolor over graphite
on paper, 10 ⅞ × 19 ⅜ in.
Collection of Samuel H.
and Robbie Vickers,
The Florida Collection

what he had always done when he went looking for solace or inspiration, whether in Gloucester, Massachusetts; Cullercoats, England; Prout's Neck, Maine; or the Adirondacks of northern New York: when he found the place that best suited his purpose, he settled in. In his travels to Florida, he visited some of the state's most picturesque spots—Jacksonville, Tampa, and Key West—and even painted them. But his favorite places in Florida were two small resort settlements known primarily to anglers: Enterprise, on the St. John's River, a celebrated fishing mecca, which he visited on his first three trips to Florida; and Homosassa, near the gulf coast, which, once he discovered it in the winter of 1903–1904, supplanted even the better-known Enterprise as Homer's favorite place to fish (fig. 82).

The St. John's River at Enterprise

Alligators sunning themselves in the creeks, and the foliage now so dense that the novelty of it is passed; also that lovely contrast of the brown masses of trees with the bright, tender green. All this, with an occasional gigantic cypress reflected in the perfectly still water of the creeks, make pictures to wonder at if not to paint.

Boston painter William Morris Hunt (1824–1879),
writing from Magnolia, Florida, on the St. John's River, 1874[3]

"This is the most beautiful place in Florida," Homer wrote to his friend and patron Thomas B. Clarke on February 16, 1890, from the Brock House, a hotel in Enterprise.[4] He had visited there four years earlier, on his first trip to Florida, when he also traveled to Tampa on the gulf coast and then went south to Key West. But of all the locales he saw on that initial tour, it was Enterprise, in central Florida, that must have impressed him most, for in 1890 he returned there to paint and to fish.

Tampa had possessed a picturesque natural charm that Homer painted in 1885–1886 in postcard-like views—shoreline scenes with moss-laden oaks and tropical birds. The island city of Key West was lively and exotic, its Cuban and Bahamian residents engaged in cigar manufacturing, sponging, and turtling, though Homer was drawn to the graceful towering palms, which seem to have dominated his view of the place. Tiny inland Enterprise was not at all like either of these seaports. Homer was not alone in appreciating its distinctive charms, however, for Enterprise was a popular destination for anglers and so-called invalids, who traveled there for rest and for the rejuvenating sulphur springs.

Nothing of the nineteenth-century resort Enterprise remains today, but it is not difficult to gauge the spirit of the place Homer knew. Though it was once the seat of Volusia County, the town was never large. "This little place consists of a hotel, a store, and two or three houses and has a population of perhaps forty," an angler visitor had described it in *Forest and Stream* in 1873.[5] Developers no doubt had pinned their hopes and fortunes on its continuing growth as a resort, but their prospects changed when Flagler began to develop Florida's Atlantic coast in the late 1880s. The small town has now all but disappeared, and a few stately private residences and a large modern Methodist orphanage stand on deep stretches of the shoreline where the impressive Brock House, the only hotel in Enterprise, once stood. The landscape, as we know it from late-nineteenth-century photographs, seems unchanged, however (figs. 83, 84). Count Frederick de Bary's (1815–1898) famous orange groves, mature by the early 1870s, have been preserved.[6] Majestic old oaks festooned with long veils of Spanish moss line the shore, sheltering the homes and shading the brilliant sunlight off the broad lake—Lake Monroe it is called, though it is actually a wide spot in the St. John's River. The shoreline road is a magnificent arcade of overarching

FIG. 83
Green Springs, Enterprise, Florida, 1870s. Stereoview photograph, photographer unknown. Florida Photographic Collection, Florida State Archives

FIG. 84
Gemini Springs, Enterprise, Florida, late 19th century. Stereoview photograph, photographer unknown. Florida Photographic Collection, Florida State Archives

FIG. 85
Deep Creek, Florida, 1880–1897. Photograph by William Henry Jackson (1843–1942), published by Detroit Publishing Company. The Library of Congress, Prints and Photographs Division

FIG. 87
An alligator hunting party, Enterprise, Florida, late 19th century. Stereoview photograph, photographer unknown. Florida Photographic Collection, Florida State Archives

oaks, their densely interwoven boughs and silken moss drapes filtering the light and transforming the roadway into a kind of glittering Gothic cathedral nave. Even with the sunlight off the large mirror lake, the colors of nature at Enterprise are dark and cool. The mood of the place is a satisfying peace. For northern tourists steamboating up the St. John's from Jacksonville in the 1870s and 1880s, lovely wooded Enterprise and the six-mile-wide Lake Monroe must have been a refreshing contrast to the narrow, swampy stretches of the lower St. John's, as picturesque as they were with overhanging cypress and palmettos, thick reeds, and patches of water hyacinths (fig. 85).

Jacob Brock and his St. John's River steamboat line put Enterprise on the map in the 1860s. The Brock line was the first to offer service south of Palatka, one of many river towns that flourished with sightseeing on the St. John's. Brock built a comfortable hotel at Enterprise in 1856 to lure passengers onto his riverboats, and Lake Monroe became the southern terminus for tourist traffic on the St. John's. There were fine resorts for travelers all along the lower St. John's—the brother of the Vermont rod and tackle manufacturer Charles F. Orvis kept a lodge at Palatka, for instance.[7] But anyone wishing to have a full experience on the romantic St. John's traveled the entire steamboat route upstream from Jacksonville to Enterprise and stayed at the Brock House. The New York artist Alexander Helwig Wyant made the trip to Enterprise in 1871 and painted the charming Brock House in its wooded setting, showing it as a large structure, three stories tall, with broad porches facing the lake (fig. 86). It offered accommodations for fifty people. Some tourists came to bathe in the sulphur springs, but Enterprise, with its pristine fishing waters and still wild woodlands, quickly became known as a sportsman's paradise (fig. 87). Ulysses S. Grant and Grover Cleveland were just two of the many famous well-heeled sportsmen who traveled

FIG. 86
Alexander Helwig Wyant (1836–1892), *Enterprise, at Lake Monroe,* 1871. Oil on canvas, 15 × 27 in. Collection of Samuel H. and Robbie Vickers, The Florida Collection. The subject is the Brock House hotel.

there. Hunters and anglers came in increasing numbers year after year. By the time Homer visited in 1886, the hotel had already been substantially enlarged and refined by new owners. By 1891 the proprietor of the famous Brock House could promote his grand hostel as "one of the most comfortable and homelike hotels in Florida," offering, according to his broadside (fig. 88), "Gas, Bells, Baths, Orchestra, Artesian Well, Mineral Springs, Telegraph Office in Hotel, Steam Launch for use of guests, ORANGES FREE TO GUESTS FROM BROCK HOUSE GROVE. Sailing, Hunting and Fishing. Interesting Drives. Service, Attendance and Cuisine of the highest order."[8]

Homer's first trip to Florida in the winter of 1885–1886 inspired only a few paintings, and it is difficult to chart his travels during the two months that he spent in the state. When he arrived in Florida,

FIG. 88
Broadside advertisement for the Brock House, Enterprise, Florida, 1891. Courtesy Florida Photographic Collection, Florida State Archives

FIG. 89
A Norther—Key West, 1886. Watercolor over graphite on paper, 13 ³⁄₁₆ × 19 ½ in. Fine Arts Museums of San Francisco, Achenbach Foundation for Graphic Arts. Gift of Mr. and Mrs. John D. Rockefeller 3rd

probably by ocean steamer from New York, Homer went from Jacksonville, the center for all Florida tourist travel, first to Tampa, it seems—a watercolor *At Tampa* bears the date 1885.[9] Possibly he was curious about the tarpon fishing at nearby Tarpon Springs, a place well known to anglers. He then traveled southward, settling for a time after the first of the year at Key West, a popular tourist destination, and he painted there (fig. 89).[10] Most of the watercolors from this first Florida tour were done, presumably, on the gulf coast and at Key West.

Yet, one watercolor also places Homer at Enterprise that winter: a painting the Homers referred to as *Thornhill Bar,* dated 1886 (cat. 7), an angling scene showing the prominent sandbar at Thornhill Lake, another broad extension of the St. John's, just upstream from Lake Monroe.[11] Whatever

else he might have planned to do on this trip, Homer could not have missed the opportunity to fish the fabled waters of Lake Monroe and the St. John's. Thornhill Bar is a distinct landmark that has been created by the river currents. The same currents that have built the sandbar also carry with them a rich supply of food for fish. Thornhill Bar is well known to anglers on these waters as a rewarding place to cast a line. Homer sketched the impressive sandbar in a luminous watercolor, which he presented to his brother Charles on his return from Florida, probably because he knew how much the scene of this fine fishing spot would mean to a fellow angler. Charles would fish there himself two years later.

Homer arrived at the Brock House on February 11, 1886, accompanied by his elderly father, his companion on this Florida tour.[12] Homer's uncle, Arthur W. Benson, was then in residence at the Brock House, too, as he had been every season for several years, and the Homers probably traveled to Enterprise to meet Benson there.[13] On this initial visit, the artist stayed at Enterprise for nearly two weeks. He was back in Jacksonville on February 24, his birthday, preparing to make the journey home, for the local *Florida Times Union* reported on that day that Homer and his father had arrived at the city's elegant St. James Hotel in the company of their good friend Lawson Valentine, brother Charles's business partner at Valentine & Company varnish manufacturers.[14]

Arthur W. Benson could well have figured large in his nephew's plans to embark on a fishing excursion to Florida in 1885. Benson, Homer's mother's favorite younger brother, was an avid angler, well known to serious sportsmen. His reputation as an angling enthusiast is documented in a profile written for *Forest and Stream* by no less an angling authority than Charles Hallock, that paper's founder and publisher.[15] Benson's nephews must have admired him—most everyone who knew him did.[16] He had made his fortune in the shipping

CAT. 7

Thornhill Bar, 1886. Watercolor over graphite on paper, 14 × 20 in. Museum of Fine Arts, Boston.
Gift of Mrs. Robert B. Osgood, 1939 (39.620). © Museum of Fine Arts, Boston

business by the early 1840s and used it to build the residential gaslight utility in Brooklyn, where he lived, as well as to develop Long Island beachfront properties. Thus, he could easily afford to indulge his irrepressible passion for fishing almost year-round. In summer, Benson fished at Montauk Point, where, beginning in 1879, he had developed a small, private cottage community and family compound that, remarkably, foreshadowed the development that the Homers undertook at Prout's Neck, Maine, only a few years later.[17] In winter, Benson fished at Enterprise. The amenities of the Brock House were such that it could comfortably accommodate Benson even in his later years, when, somewhat infirm, he traveled with both a manservant and a female nurse. Benson died at Enterprise on December 27, 1889, and his hometown newspaper carried a lengthy news item about his death that suggests his long association with that Florida angler's resort. On December 30, 1889, the *Brooklyn Daily Eagle* reported that Benson had suffered a heart attack while fishing on Lake Monroe:

On these trips [to Enterprise] he was accompanied by a colored attendant, who looked after his wants, which were few and simple. It was his custom to leave the Brock House . . . at an early hour in the morning and remain on the water all day. This he followed to the end. He was enjoying his favorite pastime when the summons came. On Friday morning he had, as usual, gone off with his attendant at an early hour for a day's fishing. They had not been on the water very long before the fatal attack seized him. He had his line cast and was quietly awaiting a bite when his man saw him suddenly place his hand to his heart. He turned partly around in his seat, and after a few brief struggles, fell back dead in his attendant's arms with his line still cast.[18]

Homer's return to Florida—to Enterprise—four years after his first visit in 1886 followed by only a few weeks his uncle's death there. Homer went to Enterprise for a short holiday in late February 1890. He felt no need to tour Florida this time—Homer went straight to Enterprise and stayed there. When he arrived at the Brock House, the hotel's proprietor and guests must still have been talking about his famous uncle's rather dramatic demise. Possibly Homer had planned this second visit to Enterprise to fish with Benson and, having made the necessary arrangements before his uncle's sudden death, simply proceeded with the trip as scheduled. Certainly he was in the mood to fish and to paint in the outdoors. The previous year, 1889, had been dedicated to work on what proved to be a magnificent series of watercolors, primarily on angling themes. They were the products of Homer's two extended stays that year, in spring and fall, at the private sportsmen's club known as the Adirondack Preserve Association in New York's North Country. Before leaving for Florida, Homer delivered thirty-three of the new Adirondack watercolors to the galleries of Gustave Reichard and Company in New York for a special exhibition that excited him greatly. He had developed a show of pictures for anglers—he had even encouraged his dealer to market them through the popular sporting magazines—and then went off to Enterprise to await the fishermen's response to the new paintings. The show opened in New York on February 14 and was both a critical and a commercial success; before it closed at the end of the month, all but three of Homer's new watercolors had sold.[19]

Homer was keen to maintain his creative momentum and expand his repertoire of angling subjects from those he had discovered in the Adirondacks, and thus he moved on to Enterprise for his winter's work in another angler's retreat. On February 16, 1890, having just taken up residence at the Brock House, Homer, filled with anticipation, wrote to Thomas B. Clarke in New York, "I commence work and play tomorrow. I expect to show you something when I return."[20] Clarke had been enthusiastic about the Adirondack angling water-colors and bought two from the Reichard gallery exhibition. It seems that Homer was eager to show him what else he could do with the theme or what else he might achieve in watercolor under different conditions of light and atmosphere.

Homer's two-week stay in Enterprise in February 1890 was far shorter than his lengthy fishing holidays in the Adirondacks had been in 1889, and it yielded far fewer paintings. Eleven watercolors made at or around Lake Monroe are known, most of them quick studies of the pictur-esque shoreline seen from some distance out in the broad lake—spare scenes where a far-off line of old oaks is here and there punctuated by tall, expressive palms.[21] Recording his angling experiences in para-dise, Homer emphasized the paradise over the angling, for in these watercolors Florida's distinctive landscape features and winter light are more than backdrop to dramatic angling scenes; they are the subjects themselves.

Angling subjects pushed Homer to an ever greater simplification and abstraction in his water-colors as he sketched increasingly in the open air and responded to the pictorial challenges of the transparency and reflective qualities of water. The spatial complexities and ambiguities that Homer had begun to explore in his 1889 studies of Adiron-dack trout ponds became more freely developed in his subsequent Enterprise scenes, most of which appear to have been done directly, on the spot. When Homer looked into an Adirondack trout pond and saw forms magically suspended in an indefinable space, he translated his observations into studied and riveting painted compositions unbounded by conventional figure/ground relation-ships. The transparency and mirror quality of still water plays tricks on our eyes, confusing our sense of what lies on or above the surface and what lies below, and Homer was intrigued by the pictorial possibilities of this confusion. He re-created it

masterfully in, for instance, *An Unexpected Catch* (cat. 18, ill. p. 112), in which a sunfish seems almost to hover in space as we struggle to discern where the surface of the water might be. A different kind of spatial disorientation could be observed on the broad expanse of Lake Monroe. When sitting in a boat far out on the lake, looking across the miles of its expanse, Homer's view was exceedingly spare. From this vantage point, under certain conditions of light and atmosphere, the distant horizon might seem to fall away and water and sky could appear to merge. Homer observed Lake Monroe anglers in the silver mist of a morning fog or against the bril-liant backdrop of the setting sun, and he translated such scenes into highly reductive color abstractions. In *Rowing Home* (fig. 90), for example, the anglers,

FIG. 90
Rowing Home, 1890. Watercolor on paper, 13 ¾ × 19 ⅞ in. The Phillips Collection, Washington, D.C.

CAT. 21
St. John's River, Florida, 1890. Watercolor over graphite on paper, 13 ½ × 19 ⅞ in.
The Hyde Collection Trust, Glens Falls, New York (1971.70)

only barely discernible as such in Homer's short-hand sketch of their silhouetted forms, float in a luminous field of gold and vermilion that conveys perfectly the glare of the late afternoon sun on the water. At other times Homer delighted in the hallucinatory effect of reflections. The most intricate of Homer's paintings of the play of color and light on the water at Enterprise is an angling scene entitled simply *St. John's River, Florida* (cat. 21), a study made near the shoreline of, presumably, Lake Monroe. Clearly Homer was inspired by the dazzling mirror effects created by the smooth, brilliant surface of the placid lake. In this watercolor he created a kind of flat painted tapestry of loosely interwoven forms and colors: deep green palmettos and purple oaks with long tendrils of green, blue, and lavender Spanish moss. The fluid pattern of this band of tall trees is matched top to bottom within the composition as Homer conveyed their disorienting reflection in a deep stretch of uninterrupted water. At center anglers in a white rowboat cast to a rise-form, a short streak of white light that helps to ground the viewer by establishing where on this dense, dark field of color the surface of the lake lies.

Another decade would pass before Homer traveled south again to fish and to paint. He was fishing regularly in the Adirondacks, of course, at the North Woods Club, where he was a member. And in the 1890s he also made at least three excursions to the great fishing waters of Quebec, a place that inspired an extensive series of watercolors documenting his angling experiences there in the summers of 1895 and 1897. But his travels—and his painting, too, he said—had been restricted by the demands of caring for his elderly ailing father in these years. With his father's death on August 22, 1898, Homer was free of those responsibilities and was at a crossroads in his life and art. That December he went to Nassau in the Bahamas and enjoyed a highly productive two months, painting a series of brilliant watercolors, scenes made along the white sandy coastline, many

depicting Bahamian sponge divers and turtlers. He was looking for material to develop into oil paintings, he told his friend Clarke—and, indeed, after this trip to Nassau he would bring to completion in oil his long percolating idea for *The Gulf Stream* (fig. 91), first conceived in Nassau in watercolor in 1885.[22] But more than inspiring new works in oil, this return visit to Nassau reawakened in Homer an interest in painting light-filled watercolors in tropical locales, and the next few years would find him painting in Bermuda and Florida with renewed vigor.

Satisfied by his work in Nassau, he left there in February 1899 and went to Florida— to Enterprise again—this time simply to rest and to fish. "I shall not go North until it is warmer but I am through work for the winter & desire to report myself *very well*," he wrote to Clarke from the Brock House on February 25, 1899, the day after his sixty-third birthday.[23]

FIG. 91
The Gulf Stream, 1899. Oil on canvas, 28 ⅛ × 49 ⅛ in. The Metropolitan Museum of Art, New York. Wolfe Fund, Catherine Lorillard Wolfe Collection (06.1234). Photograph © The Metropolitan Museum of Art

Over the next decade, as winters at Prout's Neck became harder and harder for the aging Homer to endure, extended trips to Florida would become more frequent. But after 1899, he would spend little time at Enterprise. Perhaps the Brock House resort had grown too popular for Homer's liking. Or perhaps he felt little need to return to Lake Monroe when he discovered better fishing elsewhere in Florida. And he did—on the Homosassa River, near the central gulf coast. On his subsequent visits to Florida, Homer would be based there; and there he would paint his last known watercolors.

THE HOMOSASSA RIVER

But for all places for anglers, Homosassa bears away the palm.

American Angler, *March 24, 1883*[24]

In November 1903, with winter on him at Prout's Neck, Homer began to consider a long stay in Florida. Now he was interested not so much in Enterprise as in other locales along the gulf coast. He decided that he would take the Mallory line ocean steamer to Key West: "I know the place quite well," he told his brother Arthur in Galveston, Texas, "and it's near the points in Florida that I wish to visit."[25]

One place that he must have intended to visit as he planned this Florida trip was Homosassa, a tiny village on the river of the same name, situated six miles from the gulf and about an hour's drive north of Tampa today. After two weeks in Key West—a short stay that nevertheless brought forth a group of extraordinarily fluid watercolor studies of fishing sloops in the harbor—Homer moved on to Homosassa, where he settled in, staying through mid-February (figs. 92, 93). Although he must have been seeing Homosassa for the first time, Homer certainly knew well its reputation as a superior fishing ground. The river's source is the Homosassa Springs, located about nine miles upstream from its mouth at the Gulf of Mexico, and its shallow waters are crystal clear. "I suppose this is one of the few places where, owing to the clearness of the water, the angler can select the specimen of fish he wishes to take," an early visitor to Homosassa reported in *American Angler* in 1883.[26] Near the mouth of the river, the fresh water commingles with the saltwater of the gulf, and, as a consequence, the Homosassa is home to a great variety of fish, both fresh- and saltwater species: channel bass, sheepshead, sea trout, back bass, sunfish, bream, and others. One enthusiastic fisherman in Homosassa noted in *American Angler* in 1886 that a record "thirteen varieties of fins, in a morning's fish, have been lifted on the feathered hook."[27]

Enterprise had been developed by the commercial steamboating entrepreneur Jacob Brock, who wished to stimulate and capitalize on tourism; Brock's grand hotel was a symbol of his aspirations for the place. Homosassa, by contrast, was developed into an angler's enclave in the late 1880s by a small group of serious northern sportsmen led by the famous down-easter Joshua Lawrence Chamberlain (1828–1914)—Civil War hero of the Battle of Gettysburg, former two-term governor of Maine, and past president of Bowdoin College; and as a resident of Portland, Maine, he was, coincidentally, something of a near neighbor to Homer at Prout's Neck.[28] Until the 1880s, Homosassa had been a deeply forested backwater known primarily for cedar lumbering and turpentine distilling. In 1886 Chamberlain and his Yankee syndicate purchased twelve thousand acres along the Homosassa River with a plan to establish a sportsmen's resort. They developed the Homosassa Inn (fig. 94) at the river's edge, enlarging an extant structure, and they hired Captain A. E. Willard and his wife, Helen, to run it. The Willards had managed the comfortable

FIG. 94
The Homosassa Inn, early 20th century. Photographer unknown. Citrus County Historical Society, Inverness, Florida

Suwanee Hotel at Cedar Keys and were the kind of experienced hostelers Chamberlain wanted to make his Homosassa Inn a favorite establishment among anglers. Their efforts and experience quickly paid off: the inn was soon filled with eminent guests who reportedly included men like John Jacob Astor and, again, that inveterate angler Grover Cleveland.[29] On January 7, 1904, Homer registered there for a stay of five weeks—his first of several visits over the next few years.[30]

As beautiful and charming as Homosassa is, there is nothing grand about the place. It is now as it has always been—a simple sportsman's retreat. It was never anything remotely like the spa that Enterprise had been. Even after Chamberlain built the Silver Springs, Ocala, and Gulf Railway, connecting Homosassa to points well inland and making the resort easily accessible at last, the settlement remained small and wholly oriented toward the river. Sport fishing is not incidental to life here; it is everything. The place has something of the appearance and

FIG. 95
The Rendezvous Sportsmen's Lodge, Homosassa, Florida, early 20th century.
Photographer unknown. Citrus County Historical Society, Inverness, Florida

social air of an American backwoods Venice: cottages and boathouses and guest hostels line the banks, each building fronting on the river. In Homer's day the principal establishments along these shores were the Homosassa Inn, on the south side, and directly opposite, the Rendezvous Sportsmen's Lodge (fig. 95). Boats move casually up and down and across the narrow passage, and the Homosassa feels like the town's major thoroughfare. And like any small-town Main Street, it is a delightful center of activity. For all the wealth and celebrity concentrated here during the winter fishing season, there has always been a distinctive informality about Homosassa, a lack of pretension, an easy exchange among everyone on the river—among the wealthy angling tourists and the local river guides, fishermen, and crabbers. Even the birds—great blue herons, egrets, brown pelicans, and anhingas—seem happy to be a part of the congenial mix.

The fishing, the climate, the simple accommodations, the people—it seems that everything about Homosassa appealed to Homer. Writing to his brother Arthur on his arrival there, Homer enthused, "Delightful climate here about as cool as our September—Fishing the best in America as far as I can find." To make his point, he sketched for Arthur the different species of fish he had already managed to land (figs. 96, 97): cavalle [*sic*], channel bass ("looks like a new $20 gold piece," Homer said), sea trout, black bass, and sheepshead.[31] At the Homosassa Inn, he was entertained by the charming Helen Willard, a worldly, independent-minded woman, who, after the death of her husband, managed the property on her own. We also know from an extant copy of Willard's accounts ledger that Homer's companions at the inn that winter comprised an array of fascinating people: James Weir Jr. of New York (who visited with his wife), a neurologist and author of several studies on sexual desire; Charles Embree Thorne, an agriculturalist and soil scientist affiliated with Ohio State University; and George B. Martin, a Philadelphia newspaper man.[32] Dinner-table conversation must have been lively, indeed. Homer seems to have particularly enjoyed the company of Captain Edward Bethel Richardson, a local, Mrs. Willard's trusted friend and adviser, the man who would become her second husband; Homer said he stayed with Captain Richardson on a subsequent visit. Richardson, ten years Homer's junior, was probably quite a contrast to everyone else the artist knew, for he was a Southerner and a Confederate veteran; he had fought with the rebel army when just a young man of fifteen or sixteen.[33]

Although luminous watercolors seemed to flow easily from his brush when Homer painted at Key West in December 1904, he was not optimistic about the prospects for selling those and subsequent paintings, and thus he was slow to pick up work again at Homosassa. "I shall fish until the 20th then my guide has another engagement & I shall take my own boat and work half the time and fish on my own hook," Homer told Arthur. "I shall only paint to see if I am up [to] it," he continued, "and with a chance of paying expenses."[34] Fishing, he seemed to be saying, was his primary objective.

Yet the fishing at Homosassa proved to be his inspiration. In these weeks of January and February 1904 Homer painted some of his most dramatic angling scenes. A few of these watercolors show picturesque landmarks along the river, sites that were well known to anglers who had fished the Homosassa near the Willards' inn: Turkey Buzzard Island, a natural rookery; Hell's Gate, an opening downstream, near the swampy mouth of the river; and a shell heap, a peculiar feature of Florida waters, a centuries-old refuse mound left by early Indians who survived on what must have been extraordinary amounts of shellfish.[35] Other scenes are not so specific but suggest the rich color and sharp, thorny textures of the deeply forested banks, which Homer aptly referred to as Homosassa jungle (cats. 51, 52). In his day, the river was lined with seemingly impenetrable woods—dense cedars, palmettos, and mangroves—which must have lent a distinct air of mystery to the river. Even today the stretches of woodland that remain in the swampy regions downstream are a source of endless fascination to boaters, for they provide an eerie panorama, which here and there reveals evidence of wild animal habitation—panthers or alligators perhaps—or the curious rotting remains of old cabins.

Most of the Homosassa watercolors function as a kind of Florida angler's travelogue. But another group, a trio of paintings of fighting fish, stands apart as arguably Homer's most stunning achievement in the trophy picture genre, if we can expand that term to include Homer's highly original fish studies. A lifetime of angling experience was brought to bear on these paintings of Florida fish, and a lifetime of experimentation with watercolor

as well, for they are deft and fluid. But there is also an element of place that underlies these dramatic compositions, an artist's response to the distinctive character of the fishing at Homosassa.

Homer had painted close-up views of brilliant leaping fish earlier, in the Adirondacks, but these Florida fish studies are different technically, formally, and conceptually. The dark hues of the North Woods had brought forth from the artist deeply saturated sheets of midnight blue, viridian, ultramarine, and violet, worked with a heavily loaded brush or laid down layer on transparent layer. Against such inscrutable backdrops, flashes of light that were the underside of a shimmering,

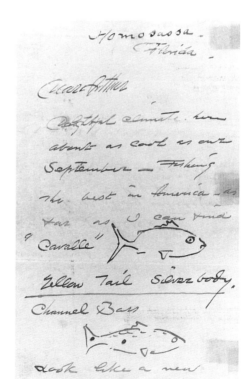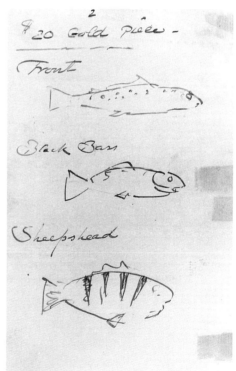

FIGS. 96 AND 97
Sketches of Fish Caught in the Homosassa River, in Winslow Homer's letter to his brother Arthur, from Homosassa, Florida, January 1904, pages 1 and 2. Bowdoin College Museum of Art, Brunswick, Maine. Gift of the Homer family, 1964.69.105/1-3

CAT. 51

Homosassa Jungle in Florida, 1904. Watercolor over graphite on paper, 13 ⅝ × 21 ⁷⁄₁₆ in. Harvard University Art Museums (Fogg Art Museum), Cambridge, Massachusetts. Gift of Mrs. Charles S. Homer, in memory of the late Charles S. Homer and his brother, Winslow Homer (1935.50). © President and Fellows of Harvard College

CAT. 52
Red Shirt, Homosassa, Florida, 1904. Watercolor over graphite on paper, 14 × 19 ¾ in. National Gallery of Art,
Washington, D.C. Gift of Ruth K. Henschel in memory of her husband, Charles R. Henschel (1975.92.13).
Photograph © 2001 Board of Trustees, National Gallery of Art

FIG. 98
Black Bass, Florida, 1904. Watercolor over graphite on paper, 10 ⅞ × 19 ⅜ in.
Collection of Samuel H. and Robbie Vickers, The Florida Collection

leaping trout or that served to signal a fish's rise on impenetrably dark waters were the result of the artist's sparing use of the white of the paper or the slightest strokes of opaque white. Florida scenes required a lighter touch, however, and a different palette—they required a sense of sunlight, clarity, tropical color, and heat. Homer's studies of Florida fish—a pair of fighting black bass pictures (figs. 98, 99) and a glittering specimen of the channel bass (cat. 50, ill. p. 87)—are all painted with fluid calligraphic strokes of thin transparent color so that the fish appear as though bathed in light, appear even to emanate light.

This trio of fish paintings suggests the sensations Homer gathered while angling in this particular locale. The extraordinary optical qualities of the still, clear, shallow water make fishing on the Homosassa a heightened visual experience because the fish are clearly visible. Homer could envision a shimmering channel bass moving along the river bottom in blue crystalline water, about to take the fly, because the shallow Homosassa offered up such visual delights and stimulated a painter's imagination. Even the discarded bottles in this strange composition, odd and amusing details that Homer included, he said, to convey an idea of the fish's

FIG. 99
Life-size Black Bass, 1904. Watercolor over graphite on paper, 17 ½ × 24 ½ in. Private collection

FIG. 100
Living room of Winslow Homer's studio-home at Prout's Neck, Maine, 1936. Photograph by the artist's nephew Charles Lowell Homer. Bowdoin College Museum of Art, Brunswick, Maine. Gift of the Homer family, 1964. A group of Florida watercolors, with *Black Bass, Florida* (fig. 98), hangs on the wall above the settee.

too, as Homer shows us. A fish's physical strength, will to live, and tortured death throes are easily felt in a fight with a fish so large, and Homer now depicted that struggle with an unprecedented emotional intensity, showing it as the simultaneously exhilarating and horrifying sight that it is. In both pictures of fighting black bass that he created at Homosassa—one a broad scene, with the fish viewed from some distance, and the other an unnerving close-up view—the fish appears beautiful and balletic as it leaps to its death. The physical and emotional impact of both studies owes much to the dramatic notes of blood red color—the fish's gills—that punctuate these near monochromatic compositions in deep tropical green tones. Within the body of Homer's late experimental work these are among the watercolors that most closely approach highly refined Japanese ink painting.[37] By virtue of his fluid calligraphic brushwork and dramatic color patterns, Homer managed to create in his wrenching studies of thrashing, contorted, death-defying black bass a pair of paintings that are, ironically, among his most beautiful and even elegant works. And with them he distilled from his Florida angling experience a singularly powerful expression of the joy and miracle of life, a profound sense of death, and the wonder and mystery of nature.

Following his stimulating first visit to Homosassa in 1904, Homer returned there in subsequent winters, in the first months of 1905, 1908, and 1909.[38] But except for the charming watercolor of a speckled sea trout that he painted in 1905 for Mrs. R. A. Watts, the wife of a fishing companion (cat. 53, ill. p. 84), he did not paint there again. By 1906 his health was deteriorating. His watercolors had not sold well. He was content now just to fish.

"I am living with Captain Richardson and *living high,*" Homer wrote to his brother Charles from Homosassa in late February 1909. This trip he was staying with his old friend, renting makeshift quarters above an old dance hall. "I was never so

large size, make sense when the viewer comprehends how shallow the river is in places.[36] His channel bass is not a literal depiction of a fish underwater by any means, but it does suggest how acutely visual Homer's angling on the Homosassa could be. On the lazy Homosassa, angling is not necessarily rigorous, but the fishing is nevertheless quite physical. Homer caught large fish there— black bass especially, fish much larger and stronger than the rainbow and brook trout he typically pursued in the Adirondacks. Imparting a sense of scale was important when he took these fish for subjects. Presenting a magnificent black bass life-size, for instance, Homer could give us only the enormous head and upper body on a fourteen-by-twenty-inch watercolor sheet. The strike of a great black bass could be an intensely visceral experience, nicely fixed in terms of air and room," he remarked to Charles with glee.[39] At Homosassa, he had found the equivalent of life at Prout's Neck, Maine, a life of simplicity, a life close to nature. At this time, Homosassa had come to fit perfectly into the pattern of his days, as he traveled with the changing seasons from Prout's Neck to the North Woods Club in the Adirondacks to Florida, satisfying his need for sport, fellowship, and a kind of easy encounter with nature that nourished him physically, spiritually, and artistically. But after his stay in Homosassa in February and March 1909, the fates would never again permit Homer to return to these warm climes. The following winter he felt too ill to travel, it seems.[40] By the summer of 1910 he seemed to be preparing for the end. In August he entertained at his studio the New York dealer William Macbeth, and the two men, in a reflective mood, "roamed over his Prout's Neck possessions, with their many wonderful views, far and near," Macbeth remembered.[41] Homer's Florida watercolors were among the pictures of far-off places that the two men reflected on that day (fig. 100). And perhaps more than any of his other tropical scenes, the Florida paintings must have stirred within the artist especially fond memories of people and events, for it was there that he often marked birthdays and renewed friendships and enjoyed memorable fishing. Though he created a relatively small number of paintings there, Homer grew to feel attached to Florida as he did to few other places. "The place suits me as if made for me by a kind providence," he wrote to Charles from Homosassa on February 23, 1909, on the eve of his seventy-third birthday.[42] For Homer, nearing the end of his life, Florida was more than a fishing retreat, and the time he spent there over a twenty-three-year period, more than a winter holiday. Simply put, Florida was to him a gift, a divine gift.

NOTES

1. Dr. J. C. Kenworthy, "Fly-Fishing in Florida," in Charles F. Orvis and A. Nelson Cheney, eds., *Fishing with the Fly: Sketches by Lovers of the Art, with Illustrations of the Standard Flies* (1883; reprint, Secaucus, N.J.: The Wellfleet Press, 1989), 311.

2. [Charles Hallock], "The Sportsman's Florida," *Forest and Stream* 33, no. 25 (January 9, 1890): 485. For a history of Flagler's development in Florida, see Samuel Proctor, "Prelude to a New Florida, 1877–1919," in Michael Gannon, ed., *The New History of Florida* (Gainesville: University Press of Florida, 1996), 266–286.

3. Hunt, to an unknown correspondent, from Magnolia, Florida, April 2, 1874, quoted in Helen M. Knowlton, *Art-Life of William Morris Hunt* (Boston: Little, Brown, and Company, 1900), 106.

4. Homer to Thomas B. Clarke, from Enterprise, Florida, February 16, 1890, William T. Evans Papers, Archives of American Art, Smithsonian Institution (hereafter AAA), microfilm reel number 2814, frame 581.

5. Piseco, "Sketches in Florida. Up the St. John's River," *Forest and Stream* 1, no. 17 (December 11, 1873): 275.

6. Count Frederick de Bary came to the United States from Germany in 1851 and became the American representative of Mumm's champagne. In the late 1860s de Bary settled in Florida, establishing a baronial estate at Enterprise, which included extensive orange groves and a hunting preserve. See Branch Cabell and A. J. Hanna, *The St. John's: A Parade of Diversities, The Rivers of America* series, ed. Hervey Allen and Carl Carmer (New York and Toronto: Rinehart & Company, 1943), 268–269. An especially rich photographic survey of the St. John's River in the nineteenth century is offered in Floyd Rinehart and Marion Rinehart, *Victorian Florida: America's Last Frontier* (Atlanta, Ga.: Peachtree Publishers Limited, 1986), 55–76.

7. Charles Hallock, publisher of *Forest and Stream*, noted sights along the lower St. John's that particularly appealed to him as an angler and mentioned the resort owned by Charles Orvis's brother. See Charles Hallock, "A Sojourn in Florida," in *An Angler's Reminiscences: A Record of Sport, Travel, and Adventure* (Cincinnati, Ohio: Sportsmen's Review Publishing Company, 1913), 39.

8. For a history of Jacob Brock's development at Enterprise, see Cabell and Hanna, *Parade*, 274. Also see *Florida: A Guide to the Southernmost State*, comp. Federal Writers' Project of the Work Projects Administration for the State of Florida (New York: Oxford University Press, 1939), 70–71. I have also relied on informative articles published in electronic form on two internet sites: see Tracy McKenna, "Steamboating," for *Antiques and Art around Florida* at www.aarf.com; and Steve Rajtar, "Enterprise Historical Trail," at www.geocities.com.

9. *At Tampa* (Canajoharie Library and Art Gallery, Canajoharie, New York) is inscribed and dated *Tampa Fla./1885*. See Helen A. Cooper, *Winslow Homer Watercolors*, exh. cat. (New Haven and London: Yale University Press for the National Gallery of Art, 1986), 150–151.

10. Cooper notes that of the Key West watercolors, none is dated 1885, but one is inscribed *January 1886*. See Cooper, *Winslow Homer Watercolors*, 150–151.

11. I am especially grateful to Robert J. Demarest, of Hawthorne, New Jersey, an angler and watercolorist who has fished and painted at Thornhill Bar, for confirming the location of Homer's 1886 watercolor view (letter from Demarest to author, December 17, 2001). Rita Gillis, Assistant Director, West Volusia Historical Society, DeLand House, DeLand, Florida, provided me with a navigational map of the St. John's River that shows Thornhill Bar. The watercolor was shown at the *Twentieth Annual Exhibition of the American Water Color Society*, at the National Academy of Design, in February 1887 as

simply *Sketch in Florida,* no. 420, lent by Charles S. Homer Jr.; see *Illustrated Catalogue, Twentieth Annual Exhibition of the American Water Color Society,* exh. cat. (New York: National Academy of Design, 1887), cat. 420. The illustration in the accompanying catalogue, a drawing made by Homer himself, identifies *Sketch in Florida* as the painting now known as *Thornhill Bar.* According to a note from Lloyd Goodrich in the documentation file on the painting at the Museum of Fine Arts, Boston, the title *Thornhill Bar* came from Mrs. Charles S. Homer Jr. when she offered the painting to Knoedler Gallery in 1932, suggesting that the Homers referred to the subject in this way, by the name of the place depicted. Surprisingly, Homer's drawing of the watercolor, made for reproduction in the catalogue, does not include the anglers in the right middle ground. It is possible that he edited this element out of the drawing to heighten the reflections of the palms in that area, but it seems odd that Homer would make his illustration appear different from the exhibited watercolor. It is also possible that Homer added the anglers to the watercolor at a later date, after he made the drawing for the catalogue. I am grateful to Sue Welsh Reed, Associate Curator of Prints and Drawings, Art of the Americas, at the Museum of Fine Arts, Boston, for her help with this question.

12. The collection of Brock House registers, though incomplete, survives in the West Volusia Historical Society, DeLand House, DeLand, Florida. These registers are more guest books than a business record, and signing in seems to have been purely voluntary. The registers include only one entry for Winslow Homer, when he arrived with his father on February 11, 1886, though we know from his extant letters written on Brock House stationery that he was there in subsequent years, too. The registers show that Charles Savage Homer Jr. stayed at the Brock House from March 24 through April 2, 1888. It was Samuel Vickers who brought the registers to my attention. I am grateful to Spring Dautel for reviewing all the extant volumes to find entries from the Homer men, for Arthur W. Benson, and for any other artists as well. The details included here are the result of Ms. Dautel's work. Rita Gillis, Assistant Director of the West Volusia Historical Society, laid the groundwork for Ms. Dautel's research by making an initial review of the registers for me and by providing photocopies of the appropriate pages.

13. Arthur W. Benson's name appears in the extant Brock House registers as early as 1876 and annually from 1884 through 1889, when he died there. In the "Brock House, Fishing Record," bound with some of the guest registers, someone dutifully entered Benson's daily catches of black bass (and made note of the occasional taking of an alligator or turtle) and at season's end computed the total weight of the large fighters he had landed: a total 3,745 pounds in 1884–1885 and an amazing 5,335 pounds in 1885–1886. The largest black bass that Benson recorded he caught on December 5, 1884—an impressive trophy weighing 13¼ pounds. On the day Benson died while fishing on Lake Monroe—December 27, 1889—someone drew a heavy black line through his entry in the fishing record for that outing. See Brock House registers, West Volusia Historical Society, DeLand House, DeLand, Florida.

14. The route of Homer's first tour of Florida is not entirely clear and has been reported variously. In early April 1886, only weeks after his return from Florida, Homer exhibited a watercolor entitled *St. John's River, Florida* at the Century Association in New York, so his travels on the river during his first Florida trip are thus clearly documented; see exhibition record in "Chronology," in Nicolai Cikovsky Jr. and Franklin Kelly, *Winslow Homer,* exh. cat. (New Haven and London: Yale University Press for the National Gallery of Art, 1995), 410. For various accounts of Homer's Florida itinerary in the winter of 1885–1886, see Patti Hannaway, *Winslow Homer in the Tropics* (Richmond, Va.: Westover Publishing Co., 1973), 88–90; Robert W. Schlageter, *Winslow Homer's Florida, 1886–1909,* exh. cat. (Jacksonville, Fla.: The Cummer Gallery of Art, 1977), 3–4; Gordon Hendricks, *The Life and Work of Winslow Homer* (New York: Harry N. Abrams, 1979), 184–185; and Cooper, *Winslow Homer Watercolors,* 150–161. Only Hendricks has placed Homer at Enterprise in 1886.

For the notice in the *Florida Times Union* of Homer's arrival in Jacksonville on his birthday, see Cooper, *Winslow Homer Watercolors,* 150–151.

15. Charles Hallock, "Two Ancient Anglers . . . Recollections of Daniel Webster, Genio C. Scott, Arthur W. Benson and Other Angling Worthies," *Forest and Stream* 46, no. 8 (February 22, 1896): 156–157.

16. The *Brooklyn Daily Eagle* report of Benson's death said that "the funeral tomorrow will be one of the largest, in point of attendance of old residents, that the city has ever witnessed. Mr. Benson was a contemporary and intimate friend of some of the best known men in the history of Brooklyn—men who helped to shape its destiny and make it what it is today." See "Died in a Boat. How Arthur W. Benson Passed Away," *Brooklyn Daily Eagle,* December 30, 1889, 4. On December 28, 1889, the *Brooklyn Daily Eagle* had this to say of Benson in a shorter obituary: "He was a strong figure in a group of sturdy men who gave scope and force to the building of Brooklyn." See "Arthur W. Benson," *Brooklyn Daily Eagle,* December 28, 1884.

17. Benson bought the eastern tip of Long Island in 1879 and formed the Montauk Point Association with like-minded moneyed sportsmen. They employed Frederick Law Olmsted to lay out a community of summer cottages, and they commissioned the firm of McKim, Mead, & White to design complementary shingle-style homes. The Homers would do something similar at Prout's Neck, Maine, four years later, and would employ the Portland architect John Calvin Stevens to build complementary shingle-style homes for them. For information on the Homer family's development of Prout's Neck, see this author's "Expressions of Art and Life in *The Artist's Studio in an Afternoon Fog,*" in Patricia Junker et al., *Winslow Homer in the 1890s: Prout's Neck Observed,* exh. cat. (New York: Hudson Hills Press in association with the Memorial Art Gallery of the University of Rochester, 1990), 34–65.

18. *Eagle,* December 30, 1889, 4. Other sources of information on Benson's life are "Arthur W. Benson Dead," *New York Tribune,* December 28, 1889, 1; obituary, *New York Times,* December 29, 1889, 5; "Arthur W. Benson's Will," *New York Times,* January 10, 1890, 8; and Samuel G. White, *The Houses of McKim, Mead, & White* (New York: Rizzoli International Publications, 1998), 85–93.

19. For a full account of Homer's 1890 exhibition of Adirondack watercolors, see my essay, "Pictures for Anglers," in this volume.

20. Homer to Clarke, February 16, 1890, AAA, microfilm reel number 2814, frame 581.

21. Cooper, *Winslow Homer Watercolors,* 160.

22. On August 29, 1898, Homer wrote to John W. Beatty of the Carnegie Institute, Pittsburgh, "My time has been so taken by overlooking my father that I have not painted anything" (quoted in Cikovsky and Kelly, *Winslow Homer,* 401). Homer wrote to Clarke on Brock House letterhead on February 25, 1899, "I have had a most successful winter at Nassau N.P. Bahamas I found what I wanted & have many things to work up into *two paintings* that I have in mind." The letter is reproduced in Schlageter, *Homer's Florida,* 26. *The Gulf Stream,* 1899, The Metropolitan Museum of Art, New York, was based on watercolors conceived in Nassau in 1885. See Cooper, *Winslow Homer Watercolors,* 142–143.

23. See the letter reproduced in Schlageter, *Homer's Florida,* 26.

24. H.F.C. [*sic;* Henry C. Ford], "Angling at Homosassa, Florida," *American Angler* 3, no. 12 (March 24, 1883): 185.

25. Homer to Arthur Homer, from Homosassa, Florida, undated [January 1904], Homer Collection, Bowdoin College Museum of Art, 1964.69.105.

26. "Angling at Homosassa, Florida," *American Angler* 3, no. 12 (March 24, 1883): 185.

27. "Old Homosassa," *American Angler* 9, no. 8 (February 20, 1886): 120.

28. I have relied on William MacDonald's extensive entry for Chamberlain in *Dictionary of American Biography,* ed. Allen Johnson and Dumas Malone (rev. ed., New York: Charles Scribner's Sons, 1958), 2:597–598.

29. For a history of Homosassa, see Ford, "Angling at Homosassa" and "Homosassa," *American Angler* 9, no. 11 (March 13, 1886): 170; Henry C. Ford, "Homosassa River, Florida," *American Angler* 9, no. 13 (March 27, 1886): 195–196; A.M.S., "Fishing in the Homosassa," *Forest and Stream* 34, no. 18 (May 22, 1890): 351; *The Encyclopedia of Florida,* 2 vols., 2d ed. (St. Clair Shores, Mich.: Somerset Publishers, 1997), 1:278–280; Hampton Dunn, *Back Home: A History of Citrus County, Florida* (Inverness, Fla.: Citrus County Bicentennial Steering Committee, 1976), 76–78, 94–95, 132–133; "Homosassa Springs of Yesteryear," unidentified clipping, vertical file, Citrus County Historical Society (hereafter CCHS), Inverness, Florida; Homosassa Springs issue of *The Florida Gathering* [periodical publication of the Florida Humanities Council] (1997), copy in vertical file, CCHS; Douglas Carpenter, "Winslow Homer at Turkey Buzzard Island," unidentified clipping in object file, Homer, *White Rowboat, St. John's River, Florida,* The Cummer Museum of Art and Gardens, Jacksonville, Florida; Lynn M. Homan and Thomas Reilly, *Citrus County, Florida,* from *Images of America* series (Charleston, S.C.: Arcadia Publishing, 2001). I am especially grateful to Kathy Turner of the CCHS for providing material on the history of Homosassa; and to Duncan and Wilma MacRae of Homosassa, whose family has owned and maintained the Homosassa Inn for two generations. They recounted to me many stories about the history and people of old Homosassa and shared with me the inn's early ledger book (hereafter Homosassa Inn Accounts Ledger, 1903–1904), which contains entries for Homer's stay there in January and February 1904. Kathy MacRae Foulks introduced me to people of Homosassa and, among other things, shared with me important material from Helen Willard Richardson's diary (for whom, see below), in her possession. Captain Jeff Beeler of Crystal River, Florida, gave me a guided boat tour of the river from Homosassa to the gulf.

30. One volume of the accounts ledger for the Homosassa Inn is extant, that which records the charges for visitors in 1903–1904; the volume is incomplete, but it does retain the page dedicated to Homer's charges. The record shows that Homer left the inn for a week, beginning January 14, returning on January 21. He departed Homosassa via the train on February 19, and he may have traveled to Enterprise again, for he was in Jacksonville on February 24. I am grateful to the MacRae family of Homosassa for sharing the ledger with me.

31. Homer, Homosassa, Florida, to Arthur Homer, [January 1904], Homer Collection, Bowdoin College Museum of Art, 1964.69.105/1-3.

32. Homosassa Inn Accounts Ledger, 1903–1904. For biographies of these figures I have consulted *Who Was Who in America,* vol. 1, *1897–1942* (Chicago: Marquis, 1968). For Weir, see 1317; for Thorne, 1236; for Martin, 783.

33. In a letter to his brother Charles, dated simply February 23 [no year], Homer mentions that he is "living with Captain Richardson" in a small room above a dance hall [in Homosassa], and he is "living well." He must have enjoyed Richardson's company. From the late February date of the letter, we can identify the year of his stay as 1909. See Homer [from Homosassa], to Charles Homer, February 23, [1909], Homer Collection, Bowdoin College Museum of Art, 1964.69.66/1-3. I am grateful to Kathy MacRae Foulks for sharing information about Captain Richardson with me, all of it gathered from Helen Willard Richardson's diary. In a memorial tribute to her husband, Mrs. Richardson gave her husband's birth date as May 6, 1846; Mrs. Richardson's diary, 149.

34. Homer Collection, Bowdoin College Museum of Art, 1964.69.105/1-3.

35. Paintings done at these sites are *Turkey Buzzard,* 1904, Worcester Art Museum, Worcester, Massachusetts; *Hell's Gate,* 1904, private collection; *The Shell Heap,* 1904, private collection. For information on Florida shell heaps I have relied on *Encyclopedia of Florida,* 1:61–64.

36. Homer wrote to his dealer, M. Knoedler & Co., in New York, "I did not explain to you the reason for the bottle in this drawing. It is to show the size of the fish." See Homer, Scarboro, Maine, to M. Knoedler & Co., April 11, 1905, original in Knoedler library, copy in AAA, microfilm reel number NY59-5, frames 571–573.

37. For a discussion of Homer's watercolor technique and Japanese ink painting, see Judith Walsh, "Innovation in Homer's Late Watercolors," in Cikovsky and Kelly, *Winslow Homer,* 283–299.

38. The chronology of Homer's visits to Homosassa is as follows, as far as can be determined from dated sources: January 7–February 19, 1904, at Homosassa Inn (Homosassa Inn Accounts Ledger, 1903–1904); after December 7, 1904–January 30, 1905 (see letters to M. Knoedler & Co., originals in Knoedler library, copy in AAA, microfilm reel number NY59-5, frames illegible); by February 10–by March 7, 1908 (see letters reproduced in Schlageter, *Homer's Florida,* 38; Homer stayed at the Rendezvous on this visit); probably February 22–after March 21, 1909 (see letters December 8, 1908, February 23, [1909], and March 21, [1909]; Homer Collection, Bowdoin College Museum of Art, 1964.69.139, 1964.69.66/1-3, and 1964.69.16). The February 23 letter has been miscatalogued as written from Quebec because it makes mention of the Island House at Roberval. But Homer offers this only as a comparison to his simple room at Homosassa, which he is sharing with or renting from, he says, Captain Richardson.

39. Homer Collection, Bowdoin College Museum of Art, 1964.69.66/1-3.

40. Homer wrote to Arthur from Prout's Neck on January 18, 1910, "I have not written as there has been no particular change in my case. But now that I know all about it I will tell you I find that there is nothing unusual the matter with me that after all it is only an acid stomach." The letter, in the collection of the Bowdoin College Museum of Art, is quoted in Cikovsky and Kelly, *Winslow Homer,* 406. By the summer of 1910 his health had begun to fail rapidly, and he suffered an internal hemorrhage.

41. Quoted in Cikovsky and Kelly, *Winslow Homer,* 406.

42. Homer Collection, Bowdoin College Museum of Art, 1964.69.66/1-3.

Before Winslow Homer
The Art of Fishing in the United States

William H. Gerdts

IN A RECENT STUDY OF THE HISTORY OF PAINTINGS depicting fishing, Tom Quinn wrote: "The earliest serious painter of angling subjects in American art history also happens to be one of the country's truly great original artists: Winslow Homer (1836–1910)."[1] Quinn is not, of course, totally mistaken, either in identifying the seriousness of Homer's fishing imagery or of that artist's greatness. Still, not only is there tremendous variety in fishing imagery before Homer, but there were a good many painters who created a considerable body of such works. This, in addition to occasional excursions into fishing and angling subjects by a large number of painters, both celebrated and obscure. And some of these works are surprisingly inventive. These works are the subject of this essay.

There are important early images of fishing made by Native Americans in the eastern half of the United States dating back as early as 1585, when John White (fl. 1577–1593), the official artist attached to Sir Walter Raleigh's colony founded on Roanoke Island in the Carolina Outer Banks, depicted Indians fishing.[2] There are images of commercial fishing, too, in the mid-Atlantic region from the nineteenth century. But these fishing subjects are beyond the scope of this essay. As later with Winslow Homer, and indeed the venerable tradition of British paintings of fishing and fishermen, the greatest emphasis in the United States was on sporting depictions, a theme that has received little study.[3]

One such picture was *The Young Waltonians* by De Witt Clinton Boutelle, which appeared in a sale of 138 paintings held under the direction of the American Art-Union in New York in December 1853. This, one of fifteen paintings in the sale by Boutelle, was five feet long, a sizable work, exceeded only by another that was six feet long, and two history paintings by Emanuel Leutze (1816–1868). The title, of course, referenced *The Compleat Angler* (original ed., 1653, subsequently enlarged), the great book by Sir Izaak Walton (1593–1683), which remained enormously popular in the English-speaking world for two centuries or more.[4] Boutelle's audience would have needed no verbal clue to identify the picture as a fishing subject. While it is possible that this now unlocated work may have been a copy after the famous English painting of that title by John Constable (1820, originally *Stratford Mill;* Tate London)[5] among Boutelle's best-known works in his lifetime and today are the set of copies he made after Thomas Cole's (1801–1848) *Voyage of Life* (1852; private collection)—the size of *The Young Waltonians,* along with the originality of all his other entries, suggests emulation rather than replication. By midcentury Boutelle was only one of many American painters producing fishing paintings; one such located work by him is his *Landscape with Fisherman* of about 1858–1867 (fig. 101).[6]

Walton's *The Compleat Angler* went through many editions in England, but the first American edition had appeared only in 1847, just six years

FIG. 101
De Witt Clinton Boutelle (1820–1884), *Landscape with Fisherman,* ca. 1858–1867. Oil on canvas, 24 × 34½ in. State Museum of Pennsylvania, Pennsylvania Historical and Museum Commission, Harrisburg, Pennsylvania.

DETAIL: FIG. 108
Henry Inman (1801–1846), *Trout Fishing in Sullivan County, New York,* ca. 1841. Oil on canvas, 25 × 30 in. Munson-Williams-Proctor Arts Institute, Museum of Art, Utica, New York. Purchase (83.14)

before Boutelle's painting was on exhibition.[7] This was the stupendous achievement of its editor, George W. Bethune (1805–1862), who provided an eighty-four-page "Bibliographical Preface," itself a highly regarded piece of scholarship. Bethune, the minister of the Dutch Reformed Church in Philadelphia, was more than an active fisherman; he esteemed the sport in terms of moral uplift, as he said when he spoke before the Literary Societies of Yale College, two years earlier. There, in an oration entitled "A Plea for Study," Bethune noted: "Among out-door recreations, none has been a greater favourite with studious men of Great Britain, because none is more suited to quiet habits, fondness for retirement, and love of nature, than angling, not in the sea, but in brooks and

rivers, where the genus *Salmo* abounds." Bethune went on to extol the salutary effects of fishing and even of the unusual age that devotees of angling such as Walton had attained. He stated,
Their pursuits by the side of running streams, whose motion imparts increased vitality to the air, their exercise regular without being violent, and that composure of mind so necessary to the health of the body, to which this amusement so materially contributes, must all have had an influence upon their physical constitution, the effect of which is seen in the duration of their lives.[8]

That Americans subscribed to Walton's estimation of the value of fishing—or rather angling (Bethune noted in his "Bibliographical Preface" that "an angler, kind reader, is not a *fisherman,* who plies his calling for a livelihood, careless in what way he gets his scaly rewards"[9])—is easily confirmed just by the number and variety of contemporary references. Bethune's 1847 edition had filled an essential gap; an earlier biographical sketch of Walton in the *United States Literary Gazette* had been inspired by a comparatively inexpensive 1824 British edition of *The Complete Angler.* The author had noted that "All the world has heard of Izaak Walton's 'fascinating little volume'. . . but few in this country have ever read it . . . [and] it has for many years been comparatively a rare book."[10] Two decades later, in 1845, another article on "Waltoniana" was published,[11] and in 1847, the year that Bethune's edition of *The Complete Angler* appeared, an article "written by an American," on *Izaak Walton's Complete Angler* appeared in *The Knickerbocker,* which described the essence of a variety of individual professions before concluding that "The soft and peaceful tenor of the angler's life was delineated with great elegance and truth, near two centuries ago, by one Izaak Walton; a name that stands almost as much alone and distinct in the eye of the English world as that of Isaac Newton."[12] And in 1855, "The Complete Susquehanna Angler" was published, a tribute-parody of Walton's famous book, involving "Piscator" and "Venator," the same principal characters who appeared in *The Compleat Angler*.[13]

Also in 1855 Henry Ward Beecher (1813–1887) published an essay he had written the previous year, "The Morals of Fishing," concerning a debate about the questionable ethics of fishing for pleasure as opposed to obtaining food for sustenance. Beecher himself seems to speak out for a catch limited to what could be used for nourishment, noting, "Isaac [*sic*] Walton . . . would say, and all true sportsmen are scrupulously at agreement with him, that no man should take a single fish, or bag a single bird, beyond the number which can be used for food by himself or his friends." And he emphasized that "If the pleasure of hunting or of fishing were in the excitement furnished by the creature's suffering, then it could no more be justified than any other form of torturing, as practiced hitherto, upon moral principles, for the good of men's souls. A benevolent man should find no pleasure in mere animal suffering." But for Beecher as for his fellow minister, Bethune, "the collateral enjoyments amount, often, to a greater sum than all the rest"—meaning here the immersion in nature and sense of freedom "in remote fields, in forest, and along the streams."[14]

These "collateral enjoyments" should be strongly considered among the pleasures of angling and were incorporated into many of the pictorial images made in the early and middle years of the nineteenth century in the United States. One should recall, too, that the subtitle of Walton's famous treatise is *The Contemplative Man's Recreation*, wording that implies the pleasures and benefits of the quiet introspection afforded by communion with nature. Of course, debates about the propriety of fishing arose even in the eighteenth century in colonial America. The Connecticut lawyer and politician Roger Wolcott (1679–1767) wrote of the pleasures of the salmon, sturgeon, crab, and eel fisherman

"With Seins, Pots, Angles, and his Tramel-pots."[15] And the Reverend Joseph Seccombe (1706–1760), under the pseudonym "Fluviatulis Piscator," a name certainly inspired by Walton's fishing representative, "Piscator," offered a sermon approving angling, which he presented in 1739 and published four years later.[16]

Seccombe, the parish minister in Kingston, New Hampshire, near Amoskeag Falls on the Merrimack River, an abundant source for shad, salmon, and eels, began his text with a quotation from the Gospel according to St. John: "Simon Peter saith unto them, I go a Fishing." Prefiguring Beecher's arguments, Seccombe stated that "He that takes Pleasure in the Pains and dying Agonies of any lower Species of Creatures, is either a stupid sordid Soul, or a Murderer at Heart," but that in catching fish for consumption, "We are taking something, which God, the Creator and Proprietor of all, has given us to use for Food. . . ." And Seccombe, too, follows the recreational line of Walton (later postulated by Bethune and Beecher), that ". . . the End of Business and Diversion . . . are the Refreshment and Support of Man in the Service of God. If I may eat them for Refreshment, I may as well catch them, if this recreate and refresh me."[17] Seccombe's twenty-two-page pamphlet approved of fishing even on Sundays, arguing that recreation, and especially fishing, which had previously been viewed as inherently wasteful of time and skill, was a necessity for hardworking colonists.

Seccombe's arguments were not won easily. Even as late as 1789, Elijah Fitch (1746–1788), in a published poem, *The Beauties of Religion*, somewhat deprecated fishing as a sport, warning his readers against taking the lives of the "finny tribe . . . with barbed hook, or the more fatal seine," judging that

What Heaven *has* given *to man,* his right to take,
The earth and all that's in it for his use,
For profit, pleasure, not to sport with death.[18]

Likewise, the New York poet Samuel Low (b. 1765) wrote in 1800 of the barbarities perpetrated "On a small FISH caught by angling,"

'Fain would I draw the barbed steel
Which makes thee pant and gasp for breath,
But, ah! 'twould sooner make thee feel
Thy final pang,—'twould be thy death;

and Low equated the enjoyment of angling with "Pleasure's Syren wiles":

If, like this captive fish you grasp
At joy on Treach'ry's hook that's hung,
Or soon or late like him you'll gasp,
And with Remorse your soul be wrung![19]

It may be in part this admonition that prevented the prevailing portrait imagery in eighteenth-century America to include attributes of fishing as recreational identification to any extent, common enough in English portraiture in paintings by William Hogarth (1697–1764), Arthur Devis (1708–1787), Johann Zoffany (1733–1810), and Sir Henry Raeburn (1756–1823)—see, for instance, the splendid likeness of Lieutenant-Colonel Bryce McMurdo (National Gallery, London) by the last.[20] Still, the proscription against the killing of creatures for sport did not prevent colonial artists such as Justus Englehard Kühn (d. 1717) and Benjamin West (1738–1820) to portray young hunters with their prey, and it may be, rather, that images of the catch simply did not project the virility associated with the hunt.[21] To my knowledge, the only such fishing portrait by a professional artist in colonial times is that of Barnard Elliott Jr. (Gibbes Museum of Art, Carolina Art Association, Charleston, South Carolina), painted by the Swiss émigré artist Jeremiah Theus (ca. 1719–1774), active in Charleston, depicting the son of a plantation owner, Barnard Elliott, who holds a fishing line and hook.[22] A few more fishing portraits, such as that of Thomas Fitch Oliver Jr., of Marblehead, Massachusetts (private collection), and his relative Peter Oliver (ca. 1801; fig. 102) of Salem, attributed to the Neapolitan émigré artist Michel

FIG. 102
Michel Felice Cornè (ca. 1752–1845), *Peter Oliver (1767–1831)*, ca. 1801. Watercolor on paper, 18 × 12½ in. Private collection. Photograph courtesy Peabody Essex Museum, Salem, Massachusetts

Felice Cornè, begin to appear at the beginning of the nineteenth century. In these portraits, the much younger Thomas is depicted actually fishing, while Peter's maturity is suggested by his abandonment of the upright fishing pole at the left, opting instead for intellectual (or commercial) pursuits, identified with the book he holds on his lap. Likewise, Thomas's still domestic situation is conveyed by the house on the far bank of the stream, while Peter's ambitions and profession as a trader are identified by the distant sailing vessel.[23]

At about the time the Oliver portraits were painted, fishing activity began to appear in a few works by the earliest professional landscape painters active in the new republic, three English-born artists who came to the United States in the last decade of the eighteenth century. Fishermen are grouped together and bathed in Claudean light on the bank of a quiet stream, supposedly the Hudson River, but actually an Edenic ideal of the new republic, in William Winstanley's *View on the North River, Evening* of 1792–1793 (fig. 103). This is one of a pair of paintings the artist had sold to George Washington, then residing in the nation's capital, Philadelphia.[24] In 1802 William Groombridge (1748–1811) painted *Ideal Afternoon* (private collection), and shortly after, Francis Guy painted *View of the Presbyterian Church and All the Buildings as They Appear from the Meadow* (1804; fig. 104). The painting depicts a group of substantial Baltimore structures on the far side of the water, but Guy emphasizes that nature and urbanism coexist happily, with the figure of a fisherman prominent on the right bank in the foreground.[25]

Fishing imagery began to come into prominence in American painting at the same time that it began to be celebrated in our literature. In 1820 Washington Irving (1783–1859) published his story "The Angler" in *The Sketch Book*,[26] though for the most part he dealt in this tale with an English, rather than an American, setting, his narrator having found that "Our first essay was along a mountain brook, among the highlands of the Hudson; a most unfortunate place for the execution of those piscatory tactics which had been invented along the velvet margins of quiet English rivulets."[27] In his story, Irving immediately paid homage to Izaak Walton, recollecting "studying his 'Complete Angler' several years since, in company with a knot of friends in America, and moreover that we were all completely bitten with the angling mania."[28] He remained very aware of the distinction between a native and a British environment, for many years later he wrote to the artist-writer-fisherman Charles Lanman: ". . . the adventurous life of the angler,

FIG. 103
William Winstanley (before 1792–after 1806), *View on the North River, Evening*, 1792–1793. Oil on canvas, 35 ½ × 59 in. Courtesy of the Mount Vernon Ladies Association, Mount Vernon, Virginia

FIG. 104
Francis Guy (ca. 1760–1820), *View of the Presbyterian Church and All the Buildings as They Appear from the Meadow*, 1804. Oil on canvas, 24 ¾ × 39 ⅜ in. The Maryland Historical Society, Baltimore

FIG. 105
Thomas Doughty (1793–1856), *Landscape with Fishermen*, 1826. Oil on canvas, 17 × 24½ in.
Museum of Fine Arts, Boston. Gift of Martha C. Karolik for the M. and M. Karolik Collection
of American Paintings, 1815–1865 (47.1244). © Museum of Fine Arts, Boston

amidst our wild scenery, on our vast lakes and rivers, must furnish a striking contrast to the quiet loiterings of the English angler along the Trent and Dove. . . ."[29]

Jennie Holliman, paraphrasing the article "Proceedings of the Cincinnati Angling Club" (1830), has written of the benefits that fishermen of the early 1800s found in the sport:

Angling . . . did not degrade or debase the faculties of either mind or body, but gave to each that salutary exercise which was considered essential to its preservation and improvement. The vigor of body and elasticity of mind derived from the exercise in the early morning air was worth the effort required in rising at dawn to pursue the finney tribe. Angling was earnestly recommended to those whose constitution had been impaired by a too sedentary life or by dissipation, for unlike other rural amusements, it did not over fatigue by the violence of exercise required. . . . In this sport

he learned lessons of wisdom, resignation, and forbearance. . . . The pastime of angling was supposed to have an influence on the temper and feeling of a man. Being in the midst of nature, in the pursuit of the fish, was sufficient to excite the feelings of the highest order of enjoyment, feelings which tended to make him, on his return to duties and his employment a more amiable and more useful man.[30]

To retreat from that sedentary life, patrons were attracted to paintings that combined the beauties of unspoiled American nature with the image of the fisherman, with which they could identify, either recreationally or conceptually. These began to appear in the 1820s, primarily in the form of fishing landscapes. The painter to be especially identified with this genre was Thomas Doughty, based successively in Philadelphia, Boston, and later in Newburgh and New York City. Often designated the earliest native-born American landscape painter and one of the "fathers" of the "Hudson River School," Doughty began exhibiting at the Pennsylvania Academy of the Fine Arts as early as 1816 and was producing hunting subjects by 1822. Identifiable fishing pictures appeared in the mid-1820s, and he continued to paint numerous examples of this theme after he moved in 1829 to Boston, where many of them appeared in the annual exhibitions of the Boston Athenæum; the majority of those located today date from the mid-1830s, including *Mountain Lake with Man Fishing* (1837; Museum of Art, Brigham Young University, Provo, Utah).[31] The figures in paintings such as these have often been seen primarily as scale modules and staffage—a way to introduce a human element into his landscapes while contrasting their minuscule form with nature's grandeur. But they are more than these. They *are* fishermen, and the Waltonian ethos of mental, physical, and moral health as well as the intimate communion with nature are very much implied in these scenes. Here, the single figure stands upright, alone on a rock with his back turned to the viewer, in contemplation of the glories of this peaceful wilderness.[32]

Doughty produced fishing landscapes in two slightly varying forms. In addition to those such as *Mountain Lake with Man Fishing,* with a single, isolated fisherman, there are what appear to be an equal number that feature several fishermen enjoying the sport together. The figures in these works tend to be more active, the two fishermen exerting their sporting efforts in different ways, but of course the pairing of these fishermen also implies human camaraderie as well as communion with nature. While not suggesting to any degree the philosophical depths of brotherhood implied in the contemporaneous work of the Dresden painter Caspar David Friedrich (1774–1840), such as his *Two Men Gazing at the Moon* (1819; Gemäldegalerie Neue Meister, Dresden), in paintings such as Doughty's *Landscape with Fishermen* (1826; fig. 105), nature provides the ideal setting for man's pleasurable interaction with his fellow man. In this work, just about the earliest fishing picture by Doughty known today, a slightly more active fisherman again stands in the foreground on an isolated rock, while a second fisherman appears on the riverbank in the distance. Because Doughty was living in Philadelphia, the setting in this case can probably be identified as the Delaware Water Gap, given the configuration of the flat, sloping hills in the distance. This was a locale where Doughty is known to have painted often at this time, the earliest American artist to investigate the region.[33]

In Philadelphia, Doughty, with his brother John, also produced one of the earliest American colorplate publications, *The Cabinet of Natural History and American Rural Sports,* appearing between 1830 and 1833 and containing the first American color sporting prints. Thomas Doughty was only involved with the *Cabinet* for its first two volumes, of 1830 and 1832, for he had moved to Boston by the former year and was not associated

with the aborted third volume (1833). Doughty designed the twenty-three lithographs for volume one, including the brilliantly colored *Trout of Silver Lake* and *Brook Trout* (fig. 106), the imprint of which reads, "Thomas Doughty on stone from a drawing by a Lady," illustrating an article on fly-fishing for trout.[34] This volume also printed a number of articles related to fishing, including "Angling," "White Fish of the Lakes," and "Bass Fishing in the West," as well as the aforementioned "Proceedings of the Cincinnati Angling Club."[35] This last, celebrating the first anniversary of that organization, leads off with a quotation from Izaak Walton and is decorated with an outdoor fishing equipment still life by Reuben S. Gilbert (fl. 1830–1850).[36] Volume two, which appeared in 1832, included articles on "Angling in Surinam,"

FIG. 106

Thomas Doughty (1793–1856), lithographer, after a drawing by "a Lady," *Trout of Silver Lake* and *Brook Trout.* Plate 13 from *The Cabinet of Natural History and American Rural Sports,* vol. 1 (Philadelphia: John and Thomas Doughty, 1830). Library, Amon Carter Museum, Fort Worth, Texas

"Natural History of the Bassae," "An Extraordinary Pike," "Pike," and "Directions for Fishing for Pike" (suggesting a particular interest of one or both brothers in pike fishing, though a good many articles in volume two were not original pieces and were taken from other sources). In addition, one chapter in volume two of the series, "Some Pages from the Diary of a Sportsman," excerpted from the *New-England Galaxy,* not only dealt with angling but included the poem "The Angler's Song."[37] The frontispieces of the two volumes that Doughty designed tendered equal homage to the two aspects of the sporting life: that for volume one depicted a hunter with his dogs, while that for volume two represented an angler.

Doughty was by far the most prolific painter of fishing landscapes in the United States in the second quarter of the nineteenth century, but hardly the only one. Alvan Fisher (1792–1863), with whom Doughty was often paired and compared after he settled in Boston in the early 1830s (though Fisher was a far more versatile artist, including portraits, rural genre, and animal painting in his repertoire), also painted numerous fishing paintings such as *Landscape with Angler* (ca. 1832; Rare Book Department, Free Library of Philadelphia). In 1829, in the same exhibition at the Boston Athenæum where Doughty first exhibited fishing subjects in Boston (*The Angler,* then owned by one of Boston's most active collectors, James Fullerton, along with his *Trout Fishing*), Fisher exhibited *The Young Angler,* though this may have been a figure or genre study, rather than a fishing landscape. That picture was owned by the prominent New York author Nathaniel Parker Willis (1806–1867), a frequent writer on fishing. When Doughty's *The Fishing Party* was exhibited at the 1830 annual at the Athenæum, a poem on trout fishing written by Willis was appended to the catalogue entry, while another poem, author unidentified, was attached to the catalogue entry for Fisher's painting *Angling*

for Trout (possibly the aforementioned *Landscape with Angler*) when that picture appeared at the Athenæum annual in 1832. Fred Adelson, the leading authority on Fisher's work, noted that "During the 1830s, sporting subjects became a new area of exploration in Fisher's oeuvre" and suggests that Doughty's example "may have inspired Fisher to try similar themes."[38]

Crossing the Stream (1827; private collection) by Thomas Cole, the greatest of the first generation of American landscape masters, is one of several early works by him to depict a fisherman in a wilderness setting. In this painting a single young fisherman placidly pursues the sporting life amid a wild tangle of trees, rocks, mountains, and a stream. *Crossing the Stream* is unusual in depicting the angler, not actively fishing, but confidently crossing a precariously sagging wooden bridge, pole and net over his shoulders. With the figure set in the exact center of the vibrantly lighted scene, Cole's picture gains dramatic intensity foreign to Doughty's more tranquil landscapes. Though Cole had painted another, more traditional fishing picture this same year set in the White Mountains, *Mount Chocorua* (formerly IBM Corporation), Ellwood C. Parry III convincingly argues that *Crossing the Stream* is a memory image of this English-born artist's early wanderings in the Allegheny Mountains of western Pennsylvania, making a "wonderful American sequel to such classicizing landscapes in the Claudean manner as J.M.W. Turner's (1775–1851) *Crossing the Brook* of 1815 (Tate Gallery, London)."[39]

For the most part, the fishing landscapes of Doughty, Fisher, and their colleagues were non–site specific, but when the artists did identify the location of their angling scenes, they were usually in the Catskills and later the Adirondacks, and, to a lesser degree, at the Delaware River and in the White Mountains. What is significant here, perhaps, is where the painters did *not* go to record their subjects. Very few fishing scenes took place along the extensive

Atlantic coast, yet this was not due to lack of such activity there. Indeed, both contemporary angling books and later histories recorded the abundance of both fish and fishing activities on the coast, especially on the streams and brooks emptying into Long Island Sound as well as those on the island's south shore. In 1862 Robert Barnwell Roosevelt wrote especially of the pickerel fishing that abounded off Long Island, while in 1869 Genio Scott (1806–1879) acknowledged that New Yorkers regarded Long Island trout as the best.[40] Paul Schullery, in fact, has noted that "it was Long Island that attracted the fisherman first, inspiring the sporting writer, Henry William Herbert (1807–1858) to describe the area as 'The Utopia of New York sportsmen.'"[41] And Charles Goodspeed, in his classic text, *Angling in America,* devotes a chapter to angling on Long Island and to the hotels there that specialized in encouraging a fishing clientele: Snedecor's in Islip, Carman's at Fireplace, and Stump Pond in Smithtown.[42] But, for the most part, the artists avoided these locales, almost surely because they could not provide the environment of thick forests, giant rocks, and rushing streams and waterfalls that would isolate their anglers and allow them full immersion in a one-on-one communion with nature.[43] By and large, sea fishing was not a popular subject for painters, though Currier & Ives issued a number of lithographs of bass fishing and blue fishing in coastal waters. Although no specific geographic location is identified, John J. Brown, in *The American Angler's Guide,* notes that the blue fish "has his peculiar grounds in Long Island Sound," while the sea bass "abound in immense quantities in the ocean outside of Sandy Hook."[44]

The association of fishing and nature was also explicit, in gentler fashion, in the lyrics of such nature poets of the period as William Cullen Bryant (1794–1878), a close friend of Cole's and to whose writings Doughty's landscapes have often been compared. In his 1820 poem "Green River," which was published in 1821 in his first book of poetry, Bryant celebrated the stream that he would visit and savor while practicing law in Great Barrington, Massachusetts. In this poem, Bryant wrote of the beauty of unspoiled nature, into which the lone fisherman might find welcome:

> *Yet fair as they art, thou shunn'st to glide,*
> *Beautiful stream! by village side;*
> *But windest away from haunts of men,*
> *To quiet valley and shaded glen;*
> *And forest, and meadow, and slope of hill,*
> *Around thee are lonely, lovely, and still,*
> *Lonely—save when by thy rippling tides,*
> *From thicket to thicket the angler guides;*[45]

The majority of the early fishing landscapes such as those by Cole, or *Landscape* (New-York Historical Society) by his contemporary Jesse Talbot (1806–1879), feature a single fisherman, or at most two anglers, enfolded within a wilderness landscape. *The Blue Hole, Little Miami River* (Historic Cincinnati Collection, Proctor & Gamble Co., Cincinnati), painted in 1839 by the German-born Cincinnati artist Godfrey Frankenstein (1820–1873), is a most unusual work, not only because it includes a group of four persons fishing but especially as one of these is a woman in a long, fashionable silver dress.[46] The formality of the costumes of all the figures is, in fact, in contrast with the wildness of the scenery, with dense foliage and a large tree uprooted in the foreground amid rocks, weeds, and vines.[47] It seems unlikely that women, when they did fish, wore their finest apparel. The Boston clergyman William Henry Harrison Murray (1840–1904), in his celebrated 1869 guide to the Adirondack wilderness, an admittedly somewhat later publication, describes the proper "Ladies' Outfit" for such outings, which included buckskin gloves, a soft felt hat, a short walking dress, and pairs of camp shoes and balmoral (laced) boots.[48]

Blue Hole on the Little Miami River, a tributary of the Ohio River east of Cincinnati, with its

FIG. 107
Robert S. Duncanson (1821–1871), *Blue Hole, Little Miami River,* 1851. Oil on canvas, 28 ½ × 41 ½ in.
Cincinnati Art Museum, Ohio. Gift of Norbert Heerman and Arthur Helbig (1926.18)

romantic wilderness scenery, had tremendous appeal for Cincinnati artists of the period; in his journal, the Cincinnati painter Miner Kellogg (1814–1889) described Blue Hole (now in John Bryan State Park) and noted that it was popular among the regional artists for its great beauty.[49] In 1851 the African-American Cincinnati artist Robert S. Duncanson, who painted a number of fishing landscapes, depicted a more casually dressed fishing party on its banks in *Blue Hole, Little Miami River* (fig. 107), one of that artist's finest wilderness landscapes.[50] Wendy Katz has recognized that the figures here

are more than generic props; they are an image of the desired effect of nature on the often socially mixed residents of the river bottoms, and of Cincinnati in general. The rustic fisherman absorbed and at ease amid a rugged Western landscape loses himself in

nature, but instead of making him wild, the experience refines as it acts. . . . Nature, in this concept, exert[s] a softening, soothing influence on those who experience it. . . .[51]
And of course, fishing is the context in which this experience is set. Two years later, Duncanson's friend and colleague William L. Sonntag (1822–1900) painted fishermen in his *Scene on the Little Miami River* (Cincinnati Art Museum).

Probably the most acclaimed fishing landscape painted in this country in the first half of the nineteenth century is Henry Inman's *Trout Fishing in Sullivan County, New York* (ca. 1841; fig. 108), also the most celebrated landscape painted by that artist, otherwise New York's premier portraitist of the period.[52] In addition, it is Inman's most autobiographical landscape, as he was almost as well known for his piscatorial ardor as he was for his artistry.

Here, the figures, actively engaged in angling, may be identified as the artist and his fellow sportsman Richard T. Fosdick, with whom Inman had ventured into Sullivan County to fish in June 1841. Since the present work was painted the preceding winter, it most probably documents a similar expedition made the previous year when Fosdick and Inman are known to have fished together in Sullivan County. The boy seated on the bank appears to be about twelve years old and may represent Inman's son, the future painter John O'Brien Inman, born in 1828. *Trout Fishing in Sullivan County, New York* was exhibited frequently during the next five years in New York, Boston, and Philadelphia, including the *Inman Memorial Exhibition* held in the rooms of the American Art-Union in February 1846, almost always to considerable acclaim.[53] When the work was shown in the *Inman Memorial Exhibition,* the entry in the catalogue was accompanied by the poem "Angling," written by the once-eminent nature poet Alfred B. Street (1811–1881).[54] And in Inman's obituary published in *The Spirit of the Times,* his good friend William T. Porter (1809–1858) wrote:

In trout fishing, especially he excelled. . . . And a more accomplished disciple, good old Izaac Walton never had. In throwing a fly or spinning a minnow, he had few equals. He was ready to say with [Thomas] Hood that "of all the sports ever sported, commend me to angling!" it being in the opinion of both, the wisest, virtuousest, discreetest, best; the safest, cheapest, and in all likelihood, the oldest of pastimes. . . . His experience, like our own, was, that he certainly became acquainted with the angling rod next after the birchen one![55]

Sullivan County was a popular fishing ground for New York fishermen and artists. Inman may well have been familiar with the poems "Trout Fishing, Sullivan County, N. Y." by F. L. Waddel and/or "Trout Fishing in Sullivan County," another poem by Street,[56] the latter soon to be reprinted with a woodcut decoration as the frontispiece to John J. Brown's *The American Angler's Guide*

(1845).[57] Both poems refer to angling on "the bright Callikoon." Other favorite areas for angling in Sullivan County for Inman, Fosdick, and their associates were the Beaverkill and the Willowwhemack (spelling constantly varying and now Willowemoc) Rivers, in the northeast corner of the county.[58] Inman and his friends were pioneer fishermen in this region; in 1838 the *American Turf Register* noted that only just then

Two or three parties, made up principally of "old hands," have lately made a descent upon the rivers of Sullivan and Montgomery counties, in this state, with immense success. The Williewemauk, Calikoon, and Beaver-kill, are three of the finest trout streams in this country; they are comparatively unknown to city anglers and are less fished than others of like pretensions within our knowledge. The trout are large, very numerous, and of the most delicious flavour. The rivers referred to lie between 30 and 60 miles back of Newburgh. To reach them from town, take any of the North River steamers to Newburgh, and the stage to Monticello, where you will find some good trouting. Five miles farther on, at Liberty, you will reach Big Beaver-kill. Make your headquarters at Mrs. Darby's [sic], and you will be sure to find excellent accommodations, and capital fishing. You will reach the Williewemauk seven miles further on, where Mrs. Purvis will take very good care of you.[59]

Inman and Fosdick did, in fact, stay at Chester Darbee's, at what was then Westfield Flats, later Roscoe. This was situated just five minutes from Junction Pool or the Forks, one of the most celebrated pools in angling literature, where the Beaverkill and Willowemoc Creek join. This would seem to be the site of Inman's painting, though if so, the artist has dramatically increased the topographical scale.[60] Darbee's inn, later known as the Boscobel, was subsequently referred to as "the little club of Houseless Anglers" in the dedication of *The American Angler* by Thaddeus Norris (1811–1877), the best-known American fly fisherman of the nineteenth century. Norris noted, *All the members (their number never exceeded ten) were fly-fishers, some of whom had met for the first time on the stream and had become acquainted without any conventional introduction. We chose the unassuming name of the "Houseless Anglers" in contradistinction to the old Fish-House clubs—associations rather of a convivial tendency than that of pure angling.*[61] This club was probably formed subsequent to Inman and Fosdick's angling activity there, but their presence was preserved in a picture of life-size trout that Inman drew on a window shutter on the porch of Darbee's inn, a picture that was still there almost twenty years later.[62] This was the largest fish, three pounds, three ounces, that Inman and Fosdick netted during a six-day fishing trip to Sullivan County in June 1841.[63]

Though great trout fishing country (Trout Brook runs off the Beaverkill at Peakville), this region was difficult to reach in the 1840s and remained so until the Ontario & Western Railroad reached the town of Roscoe in 1872, while the Callicoon was even farther distant; still, Inman is known to have fished on both the Beaverkill and the Callicoon, as well as on Long Island and at Lake Pleasant. On hearing news of Inman's planned journey abroad, his good friend William T. Porter, the editor of the sporting journal *The Spirit of the Times,* wrote in 1844:

Personally, and purely from selfish impulses, we hate to hear of his going abroad at all! Who shall now put us up to the trick of hornswoggling a salmon trout of forty pounds? Who will teach us the art and mystery of fabricating a fly that will induce a sockdollager to "rise" at its first pirouette, though living over a spring hole in ten feet of water? . . . Well may there be a "sound of revelry by night," and by day, too, among the small fry of the Kalikoon and Beaver-kill at his departure! Rejoice ye speckled denizens of the Long Island water, and leap with joy ye spotted cannibals of Lake Pleasant![64]

The journey to these fishing rivers of Sullivan County became somewhat easier by 1850, when *The Spirit of the Times* announced that the Beaverkill was "now easy of access, being within six hours of Chehocton (or Hancock), the most beautiful village on the line of the Erie road. And still nearer to that town, crossed by the new plank road leading to Walton, is the Cadosea, a brook wherein Mr. N. P. Willis took a hundred trout (or less) in three hours (or more) last June."[65] This article recognized the important Knickerbocker author and wit Nathaniel Parker Willis, who was one of the most prolific writers of the time, as well as an active fisherman. We have already seen that he was the owner of one of Doughty's fishing landscapes and the author of a poem on trout fishing associated with another of Doughty's pictures. Beginning with *Al' Abri, or the Tent Pitch'd,* published in 1839, some of Willis's very popular books contained references to fishing; indeed, in his *Hurry-Graphs,* a series of letters written to his friend the editor George Pope Morris, Willis wrote of catching a hundred trout, having taken exactly the route described in *The Spirit of the Times.*[66]

The artists, writers, and fishermen of New York at midcentury made up a close community— sometimes too close, for in 1851 Willis was involved in a scandal over some letters written by a young woman whom he was reported to have seduced, which had driven her father to an early grave. The press alleged that the girl was Mary Inman (now Mary Inman Coddington), the daughter of Henry Inman, who had died in 1846 at the young age of forty-five.[67] Henry William Herbert, a frequent contributor to *The Spirit of the Times* who wrote extensively on hunting and fishing subjects[68] and another close friend of Inman, was known to have been enamored of Mary Inman. Inman, Herbert, and Fosdick were "the shining lights" of a famous piscatorial club that met at Tom Ward's hostelry in Warwick, New York.[69] For his books, Herbert learned methods of fishing and the customs of

fishermen from William T. Porter and Inman, noting that the latter "worshipped Isaak Walton almost as a demigod."[70] And, as New York's leading portrait painter, Inman painted likenesses associated with his angling avocation, including those of Porter and Herbert's wife.

Porter, in turn, through his editorship of *The Spirit of the Times,* is given credit for starting the first rush of sportsmen to the Adirondacks in the 1840s and 1850s. This can, in fact, be pinpointed to his article "Sporting Expedition to Hamilton Co., N.Y.," which appeared in the paper on September 5, 1840.[71] Charles Fenno Hoffman (1806–1884), though, had popularized the region earlier in a series of articles entitled "Scenes at the Sources of the Hudson," which appeared in the *New-York Mirror* late in 1837.[72] That same year, Thomas Cole and Asher B. Durand had visited the area around Schroon Lake. Then, in 1846, Cole, with his pupil Benjamin McConkey and Cole's friend, minister, and ultimately his biographer, Louis Legrand Noble (1813–1882), traveled to Raquette Lake and Mount Marcy, at the time among the most remote regions of the Adirondacks. The popularity of the area for sportsmen would have gained additional celebrity in the description of trout fishing there in Joel Tyler Headley's (1813–1897) popular 1849 book, *The Adirondack.*[73]

In his magisterial tome *Angling in America,* Goodspeed dealt with writers such as Fitch, Irving, Willis, Brown, and Herbert,[74] as well as Henry David Thoreau (1817–1862) who expressed, in his *Journals* and in *Walden,* his distaste for fishing as sport, though he indulged in fishing for sustenance.[75] In his discussion of "Angling Literature before 1850," Goodspeed concluded: "One more writer of this period, Charles Lanman, remains to be mentioned."[76] Lanman has been recognized as the pioneering figure in American angling publications, not as scientific treatises or journalism, but in terms of literature. Lanman was primarily a travel writer as well as an avid angler and, unique in the context of this essay, a professional artist.[77] It is significant that in *The Angler [Portrait of Charles Lanman]* (fig. 109), the marvelous cabinet portrait that William James Hubard painted of him, Lanman is identified, not with brushes and easel, but with rod and wicker creel.[78] Lanman traveled and fished in the Adirondacks, Lake George, the White Mountains, and Maine, and preceded Winslow Homer in exploring and fishing the Saguenay River in Quebec in 1847, about which excursion he wrote *A Tour to the River Saguenay in Lower Canada* in 1848, a locale to which he returned in 1859.[79]

One of the essays in Lanman's later *Haphazard Personalities*, 1886, is devoted to George W. Bethune, who had requested a treatise on fly-fishing from Lanman for his celebrated edition of *The Complete Angler* in 1847;[80] most of this essay is devoted to a letter from Bethune concerning fishing at Lake George.[81] This publication received praise from Washington Irving and Charles Dickens (1812–1870). Lanman also served for a time as private secretary to Daniel Webster with whom he shared a passion for angling and who, during a serious illness, wrote on the flyleaf of a book he was presenting to Lanman: "To my respected friend and junior brother angler, Charles Lanman."[82] "To Charles Lanman," a poem by William Lukens Shoemaker (b. 1822), contained these lines: "Worthy disciple of old Walton meek, Not angler only, you are artist, eke. . . ."[83] Lanman was also very much involved with the American art world, a close associate of such painters as William Sidney Mount and Asher B. Durand, and wrote about contemporary artists.[84] Strangely, though Lanman painted and sketched over 350 landscapes, relatively few of them were fishing scenes.[85] He did, however, paint trout, bass, blue, and trout fishing,[86] as well as *Salmon Fishing in Canada* (fig. 110), one of his finest works. Here, the wild scenery of the

FIG. 110
Charles Lanman (1819–1895), *Salmon Fishing in Canada*, ca. 1850. Oil on canvas, 14 ½ × 20 in. Courtesy David D. McNeilly

Saguenay River all but overwhelms the two fishermen who appear dwarfed by the giant rocks, the distance screened by a forest of fir trees.[87]

Asher B. Durand was not only a close colleague of Lanman's but also, briefly at least, his teacher,[88] and for a decade the heir to Thomas Cole as the leading landscape painter of the Hudson River School. Durand, too, was an angler, though not to the extent of Lanman or Inman, and he, too, enlivened a number of his late landscapes with active fishermen.[89] *The Sketcher* (1870; fig. 111) is a typical scene by Durand, with its emphasis on botanical and geological precision as seen in peeling tree bark and well-defined rocks, bathed in the softening haze that characterizes the artist's late style.[90] In the middle distance a small angler fishes in an active stream, but what is unusual about this work is the second figure of an artist in the right foreground, a counterpart, perhaps, of

the artist-angler himself, as well as a companion to the fisherman.[91] In this way, Durand also identifies two basic options, active and sedentary, offered by total immersion in the natural environment.

Thus, the tradition of the fishing landscape was alive and well in the decades before Winslow Homer began his career. Worthington Whittredge (1820–1910), for instance, after his years studying and working abroad, committed himself to rendering the scenery of his native land and was often at his best depicting intimate glades and trout pools within a forest setting, not unlike Durand's preferences. Whittredge had painted a number of angling scenes in Cincinnati in the early 1840s, at the beginning of his career, and he painted trout fishermen again, after his return to this country. Whittredge wrote of fishing for trout in the Catskills with his close friend and colleague Sanford Gifford (1823–1880) in the memorial address he presented on the latter's death.[92] But artists increasingly sought out the wilder country of the Adirondacks, as Samuel Colman did in his *Untitled: Ausable River* (ca. 1869; fig. 112), where a small fisherman confidently casts his line into the pool below the rushing waterfall and among the forbidding, giant boulders. Keene Valley and the Ausable River began to attract artists in droves immediately after the Civil War; Colman, another pupil of Durand's, was there with his colleague James David Smillie (1833–1909), in August 1869.[93] George H. Smillie (1840–1921), James's brother and fellow artist, was also there in 1869 and described the region just as Colman painted it: "We are on the Ausable River, near where it enters the Upper Ausable Lake. It winds through a rocky gorge full of the wildest scenery—towering rocks, with a succession of water-falls, rapids, and quiet pools—places almost impassable, that test the strength and nerve."[94]

White Mountains with Fisherman (fig. 113), an especially splendid fishing landscape, was painted by Alfred Thompson Bricher in 1864 while residing in Boston. At this time, Bricher was primarily devoted to scenic New England landscapes, spending some of his summers in the White Mountains;[95] this was before he painted his better-known views of coast, rocks, and water. Although he was not a member of the contemporary American Pre-Raphaelites, Bricher's picture reveals their influence in the bright clarity and specificity of his loving rendition of the natural setting, which almost overwhelms the red-shirted fisherman on the riverbank at the left. And Bricher was careful to be specific about that setting, too, for the well-known outline of Mount Chocorua, the most famous peak in the White Mountains, is distinguishable in the far summit.[96] Bricher's work is relatively unusual, for as Robert McGrath has pointed out, "the White Mountains were seldom considered a haven for sportsmen," noting that none of the major writers on the region focused on fishing as a major attraction and that "scenery rather than sport constituted the dominant thematic of the White Mountains for painters from such urban centers as Boston and New York."[97] When Durand visited North Conway in August 1855, he had been excited by the promise of abundant trout fishing but found "as on other occasions within my recollection . . . go where you will for trout, the best fishing is always some seven or ten miles further off."[98]

●

In 1836, five years before Inman completed *Trout Fishing in Sullivan County,* another fishing scene by him, simply entitled *Landscape,* had appeared at the National Academy of Design annual held that March. The following year, an engraving after the picture was published in *The Magnolia for 1837,* as "Storm Coming On." *The Magnolia* series of annual gift books was edited by Henry William Herbert, who also wrote the poem which the engraving accompanied.[99] This now unlocated landscape is unusual in the range of fishing landscapes for the

FIG. 113
Alfred Thompson Bricher (1837–1908), *White Mountains with Fisherman,* 1864. Oil on canvas, 16 × 26 in. Location unknown. Photograph courtesy Sotheby's, New York

relative size and importance of the youthful fisherman on the bank; in almost all the paintings previously considered, the fishermen have been dwarfed by the immensity of the natural setting in which they are immersed. Inman's *Landscape,* however, in typically romantic fashion, is really concerned with the upright, stalwart figure confronting nature's stormy powers; his status as a fisherman, identified by the long fishing pole he holds, is almost irrelevant.

Still, piscatorial paintings in which there is a fairly even balance between figure and natural setting are rare before Winslow Homer. Perhaps the finest of these is that by the New York genre painter Jerome Thompson, *Fishing in the Adirondacks* (also known as *Fisherman,* 1863; fig. 114), in which a determined fisherman in proper sporting garb, older than Inman's adolescent, actively casts his line into a pool he is entering. Lee Edwards, the one scholar who has written on Thompson in recent years, suggests that the figure is probably a self-portrait and notes that Thompson shared the pleasures of trout

FIG. 114
Jerome Thompson (1814–1886), *Fishing in the Adirondacks* [or *Fisherman*], 1863. Oil on canvas, 41 × 50 ½ in. Courtesy The Berkshire Museum, Pittsfield, Massachusetts

FIG. 115
Henry Inman (1801–1846), *The Young Fisherman,* 1829–1830. Oil on panel, 13 ¼ × 9 ⅝ in. The Metropolitan Museum of Art, New York. Gift of Samuel P. Avery, 1895. Photograph © The Metropolitan Museum of Art

fishing with his friend and colleague Asher B. Durand.[100] That it is specifically trout fishing that engages the fisherman here is attested by the exhibition of the work as *Trout Fishing in the Mountains* at the National Academy of Design annual in 1864.[101]

In addition to fishing landscapes, the 1820s also saw the rise of figure and genre paintings depicting fishermen, especially young fishermen, and fisher boys.[102] This theme seems to have been introduced, again by Inman, with *The Young Fisherman* (also known as *The Fisher Boy* and *The Sailor Boy;* 1829–1830; fig. 115).[103] The boy picks fruit from an overhanging branch in this American Eden, as he moves toward his goal of a fishing pond. In this, Inman's earliest known genre painting, the artist equates carefree youthfulness with wild but beneficent, even bountiful nature, and fishing as the diversion most harmonious with this correlation. Given Inman's devotion to fishing, the work may also carry nostalgic implications for his own youthful pastimes while growing up outside Utica, New York, piscatorial pleasures that lasted the artist's entire short lifetime.[104]

Inman's *Young Fisherman* inaugurated a spate of youthful fishermen in American art, as we can see from exhibition records, but most of these canvases are unlocated today.[105] Among the fisher boy images of the period that are known is John Gadsby Chapman's 1844 *The Lazy Fisherman* (fig. 116), which inverts Inman's spirited youth to a faintly comic, but also sullen, somewhat slothful representation, proposing fishing, not as an engagement with nature's freedom and beauty, but rather as a pretext for inaction, perhaps truancy. And correspondingly, the boy does not stand erect, but rather lies prone on some rocks by the shore of a languid river, far from the invigorating forest environment of Inman's *Young Fisherman*. When Chapman, himself an avid angler, first exhibited the painting at the National Academy of Design annual of 1844, where

FIG. 116

John Gadsby Chapman (1808–1889), *The Lazy Fisherman,* 1844. Oil on canvas, 25 ¼ × 30 ¼ in.
The Nelson-Atkins Museum of Art, Kansas City, Missouri. Purchase: Nelson Trust (58–12)

FIG. 117
William Sidney Mount (1807–1868), *Eel Spearing at Setauket* [or *Recollections of Early Days—"Fishing Along the Shore"*], 1845.
Oil on canvas, 28 ½ × 36 in. Fenimore Art Museum, Cooperstown, New York. Photograph: John Bigelow Taylor, New York.

it was generally admired, one writer identified the work as "Laziness personified."[106] Chapman had earlier delineated a more idyllic image of a fisher boy for an illustration in the gift book *The Magnolia for 1837*.[107]

The celebrated Long Island genre specialist, William Sidney Mount, created what is certainly the most notable example of the fisher boy type and probably the most celebrated American painting depicting fishing of the first half of the nineteenth century: *Recollections of Early Days—"Fishing Along the Shore,"* now, *Eel Spearing at Setauket* (1845; fig. 117). The picture has been copiously discussed, viewed as a nostalgic image of the artist's youth; as a serious investigation of both racial and gender issues, given the prominence of the powerful black woman actively spearing fish; as confirmation of Mount's mastery of landscape painting; and for its innovative treatment of light, prefiguring the work of the luminist painters of the 1850s and 1860s.[107] But it is also a painting of fishing, one common on the North Shore of Long Island, where Mount resided all his life. Mount here depicts eleven-year-old Thomas Strong, son of Selah B. Strong 3rd, quietly rowing the boat, while Strong's housekeeper, Rachel Holland Hart, vigorously engages in eel spearing, in front of St. George's Manor, the Strong homestead on Long Island.[108] The scene was commissioned by George Washington Strong, young Thomas's uncle, to recall his childhood pleasures.

In addition to his artistic profession, Mount was an active fisherman, the closest colleague and artist-friend of Charles Lanman. In a letter to Lanman, written in 1847, Mount recalled an experience similar to the scene depicted here from his own childhood, when "An old negro by the name of Hector gave me the first lesson in spearing flat fish, & eels." Mount's description of the event re-creates the setting of his two-year-old picture: *Early one morning we were along shore by appointment—it was calm, and the water was clear as a mirror. . . . "Steady there at the stern," said Hector, as he stood on the bow (with his spear held ready) looking into the element with all the philosophy of a Crane, while I would watch his motions, and move the boat according to the direction of his spear.*[109] The correspondence between Mount and Lanman, some of it devoted to fishing, began in 1841 and was extensive. In September 1847 Lanman requested from Mount information on Long Island fish, for a book he was planning on American fish and fishing; Mount replied with descriptions of a tremendous variety of fish, writing: "If you will allow me to speak of eels, one was taken some years since in Stony Brook harbour by Capt. John Oaks, weighing 21 pounds, and was presented by him to one of the N. Y. Museums, and received a ticket of life membership." And he added a postscript indicating his preference for eel and eel fishing: "It runs in my noddle that if you should feel disposed to publish a chapter on spearing flat-fish—the breed will be used up and I shall have to mourn the pleasures of the past."[110] In turn, Lanman celebrated Mount's pictorial achievements in his writings a number of times.[111]

A contemporary of Mount's who was more concerned with the fishing genre but about whom relatively little is known is James Goodwyn Clonney. Clonney was born in England but was in this country by 1830. He lived successively in New York City, Peekskill, and New Rochelle, New York, and then after 1852, in Cooperstown, owning property bordering Lake Otsego.[112] Specializing in rural genre scenes similar to Mount's, he probably found his subject matter at his front door, and he may have been an aficionado of fishing, though this cannot be verified.[113] A number of his fishing genre paintings, such as *Boys Fishing* (1845; The Warner Collection of Gulf States Paper Corporation, Tuscaloosa, Alabama), involve young boys, but in this and other pictures he contrasted African-Americans with white males. Here, the young black boy is fishing and has caught some porgies; the white lad is the more lethargic, though he has gathered a hatful of apples, but it is not clear whether Clonney implies friendship or barter.[114] An adult African-American who was fishing but fell asleep is tormented by two white youths who are fishing in a later picture, *Waking Up* (1851; Museum of Fine Arts, Boston), but the identification of the black with lethargy theoretically precludes the viewer's extended sympathy. Compared with Mount's works, there is a crudeness to Clonney's

paintings both formally and ideologically which makes them less than attractive to audiences today, features that did go unnoticed in his own time.[115]

Clonney depicted other adult fishermen, though this theme seems comparatively rare among American figure painters of the period, compared with the popularity of fisher boys. The clams placed alongside the sleeping African-American in *Waking Up* suggest a saltwater location, probably Long Island Sound, and this would seem to be the locale also for the triumphant older man holding high his catch in *The Happy Moment* (1847; fig. 118). Clonney painted several multifigured fishing scenes such as *Fishing Party on Long Island Sound off New Rochelle* (ca. 1847; Thyssen-Bornemisza Collection, Madrid, Spain) and *What a Catch* (1855; Museum of Fine Arts, Boston),[116] each of which again combines black and white males, the latter work probably painted on Lake Otsego, and on a much smaller scale than his earlier paintings.

Clonney's adult fishermen actually pursue the sport, whereas his children follow an interpersonal narrative thread in which fishing is relatively incidental. A few other figure painters of the period appear to have painted adult anglers, though most of these works are unlocated; from the titles alone, several, such as Martin Johnson Heade's (1819–1904) early *Sleepy Fisherman* and William Tylee Ranney's (1813–1857) *The Lazy Fisherman,* suggest that anecdote, not sport, was their primary emphasis.[117]

As one moves westward, fisher boys seem to have had no place at midcentury, perhaps because the idyllic aspects of the natural environment did not appeal to inhabitants actually living close to the rugged frontier, and also, of course, because Catskill, Adirondack, and White Mountain forested scenery was not there to shelter and nourish them. Nevertheless, the most celebrated of midwestern (then, western) painters of the midcentury, George Caleb Bingham of Missouri, painted fishermen a number of times. These

FIG. 118
James Goodwyn Clonney (1812–1867), *The Happy Moment,* 1847. Oil on canvas, 27 × 22 in. Museum of Fine Arts, Boston. Gift of Martha C. Karolik for the M. and M. Karolik collection of American Paintings, 1815–1865 (47.1222). © Museum of Fine Arts, Boston

included several fishing landscapes, the Doughty-and-Cole-like wilderness scene, *Mountain Landscape with Fisherman* (ca. 1850; Missouri Historical Society, St. Louis), and the more pastoral *Landscape with Waterwheel and Boy Fishing* (1853; Museum of Fine Arts, Boston), as well as two genre scenes. One of these is his *Mississippi Fisherman* (ca. 1851; private collection), an image of a single fisherman in the woods, quietly but intently concentrating on

the sporting activity, oblivious to a fish that has broken the river's surface in the left foreground.

As Michael Shapiro has noted, "inaction" is a central theme of a number of Bingham's river paintings, including *Mississippi Fisherman*.[118] This holds equally true of his more ambitious picture, *Fishing on the Mississippi* (1851; fig. 119), where three fishermen remain morose and motionless on a rocky outcropping at the left, balanced by three

Arthur Fitzwilliam Tait (1819–1905), *A Good Time Coming,* 1862. Oil on canvas, 20 ½ × 30 in.
The Adirondack Museum, Blue Mountain Lake, New York

other figures on a flatboat in the far distance. Only one fishing line is extended into the river, and even that pole is propped among rocks, while its owner stares glumly into the water. Though both works may be categorized as "sporting pictures," they convey no sense of the joy of the activity, let alone the pleasures of the communion with nature. Rather, their appeal, such as it was, must have been in their definition of "representative types."

The figural artists discussed so far who dealt with fishing themes were concerned with sporting subjects per se only in passing. Soon after he arrived in New York in 1850 and then ventured to the Chateaugay Lakes in the Adirondacks in 1852, English-born Arthur Fitzwilliam Tait became recognized as his adopted nation's premier sporting artist. Living first in New York City and then, with increasing success, moving to Morrisania,

Tait found his subject matter along the various Adirondack lakes: Loon, Rainbow, Raquette, and Long, where he stayed year-round in the mid-1870s. But whether on the lakes or in the woods, Tait devoted himself primarily to hunting scenes; fishing subjects are rare in his oeuvre. In addition to a number of fishing still lifes, he painted several scenes on Chateaugay Lake in 1854, *Trout Fishing* (unlocated; compare fig. 121) and *Fishing through the Ice* (private collection), sometimes at different seasons in the year. *Fishing through the Ice* is a rare pictorial subject, though Edward Hill (1843–1923), an artist resident in Littleton, New Hampshire, painted *Ice Fishing* (private collection), and the young David Neal (1838–1915) painted a small, similar scene, *Winter Fishing, Charles River, Massachusetts,* in 1857 (private collection), both multifigural.[119] There has been considerable discussion as to the identity of the successful fisherman depicted in Tait's *Fishing through the Ice,* while his "Register" identifies the three fishermen in *Trout Fishing* as "Portrait of Mr. Mosher, J. H. Clark [on the right] & Paulus Enos (Darky)."[120] James H. Clark, who acquired this work, was one of Tait's most important patrons at this time and had already been depicted by Tait in another sporting painting. In 1862 Tait also painted a now lost picture of trout fishing on the Raquette River, between Forked and Long Lakes, entitled *An Anxious Moment.*[121] In 1849 Joel Tyler Headley had written of Raquette Lake: "The most beautiful and savory trout that ever swam are found in such quantities that you can take them without even a fly, or bait of any description."[122]

More complex and unusual are Tait's several paintings of Adirondack camps. *With Great Care* (1854; private collection) depicts four fishermen and guides, unidentified except for Tait himself who stands under the shanty roof in the center of the composition, surrounded by hunting dogs and the trophies of their sport, including both game and fish. The painting was immediately purchased by Tait's most ardent patron of all, John Osborn, a wine and liquor dealer in New York; the empty wine bottle Tait holds may be a pointed reference to his benefactor. A later work, *A Good Time Coming* (1862; fig. 120), depicts Tait's shanty on Constable Point at Raquette Lake, again with four fishermen and guides, this time acknowledging the commanding presence of the standing figure of John C. Force holding a bottle of champagne (though pouring it into a tin cup). Freshly caught trout sizzle in the frying pan, while the figure striding up from Raquette Lake carries with him some more of the day's catch. Force, another successful Brooklyn restaurateur, was one of Tait's major patrons, purchasing between 1860 and 1863 a total of sixteen works.[123]

By the time Winslow Homer investigated the theme, fishing imagery had become pervasive throughout American visual culture. While only the well-to-do could own most of the paintings described here, graphic reproductions were plentiful. This was true, for instance, of Tait's fishing pictures. *Trout Fishing* appeared as a hand-colored lithograph published by Nathaniel Currier (1813–1888) as *Catching a Trout, "We hab you now, Sar!"* (1854), and *Fishing through the Ice* was published two years later as *American Winter Sports: Trout Fishing "On Chateaugay Lake" (Franklin Co., N.Y.)* (fig. 121). Currier & Ives reproduced *An Anxious Moment* in 1862 as *Brook Trout Fishing: "An Anxious Moment"* (fig. 122), and *A Good Time Coming* in 1863 as *Camping in the Woods: "A Good Time Coming."*[124] Currier & Ives, of course, published many other fishing lithographs by artists such as Frances ("Fanny") Palmer (1812–1876) and Thomas Worth (1834–1917) as well, about thirty prints in all, and others appeared with firms such as Thomas Kelly of New York.[125] Books, such as Murray's 1869 *Adventures in the Wilderness* and Seneca Ray Stoddard's (1844–1917) 1874 *The Adirondacks: Illustrated,* were enhanced with sporting, including

FIG. 121
Charles Parsons (1821–1910), lithographer, after Arthur Fitzwilliam Tait (1819–1905), *American Winter Sports: Trout Fishing "On Chateaugay Lake" (Franklin Co., N.Y.),* 1856. Lithograph, hand-colored, published by Currier & Ives, New York, 21¾ × 29½ in. Amon Carter Museum, Fort Worth, Texas (1970.207).

fishing, images.[126] Even less expensive and far more plentiful were the illustrations that accompanied the many articles on hunting and fishing sports that appeared in both monthly magazines and the new weekly pictorial magazines of the 1850s and 1860s.[127] Fishing scenes even turned up on a number of sheet music covers such as that lithographed by Sarony & Co. of New York to accompany William Vincent Wallace's ballad "The Angler's Polka," 1854, dedicated to William T. Porter.

•

About half of Tait's fishing paintings, including *American Speckled Brook Trout* (Princeton University Library, Princeton, New Jersey), were figureless pictures, still lifes of fish piled on the shore, representing the trophies of the catch. The fishing still life had been inaugurated into the American artistic

repertoire a generation earlier by William Sidney Mount's older brothers, Henry and Shepard Alonzo Mount. Henry (1802–1841), the oldest, who died young, had begun a sign painting business in New York in 1824, and his *Still Life: Fish* (ca. 1831; Long Island Museum of American Art, History & Carriages, Stony Brook, New York) is a bold, simplified composition of fish against a wall, which might have hung outside a fishmonger's store. This, however, is an easel painting, probably the picture *Fish* that he exhibited in the annual exhibition of the National Academy of Design in 1831; Henry Mount had previously exhibited a picture entitled *Fish* at the academy in 1827.[128]

Henry Mount obviously sought to be connected with the fine arts and was made an associate member of the academy in 1828, but he remained tied to commercial interests. His brother, Shepard Alonzo, was primarily a portraitist, but he was also the nation's first specialist in fish still lifes, which he exhibited sporadically at the academy between 1832 and 1864.[129] Shepard's fish still lifes are more explicitly associated with fishing than Henry's, for they always appear in a landscape setting in the two basic modes of presentation. They may, like Tait's later examples, be set on the bank of a stream or pool, or they may be hung as fishing trophies, as in his *Fish* (Long Island Museum of American Art, History & Carriages, Stony Brook, New York), looking forward to Homer's several examples of hanging fish. This work is specifically dated to "July 1847," bespeaking Shepard Mount's avid angling activities and almost certainly documenting an actual catch. Shepard traveled deep into the American landscape for his fishing sites, painting on the Susquehanna River at Athens, Pennsylvania, near the border of New York State, in 1842, and again in 1847 when he painted *Fish,* a work of which he was especially proud, and rightly so. Mount wrote his brother William from Factoryville, New York (near Athens), saying that "for truth of representation and transparency of color I have never approached it," concluding, "You must allow me to brag a little on fish as I sometimes think (and not without some reason) that they are the only subjects I can paint really well."[130] On his return to Stony Brook, Shepard gave the picture to William, who exhibited it to great praise at the National Academy, where one critic noted that the fish "seem to breathe and move, so exquisitely life-like, so admirably drawn, and so richly colored are they. We have often seen pictures of trout, but none as perfect a one as Mr. M. seems here to have thrown off, in some few happy moments. Old Walton would revel in it."[131] As with his brother William, Charles Lanman was a friend and admirer of Shepard Mount, especially during the 1840s.[132]

Fishing still lifes were not prominent in the American artistic repertoire until the 1860s. After the Civil War, however, numerous specialists appeared, and their work became popular, though most of the artists are little known today. The explanation for this phenomenon is probably complex, but several reasons may be suggested here. One may have been the association of this subject with the growing celebrity of Arthur Tait as the country's premier sporting artist; Tait had already produced a number of dead game still lifes, and he turned to their fishing equivalents in 1860. In 1863 he painted *American Speckled Brook Trout*, which in turn became the basis the following year for a Currier & Ives lithograph. The firm subsequently produced numerous other fishing still-life lithographs, though none of equal quality.

Another factor here may be the fishing still lifes of the British painter Henry Leonidas Rolfe (fl. 1847–1881), a member of a family of artists devoted to angling subjects.[133] Rolfe's fish still lifes were in this country as early as 1854, when his *Fish* was shown at the Rhode Island Art Association in Providence. Also in that decade, a *Fish Piece* by Rolfe was shown in 1856 at the Brooklyn

FIG. 122
Charles Parsons (1821–1910), lithographer, after Arthur Fitzwilliam Tait (1819–1905), *Brook Trout Fishing: "An Anxious Moment,"* 1862. Lithograph, hand-colored, published by Currier & Ives, New York, 22 ½ × 30 in. Amon Carter Museum, Fort Worth, Texas (1970.207)

Atheneum, while in 1857 one appeared in the first major exhibition of contemporary British paintings, held in New York. During the Civil War, a number of Rolfe's works were included in the various Sanitary Fair art exhibitions in support of medical war relief, and during the 1860s Rolfe's fishing still lifes were shown at the Brooklyn Art Association, the Pennsylvania Academy of the Fine Arts, the Boston Athenæum, the Chicago Interstate Industrial Exhibition, and at the Metropolitan Museum of Art in New York.

A logical question, in connection with the appearance of so many fishing still lifes by Rolfe and his American contemporaries, is the nature of patronage for such work in post–Civil War America. Fishing still lifes, of course, may have been hung in the dining rooms of the homes of well-to-do art patrons,[134] along with pictures of fruit and other

FIG. 123
Walter Brackett (1823–1919), *The Rise,* 1872. Oil on canvas.
Location unknown. Photograph courtesy the author

FIG. 124
Walter Brackett (1823–1919), *The Leap,* 1872. Oil on canvas.
Location unknown. Photograph courtesy the author

FIG. 125
Walter Brackett (1823–1919), *The Last Struggle,* 1872. Oil on
canvas. Location unknown. Photograph courtesy the author

FIG. 126
Walter Brackett (1823–1919), *Landed,* 1872. Oil on canvas.
Location unknown. Photograph courtesy the author

edibles, but the fish would not have had comparable decorative qualities. But presumably they were often acquired by sportsmen and may have been installed in game rooms, the quarter privileged as a male preserve within the house, which was otherwise designated as a female domain.[135] This, in turn, reflects the growing distinction in post–Civil War America between the private, internal space dominated by women and the outside world of business and commerce, which was reserved solely for men. Fishing and hunting still lifes may also have been hung in the plethora of men's clubs that sprang up after the Civil War, again exclusively male preserves. And fishing and game still-life prints may have ornamented the walls of summer homes.

A prime example of a fishing still-life specialist is the Dutch-born Arnoud (or Arnoldus) Wydeveld, who arrived in this country about 1855, settling in New York. He originally painted and exhibited fruit pictures and an occasional floral piece, but after a trip to his native Nijmegen in the mid-1860s, he was back in New York in 1867 as a master of the fish still life.[136] His Dutch experience very likely contributed to this thematic change, but the new popularity of Rolfe's work may also have been a stimulus. Among the fishing still-life specialists who came to the fore in the decade following the Civil War were several from Hartford, Connecticut, Gurdon Trumbull (fig. 17, ill. p. 47) and Thomas Sedgwick Steele (1845–1903). In 1874 a critic wrote of two of Trumbull's works as "the most remarkable pictures of fish ever yet produced by an American artist," while five years later Trumbull was praised as "The finest fish-painter of America."[137] Steele's first trout picture was favorably received in 1875 at the Brooklyn Art Association, and *Forest and Stream* published a series of Steele's letters in 1877 on the scenery as well as the fishing at the Rangeley Lakes in northern Maine in 1877, the base for the Oquossoc Angling Association.[138]

Perhaps even more favored was the work of Samuel A. Kilbourne, who was born in Maine but lived much of his life in Morrisania, New York (as did Tait). Kilbourne practiced landscape painting

until the late 1850s, when a study of a trout was received so successfully that he made fish painting, such as his *Speckled Trout* (fig. 19, ill. p. 50), his specialty.[139] What brought him the greatest acclaim, however, was the publication of a large folio, *The Game Fishes of the United States,* beginning in 1879, two years before his death. This was a portfolio of twenty splendid chromolithographs of different American fish, some shown in the water, others being caught by rod and hook, and still others depicted as a "catch" on a riverbank.[140]

Even more celebrated as a painter of fish, usually in still lifes but also active in the water, was Walter Brackett; indeed, Brackett was one of the few painters discussed in this essay who achieved international renown. Though like Kilbourne born in Maine, Brackett spent his professional life in Boston and was an active member of the art community there. He began his professional career as a portrait painter, showing in the annual exhibitions held at the Boston Athenæum beginning in 1846. His biographer wrote that when Brackett was thirty years old, in 1853, he spent a summer near Conway, New Hampshire, and there painted a brook trout so successfully that he was flooded with commissions for pictures of trout. Subsequently, in 1861, on a trip to Schoodic Lake, Maine, he began to paint salmon.[141]

In 1863 he appeared at the Boston Athenæum with the painting *Brook Trout* and never looked back (Rolfe was to exhibit two paintings entitled *Fish* in the Athenæum's annual the following year). The painting of fish, salmon and trout especially, became the subject with which Brackett was overwhelmingly associated, though he never ceased painting portraits. He continued to exhibit his fish paintings at the Athenæum, at the Sailor's Fair in Boston in 1864, organized for Civil War support, and at the Boston Art Club from 1874, when that body took over the principal exhibition activities in the city from the Athenæum. But Brackett's most acclaimed work was a series of four pictures of salmon, taken from the lakes in Maine, which he painted in 1872: *The Rise* (fig. 123), *The Leap* (fig. 124), *The Last Struggle* (fig. 125), and *Landed* (fig. 126; all unlocated).[142] These pictures were shown at the Goupil Gallery in New York that year and then were taken abroad and exhibited in Liverpool and at the Crystal Palace in London in 1873.[143] They were acquired by Sir Richard Potter of Gloucestershire, and Brackett replicated this set a number of times.[144] One series was displayed in his Tremont Street studio in Boston in 1875,[145] before being shown that year at the Chicago Interstate Industrial Exhibition, at the Boston Art Club in

FIG. 127
Samuel Marsden Brookes (1816–1892), *Salmon Trout and Smelt*, 1873. Oil on canvas,
40 ⅜ × 32 ⅛ in. Fine Arts Museums of San Francisco. Gift of Collis P. Huntington (7115)

April 1876, and at the Philadelphia Centennial that same year. In these works, only the fish, not the fishermen, are depicted, but they provide a complete review of a successful angling experience, and in that regard they foreshadow the work of Homer.[146] Brackett's work was shown abroad again when several of his fish pictures were displayed at the International Fisheries Exhibition in London in 1883.[147] For a number of years, Brackett spent his summers on the St. Marguerite River, a tributary of the Saguenay River in Canada, where he had a camp in salmon region, and salmon were the fish that he especially favored.[148]

One further specialist in fish still life deserves discussion here. Samuel Marsden Brookes was the most celebrated master of that genre for thirty years in the late nineteenth century in San Francisco, where the prejudice against the theme of still-life painting as imitative and uninspiring appears not to have taken hold as it had in Europe and the eastern United States. Brookes was born and grew up in England, but in 1833 his family settled in the Midwest of this country, where he developed as a portrait and landscape painter. Brookes painted his first still life in 1858 and moved to California in 1862. He continued to paint portraits, and his range in still life was wide, from depictions of objets d'art to fruit and vegetable painting, but fish, especially salmon, was his forte, a subject to which he had turned by the late 1860s. He painted the fish in both of the usual formats—on the banks of a stream or hanging, either from a string out-of-doors or from a hook on a stone wall, as in *Salmon Trout and Smelt* (1873; fig. 127). Brookes's fish, however, were not the end result of angling in the rivers and streams of California; they were acquired in the local markets.[149]

The finish on Brookes's fish is almost microscopic; this, together with his ability to capture the delicate colors, polish, and sheen of the fish, gives his work the quality of an optical illusion. Indeed, a minor mythology grew up in San Francisco concerning Brookes's impressive achievements, with the local newspapers replete with both prose and poetry affirming his singularity and greatness. Brookes was patronized by such distinguished collectors as Edwin Bryant Crocker and Mrs. Mark Hopkins, and in his heyday his financial success was greater than that of all other California artists. Perhaps in no other place and at no other time during the nineteenth century did a still-life painter, let alone one specializing in fishing trophies, achieve such stature.[150]

•

One of the best-known and most often reproduced American fishing still lifes is *Still Life with Fish and Fishing Tackle* (fig. 128), painted in 1852 by Junius Brutus Stearns.[151] This is an unusual variant of the motif, insofar as it includes a fisherman in a stream in the distance, though the focus is on the fish already caught, along with a rod and reel, a creel, and a fly book, as well as a glass flask. Though he is best known for his series of paintings on the life of George Washington (Virginia Museum of Fine Arts, Richmond; and Dayton Art Institute, Ohio),[152] Stearns is the American painter most associated with fishing and pictures related to the sport before Winslow Homer, and he is certainly the most versatile (he is also the only painter of his time whose fishing subjects have been the object of modern scholarship[153]). That contemporaries also so viewed him is attested by the reproduction of Stearns's *Striped Bass* as the frontispiece for Genio Scott's important 1869 publication, *Fishing in American Waters*. Of 174 illustrations, only this, along with Brackett's *Brook Trout* and *Whitefish,* were not sketched by the author.[154] A good-size painting by Stearns entitled *Fish* had been acquired for distribution by the American Art-Union as early as 1849.[155] *Still Life with Fish and Fishing Tackle* may be the picture Stearns exhibited at the National Academy annual in 1853 as *Trout;* in 1860 he showed

the painting *Fish* there, and in 1863, *Four Pounder.* Such fishing trophies may well be the result of Stearns's own angling; in his will Stearns carefully detailed the disposition of his fishing rod and reels to three of his sons.[156]

The majority of Stearns's fishing pictures, however, are figural works. He made several significant contributions to the genre of the fisher boy: *Children Fishing* of 1850, *Two Children Fishing* of 1878, and *The Old, Old Story* of 1882.[157]

But Stearns's most distinctive and fascinating fishing paintings are the group of individualized images of fishermen in outdoor settings that have come to light, some of which, at least, are specific portraits. They document their subjects' attraction to the sport, shared by the artist himself. It is not

FIG. 128
Junius Brutus Stearns (1810–1885), *Still Life with Fish and Fishing Tackle,* 1852. Oil on canvas, 22 × 26 15/16 in. Toledo Museum of Art, Ohio. Museum Purchase Fund (1951.410)

FIG. 129
Junius Brutus Stearns (1810–1885), *Trout Fishing*, 1853. Oil on canvas, 37 ⅜ × 50 ¼ in.
Location unknown. Photograph courtesy Christie's, New York

known what led Stearns to take up this amalgam of portraiture and sporting painting, or if any of them were commissioned by the subjects, and if so, what induced them to choose Stearns. But whatever the circumstance, Stearns made a unique contribution to the American fishing picture genre with this group of portraits. They include *Trout Fishing* of 1853 (fig. 129), which may depict Deming Jarves of Boston and his son. *A Fishing Party off Long Island* of 1860 may portray the artist's coterie of Brooklyn fishing friends or it may show the angler who perhaps commissioned the painting, a Mr. Hone, with his fishing companions. A late example is Stearns's 1871 picture *A Fishing Party in a Catboat on Great South Bay, Long Island, New York*.[158]

Stearns's 1853 *Trout Fishing* was obviously the model for one of the artist's best-known paintings, *Elliott and His Friends* (fig. 130), painted five years

FIG. 130
Junius Brutus Stearns (1810–1885), *Elliott and His Friends,* 1858. Oil on canvas, 37 × 54 in. Keinbusch Angling Collection,
Department of Rare Books and Special Collections, Princeton University Library, Princeton, New Jersey

later, in 1858, and exhibited at the National Academy of Design annual that year. The celebrated New York portrait painter Charles Loring Elliott (1812–1868) is at the left. Lewis Gaylord Clark (1808–1873), the editor of the *Knickerbocker* magazine, is standing on a large rock in the center, fishing, while the noted author Frederick Swarthout Cozzens (1818–1869), the writer of the recent and popular *Sparrowgrass Papers* (1856), is seated on the same rock, at the right, holding a gun rather than a rod. The compositions of the two pictures are identical, as are the waterfall setting and the distant landscape, though Stearns has substituted birch trees at the left for the fir trees in the earlier painting. Clark is posed identically to the central figure in *Trout Fishing,* though the other sportsmen are posed differently, and both fish and game are depicted, signifying the sportsmen's intent and their success.

Unlike *Trout Fishing,* this is a well-recorded picture, noted in the *Crayon* magazine in March 1858, where it was erroneously stated that Stearns was depicting the figures of "a well-known editor, with two artist companions, angling at the base of a water-fall," while James Renwick Brevoort (1832–1918) was painting the landscape; the magazine later issued a retraction, crediting Stearns with the whole.[159] Surprisingly, the picture appears not to have been commissioned by any of the three subjects and seems to have been for sale at the National Academy. But within the decade, it had found a place in the collection of James C. McGuire, one of the most distinguished collectors in Washington, D.C.[160] The landscape is obviously related to that found in Stearns's earlier painting, and Lewis Gaylord Clark had written of a fishing excursion in October 1857 to "John Brown's Tract," passing through Utica, near Trenton Falls.[161]

The painting garnered a good deal of critical attention when it was shown at the National Academy.[162] Not surprisingly, the longest and most flattering piece came from the "Editor's Table" in the *Knickerbocker:*

. . . we made directly for a certain picture, in the Sixth Room, the title whereof had struck our chance-look at the Catalogue: "Elliott and his Friends": No. 608. It is a very spirited picture, and remarkably well done as to the likenesses. It is just the picture we should like to have in our "Sanctum," placing before us, as it does, three individuals, remarkable each in his particular sphere: and here they are, all shown to be united in that one "gentle art" which old Izaak Walton has so quaintly eulogized. They are evidently enthusiastic devotees of angling—the Artist and the Editor more especially— as their bold and characteristic attitudes sufficiently indicate. It was a very difficult undertaking to paint three men in the position and with the "surroundings" which Mr. Stearns has chosen for his favorite trio: but we are glad to see that he has succeeded so well. That two of the portraits, Elliott and your veritable self, friend

Knickerbocker, are excellent entirely, we can unhesitatingly testify. We made critical comparison, and agreed that it was "all right," barring your white hat and leather sporting-coat. A few days after, we chanced upon the well-bearded Elliott in the same room, and found that he, too, was equally well taken. We may naturally infer, therefore, that the other subject (Mr. Frederick Cozzens) is likewise "all right," although we are not personally familiar with his lineaments."[163]

Elliott and His Friends is thus evidence both to the friendship that existed among the three men and to their mutual devotion to sport, for Elliott and Clark at least, specifically to angling. A dozen of Elliott's portraits were engraved for *The Knickerbocker Gallery,* published in 1855 as a testimonial to Clark and his contributions to New York culture; among these were the portraits of Cozzens and Clark himself.[164] Clark had been instrumental in furthering Elliott's career, praising his work in the columns of the magazine and in his 1852 reminiscences, where he wrote: "We know of no American portrait-painter who has advanced with more rapid strides toward perfection; a fact sufficiently evinced by the patronage which he has secured from the best sources in the metropolis."[165] Moreover, Clark named one son John Elliott Clark, after his esteemed friend and fishing companion.[166] Cozzens, in turn, was a frequent contributor to the *Knickerbocker.* Also, it should be noted that both Stearns and Elliott had studios on the top floor of the old Art-Union Building at 497 Broadway in New York at this time;[167] Stearns, in an autobiographical letter, acknowledged of Elliott that he "enjoyed the benefits of his judgement and instruction."[168] It may not be without significance that Elliott had, in his personal art collection, a painting entitled *Fish* by Henry Leonidas Rolfe.[169]

Two years later, Stearns took a very different approach to fishing portraiture in *A Fishing Party off Long Island* (1860; The Minneapolis Institute of Arts, Minnesota). Here, he has moved to open-water fishing; with a minimal setting, the concentration is on both the individual likenesses and the group activity, expressing varying degrees of excitement on making a major catch. In the distinct and diverse expressions and poses of the seven figures in the two boats, along with the immediacy of the moment, the work takes on the character of a genre painting, and yet the likenesses appear extremely portraitlike. An obituary for Stearns in September 1885 named George C. Bennett, Martin Kalbfleisch (mayor of Brooklyn in 1861 and again in 1867), William G. Bishop, Caspian Sparks, E. J. Butterfield, William Marshall (perhaps the engraver of portraits of George Washington and Abraham Lincoln), and Charles Goodwin as members of a "circle of men united by the strongest ties of friendship," which had existed twenty-five or thirty years earlier in Williamsburg, Brooklyn; it was also noted that Stearns "in many ways made the coterie famous in this vicinity by transferring to canvas some of its principal reunions."170 This may be one such transfer. Stearns is known to have painted an official portrait of Kalbfleisch,171 who was president of the Oceanus Boat Club, organized in Brooklyn in 1871, with headquarters at Rockaway Beach; George Bennett was also a member of the club. It is possible that Stearns and the subjects depicted in this painting were subsequently involved with this organization.172 Stearns himself was a longtime resident of Brooklyn, and he died there. Alternatively, the picture may include Stearns's patron for this work, a Mr. Hone, along with a group of Hone's fishing companions.173

A later painting by Stearns is his 1871 picture *A Fishing Party in a Catboat on Great South Bay, Long Island, New York* (The New-York Historical Society, New York). This, again, depicts seven people but appears even more a genre painting, with the figure at the right appearing to be seasick, and that on the far left holding the rudder and turned away from the viewer. This group seems considerably younger than the seven men depicted

in *A Fishing Party off Long Island;* notable here is that three of the figures in the sailing vessel are women, two of whom are fishing, though it is the young man whom the third woman accompanies who appears to have made a catch. In this group of pictures, Stearns has made a unique contribution to the American fishing painting genre. Stearns's death in a carriage traffic accident on September 17, 1885, was reported to have removed "nearly the last of the coterie of old settlers who were so well known" in the Eastern District of Brooklyn, also known as the "Old Williamsburgers."174

·

In 1878 Charles Dudley Warner (1829–1900) published an essay, "A Fight with a Trout":
The trout is a retiring and harmless animal, except when he is aroused and forced to combat; and then his agility, fierceness, and vindictiveness become apparent. No one who has studied the excellent pictures representing men in an open boat, exposed to the assaults of long, enraged trout flying at them through the open air with open mouth, ever ventures with his rod upon the lonely lakes of the forest without a certain terror, or even reads of the exploits of daring fishermen without a feeling of admiration for their heroism.175
Hyperbole aside, while angling imagery in America had a long and quite fascinating history, it was precisely this spirit of contest and the vitality implicit in the sport that had not been expressed in even the finest such paintings. In addition to Winslow Homer's incalculable technical skill and sophisticated handling of both the oil and watercolor media, it is this sense of raw energy that he introduced into American piscatorial art. Or, in the words of a later critic of Homer: "He deals with trout-fishing and deer hounding . . . and the difference between these pictures and the conventional painting of outdoor sports is like the difference between George Inness at his best and the old time topographical art of the Hudson."176

NOTES

1. Tom Quinn, *Angling in Art* (London: The Sportsman's Press, 1991), 103. Quinn's book is almost totally concerned with British angling imagery, devoting but a short chapter to the United States and featuring only Homer, Norman Rockwell, and a few contemporaries. There is much previous literature on British paintings of angling, including one venerable but still immensely useful and important tome: Walter Shaw Sparrow, *Angling in British Art* (London: John Lane/The Bodley Head, 1923). Given the veneration of Izaak Walton in Great Britain (and in the United States), this is not surprising, but one should consider the possible range of angling imagery among artists of other Western nations (depictions of commercial fishing fleets, at least, being not uncommon).

2. Paul Hulton and David Beers Quinn, *The American Drawings of John White, 1577–1590, and Drawings of European and Oriental Subjects*, 2 vols. (London: British Museum; Chapel Hill: University of North Carolina Press, 1964), vol. 1, 102–104; vol. 2, pls. 42, 129. See also Paul Hulton, *America 1585: The Complete Drawings of John White* (Chapel Hill: University of North Carolina Press; London: British Museum Publications, 1985), 73, 181. White also depicted the Native Americans cooking fish, as well as a number of single images of identifiable fish.

3. To my knowledge, there is only one publication dealing exclusively with this topic, the small but informative catalogue for the exhibition *Piscatorial Pictorials of America* (Montclair, N.J.: Montclair Art Museum, 1973). A number of publications on American sport, all exhibition catalogues, incorporate considerations of fishing, such as *Sport in American Art* (Boston: Museum of Fine Arts, 1944); *Shooting and Fishing in Art* (Baltimore: The Baltimore Museum of Art, 1958); *"Sportscapes": Hunting, Fowling, Angling* (Southampton, N.Y.: Parrish Art Museum, 1959); *Sport in Art from American Museums* (New York: Universe, 1991); *Call of the Wild: A Sportsman's Life* (New York: Hirschl & Adler Galleries; Houston: Meredith Long & Co., 1994). In each case, however, fishing receives fairly minimal discussion compared with hunting and field sports.

4. Charles Lanman wrote in 1868: "More than two hundred years have elapsed since the appearance of the 'Complete Angler and Contemplative Man's Recreation' . . . [It] is yet without an equal in any of the modern languages." "The Annals of Angling," *Galaxy* 6 (September 1868): 307.

5. Boutelle may or may not have had the opportunity of seeing Constable's original work, but American audiences, generally, could have been familiar with this and other paintings by Constable through David Lucas's engravings of 1840. Lucas engraved *Stratford Mill* and published it under the title *The Young Waltonians*. Andrew Shirley, *The Published Mezzotints of David Lucas after John Constable, R.A., a Catalogue and Historical Account* (Oxford: Clarendon Press, 1930), 113, correspondence no. 152, n. 1.

6. For Boutelle, see Carol E. Faill, "De Witt Clinton Boutelle Hudson River School Painter," M.A. thesis, Pennsylvania State University, Capitol Campus, 1983.

7. [George W. Bethune], ed., *The Complete [sic] Angler* (New York: Wiley & Putnam, 1847). *The Complete Angler* had previously appeared with American imprints, those of T. Wardle, Philadelphia, in 1837, and J. B. Lippincott and Co., Philadelphia, in 1844, but these were reprints of British editions of the same year. See Bernard S. Horne, *The Compleat Angler, 1653–1967: A New Bibliography* (Pittsburgh: The Pittsburgh Bibliophiles, 1970), passim; and Rodolphe L. Coigney, *Izaac Walton: A New Bibliography 1653–1987* (New York: James Cummins, 1989), passim.

8. George W. Bethune, *A Plea for Study: An Oration before The Literary Societies of Yale College* (Philadelphia: John C. Clark, 1845), 40–41.

9. [Bethune], *The Complete Angler*, iii.

10. "Izaak Walton," *United States Magazine and Literary Gazette* 1 (November 15, 1824): 233–234. See a review of a 1764 British edition, "Izaak Walton's Complete Angler," *American Turf Register and Sporting Magazine* 9 (February 1838): 65–73.

11. "Waltoniana," *American Review* 1 (April 1845): 383–392. This periodical was especially favorable to fishing; see also P. P., "Angling," *American Review* 25 (January 1850): 32–46.

12. "Izaak Walton's Complete Angler," *Knickerbocker* 30 (November 1847): 385.

13. Charles A. Munger, "The Complete Susquehanna Angler," *Knickerbocker* 45 (June 1855): 598–609.

14. Henry Ward Beecher, *Star Papers; or, Experiences of Art and Nature* (New York: J. C. Derby, 1855), 231–239. In this same spirit and in the same collection of essays, Beecher wrote a piece on "Trouting," 144–151.

15. Roger Wolcott, "Some Improvement of Vacant Hours," in *Poetical Meditations, Being the Improvement of Some Vacant Hours* (New London, Conn.: L. Green, 1725), 32.

16. [Joseph Seccombe], *Business and diversion inoffensive to God . . . A discourse utter'd in part at Ammauskeeg-Falls, in the fishing season, 1739. . . .* (Boston: S. Kneeland and T. Green, 1743). This was the earliest American book on angling. For an excellent survey of American fishing literature before 1860, see Robert W. Henderson, comp., *Early American Sport* (New York: A.S. Barnes & Co., 1953). For a contemporary listing of the most influential British literature on fishing in the period before Winslow Homer, see Charles Lanman, "The Annals of Angling," *Galaxy* 6 (September 1868): 308. Lanman deprecates the small number of American books on fishing, while lauding the incidental contributions by writers such as Bethune, Beecher, and others.

17. I have drawn here, and elsewhere throughout this essay, on the incomparable study of American fishing by Charles Eliot Goodspeed, *Angling in America: Its Early History and Literature* (Boston: Houghton Mifflin Company, 1939). His treatment of Seccombe's sermon is on 58–64.

18. Elijah Fitch, *The Beauties of Religion. A poem addressed to youth* (Providence, R.I.: John Carter, 1789). See Goodspeed, *Angling in America*, 143.

19. Samuel Low, *Poems*, 2 vols. (New York: T. & J. Swords, 1800), vol. 2, 152–154.

20. Fishing attributes in British portraiture actually extend back to the sixteenth century; see the fascinating, very formal likeness of the famous Oxford divine Alexander Nowel (Brasenose College, Oxford), the dean of St. Paul's Cathedral in London, with a bag of fishing hooks on the table in front of the subject and a fishing rod hanging on the wall behind. Nowel, who lived to ninety-five, was one of those about whom Walton had written concerning the longevity of fishermen.

21. Examples are Justus Englehardt Kühn's portrait of *Henry Darnall III*, ca. 1770 (Maryland Historical Society, Baltimore), and Benjamin West's *Thomas Mifflin*, ca. 1758–1759 (Historical Society of Pennsylvania, Philadelphia).

22. My deep appreciation to Ellen Miles, Curator, National Portrait Gallery, for drawing this painting to my attention. For Theus and the Elliott family portraits, see Margaret Simons Middleton, *Jeremiah Theus: Colonial Artist of Charles Town* (Columbia: University of South Carolina Press, 1953), 127–130. Middleton notes (9) that "Much can be learned from Theus' pictures of the games and sports of colonial days. Barnard Elliott carried a gun, and his small son Barnard, Jr., has a fishing line."

23. Corně is far better known, in any case, for his ship portraits and marines than for his portraiture. See Nina Fletcher Little, introduction to *Michele Felice Corně, 1752–1845: Versatile Neapolitan Painter of Salem, Boston and Newport*, exh. cat. (Salem, Mass.: Peabody Museum of Salem, 1972). Corně's activities in Salem during the decade when he painted the Olivers are mentioned numerous times by his patron, William Bentley; see *The Diary of William Bentley, D.D.* (Gloucester, Mass.: Peter Smith, 1962), passim.

24. The scene is identified as the North (Hudson) River in the entry of April 6, 1793, in the Manuscript Household Account Book of George Washington, Library of Congress, and in a letter written four days later from Alexander Hamilton in Philadelphia to his wife mentioning "two views of situations on Hudson's River painted by Mr. Winstanley in the drawing room of Mrs. Washington. . . ." See J. Hall Pleasants, "Four Late Eighteenth Century Anglo-American Landscape Painters," *Proceedings of the American Antiquarian Society* 52 (Worcester, Mass.: American Antiquarian Society, 1943), 302–303, 321–322.

25. Stiles Tuttle Colwill, *Francis Guy, 1760–1820*, exh. cat. (Baltimore: Maryland Historical Society, 1981), 53. The work appeared in Guy's lottery held on October 23, 1804, at Bryden's Assembly Room, Baltimore.

26. [Washington Irving], *The Sketch Book of Geoffrey Crayon, Gent.* (New York: C. S. Van Winkle, 1819–1820); 4th ed., 2 vols., 1824, 239–253. See also Irving, "The Angler," *American Turf Register and Sporting Magazine* 11 (January 1838): 13–14.

27. [Irving], *Sketch Book*, 240.

28. [Irving], *Sketch Book*, 239.

29. Charles Lanman, *Adventures in the Wilds of the United States and British American Provinces*, 2 vols. (Philadelphia: John W. Moore, 1856), vol. 1, iv, quoted in Goodspeed, *Angling in America*, 145.

30. Jennie Holliman, *American Sports (1785–1935)* (Durham, N.C.: Seeman Press, 1931), 55–56, paraphrasing the article "Proceedings of the Cincinnati Angling Club," *The Cabinet of Natural History and American Rural Sports*, (Philadelphia, 1830), vol. 1, 258. The following year saw the publication of *The Proceedings of the Cincinnati Angling Club* (Cincinnati: Chronicle Press, 1831).

31. The principal published source on Doughty is *Thomas Doughty, 1793–1856: An American Pioneer in Landscape Painting*, exh. cat. (Philadelphia: Pennsylvania Academy of the Fine Arts, 1973), with an essay and catalogue by Frank H. Goodyear Jr. Goodyear had prepared his master's thesis on Doughty, "The Life and Art of Thomas Doughty," University of Delaware, Newark, 1969. See also the checklist of Doughty's paintings in John Alan Walker, "Thomas Doughty (1793–1856)," *Fine Art Source Material Newsletter* 1 (1971), and the typescript by Howard M. Doughty, "Biographical Sketch of Thomas Doughty (1793–1856)," New York, New-York Historical Society, 1941.

32. This, as many of Doughty's wilderness landscapes, is not site-specific. In regard to this work, Linda Jones Gibbs has sensitively noted: "Not merely looking at but contemplating nature required a surrender of self in the face of God's handiwork and thus was deemed an act of devotion." *150 Years of American Painting, 1794–1944*, exh. cat. (Provo, Utah: Museum of Art, Brigham Young University, 1994), 20.

33. See Doughty's *Delaware Water Gap* of 1826, reproduced in *Thomas Doughty, 1796–1856*, pl. 10.

34. R.H.R., "Communication from Susquehanna County. With a Drawing of Trout," *The Cabinet of Natural History and American Rural Sports* (Philadelphia, 1830), vol. 1, 145–149.

35. Formally organized fishing clubs such as the Cincinnati Angling Club first appeared in colonial times with the Schuylkill Fishing Club founded in Philadelphia in 1732. Two more fishing clubs were formed in Philadelphia before the Revolution; by 1837 there were also fishing clubs in New York, Boston, Baltimore, and Pittsburgh (The Walton Club), as well as Philadelphia and Cincinnati. Goodspeed, *Angling in America*, 29–54, 95–117.

36. *The Cabinet of Natural History and American Rural Sports*, vol. 1: "Angling," 111–116; "White Fish of the Lakes," 141; "Bass Fishing in the West," 260–261; "Proceedings of the Cincinnati Angling Club," 254–259. For Thomas Doughty's artistic contributions to the *Cabinet*, see Robert F. Looney, "Thomas Doughty, Printmaker," *Philadelphia Printmaking: American Prints before 1860* (West Chester, Pa.: Tinicum Press, 1976), 130–148.

37. *The Cabinet of Natural History and American Rural Sports*, vol. 2: "Angling in Surinam," 112–113; "Some Pages from the Diary of a Sportsman," 113–116; "Natural History of the Bassae," 138–139; "An Extraordinary Pike," 167–168; "Pike," 175–180; "Directions for Fishing for Pike," 286–288.

38. Fred Barry Adelson, "Alvan Fisher (1792–1863): Pioneer in American Landscape Painting," Ph.D. diss., Columbia University, 1982, 417–418. Adelson also suggests that *Angling for Trout* may be the painting now known as *Landscape with Angler*.

39. Ellwood C. Parry III, *The Art of Thomas Cole: Ambition and Imagination* (Newark: University of Delaware Press; London and Toronto: Associated University Presses, 1988), 57–58. I want to thank Dr. Parry for suggesting the inclusion of *Crossing the Stream* in this essay; Parry has noted that there is a highly finished related drawing for this work in the collection of Juniata College, Huntingdon, Pennsylvania. Another picture by Cole, *Lake with Fisherman*, is in the collection of the Bronck Museum, Greene County Historical Society, Coxsackie, New York.

40. [Robert Barnwell Roosevelt], *Game Fish of the Northern States of America, and British Provinces* (New York: Carleton, 1862), 187; Genio C. Scott, *Fishing in American Waters* (New York: Harper & Brothers, 1869), 187.

41. Paul Schullery, *American Fly Fishing: A History* (New York: Lyons & Burford Publishers, 1987), 45–46. Bethune had solicited an essay from Herbert on "Trout-Fishing on Long Island" for his celebrated edition of Walton's *Complete Angler*, published under Herbert's sportsman pseudonym Frank Forester. Walton, *The Complete Angler* (1847), 139–149; for Long Island as the utopia of New York sportsmen, 139.

42. Goodspeed, *Angling in America*, 190–204.

43. See Susan A. Popkin and Roger B. Allen, *Gone Fishing: A History of Fishing in River, Bay, and Sea*, exh. cat. (Philadelphia: Philadelphia Maritime Museum, 1987). Charles Hallock, *The Fishing Tourist: Angler's Guide and Reference Book* (New York: Harper & Brothers, 1873), devotes a chapter each to Long Island and to the Adirondacks, as well as many other regions of the United States and Canada.

44. [John J. Brown], *The American Angler's Guide* (New York: Burgess, Stringer & Co., 1845), 210, 214. Scott, *Fishing in American Waters*, 106, 119, concurs.

45. *Poems by William Cullen Bryant* (Cambridge, Mass.: Hilliard & Metcalf, 1821), reprinted as *Poems by William Cullen Bryant* (New York: D. Appleton & Co., 1847), 43–45.

46. In a sense, this anticipates the intriguing series of paintings of the end of the century depicting women standing and fishing in long, formal, often white gowns, totally inappropriate for the sport, by artists such as John Singer Sargent, Philip Hale, Thomas Dewing, and others—with the significant difference that, in these later paintings, male companions are absent. This pictorial phenomenon has yet to be addressed. It seems unlikely that Frankenstein's intention was to suggest that the principals in this scene were indulging in forbidden sexual behavior, analogous to the undisciplined nature of their context/setting—despite what contemporary art historical theorists may choose to see (Evil as well as Beauty being in the eye of the beholder). On the other hand, Elizabeth Boone, in discussion with the author (August 2, 2001), has suggested that this phenomenon might refer to the pursuit and apprehension of a male (i.e., "to hook"), made explicit in Winslow Homer's wood engraving for Will Wallace Harney's poem "Trout-Fishing," *Harper's New Monthly Magazine* 49 (August 1874): 350, depicting an amorous couple in a boat in which the woman holds the fishing pole. See also the rather humorous illustration of two women fishing who have "caught" a male in a stream, in Hallock, *The Fishing Tourist*, 79.

47. Almost all the literature on Godfrey Frankenstein, one of a family of Ohio painters, deals with his easel paintings and panorama of Niagara Falls. His

work on the Little Miami River is documented in Oscar T. Martin, "History of the City of Springfield," in *History of Clark County, Ohio* (Chicago: W. H. Beers & Co., 1881), 494–495; and in William Coyle, *The Frankenstein Family in Springfield* (Springfield, Ohio: Clark County Historical Society, 1967), 25–26. Another fishing painting by Frankenstein is *Lagonda Creek* (Wittenberg University, Springfield, Ohio).

48. William Henry Harrison Murray, *Adventures in the Wilderness; or, Camp-Life in the Adirondacks* (Boston: Fields, Osgood, & Co., 1869), 58–59. See also the depiction of a woman fishing in the illustration "Our Artist in the Adirondacks," in "The Adirondacks," *Appleton's Journal* 8 (September 21, 1872): 324. For a later guide to a woman's angling outfit, complete with description, see "Trout Fishing in California," *Overland Monthly* 18, 2d ser. (September 1891): 241–242.

49. Miner K. Kellogg, "Journal Cincinnati May 18th, 1833," *Cincinnati Historical Society* 16–17, mentioned in Joseph D. Ketner, *The Emergence of the African-American Artist: Robert S. Duncanson 1821–1872* (Columbia and London: University of Missouri Press, 1993), 39. For recent conservation efforts concerning the Little Miami River, see Ben L. Kaufman, "A Lively River Reborn," *Cincinnati Enquirer,* November 16, 1997.

50. Ketner, *The Emergence of the African-American Artist,* 38–39. For a discussion of this painting, see the essay by Lauretta Dimmick in *American Paradise: The World of the Hudson River School,* exh. cat. (New York: The Metropolitan Museum of Art, 1987), 194–196.

51. Wendy J. Katz, "Robert S. Duncanson: City and Hinterland," *Prospects* 25 (2000): 311.

52. For a discussion of this work, see the essay by the present author in Paul D. Schweizer, ed., *Masterworks of American Art from the Munson-Williams-Proctor Institute* (New York: Harry N. Abrams, 1989), 46–47.

53. See, for instance, "Fine Arts. Inman Gallery," *Anglo-American* 6 (February 14, 1846): 403; "The Inman Gallery," *Littell's Living Age* 9 (April 1846): 19. The painting was engraved to accompany Thomas Williams, "Trout Fishing," *New York Illustrated Magazine* 3 (January 1847): 36–41, though the trout fishing in this story takes place in Scotland.

54. *Catalogue of Works by the late Henry Inman* (New York: Van Norden & King, 1846), 18.

55. "Death of Henry Inman," *The Spirit of the Times* 16 (January 24, 1846): 561.

56. F. L. Waddel, "Trout Fishing, Sullivan County, N. Y.," *American Turf Register and Sporting Magazine* 6 (June 1835): 514–515; Street's poem "Angling" appeared in his collection *The Burning of Schenectady, and Other Poems* (Albany: Weare C. Little; New York: D. Appleton and Co.; Boston: Little and Brown; Philadelphia: Carey and Hart, 1842), 7–11.

57. Brown, *American Angler's Guide.*

58. Thomas Picton, "Old Time Disciples of Rod and Gun," *The Rod and Gun* 7 (February 12, 1876): 313.

59. "Fly and Bay Fishing," *American Turf Register* 9 (August 1838): 368, quoted in Schullery, *American Fly Fishing,* 44. For a thorough study of the fishing in Sullivan County, see Austin M. Francis, *Catskill Rivers: Birthplace of American Fly Fishing* (New York: Lyons & Burford, 1983), passim.

60. My gratitude to Ed Van Put of the Bureau of Fisheries for the New York State Conservation Department for his assistance and identification here. Letter from Van Put to the author, March 1999. See also by Van Put, *The Beaverkill: The History of a River and Its People* (New York: Lyons Press, 1996). Information on the Darbees by Alice D. Palen, "Historical Reminiscences," *Liberty Register,* April 6, 1923, article provided by Van Put.

61. Thaddeus Norris, *The American Angler's Book* (Philadelphia: E. H. Butler & Co., 1864), 489–494.

62. Thomas Bangs Thorpe, "A Visit to John Brown's Tract," *Harper's New Monthly Magazine* 15 (July 1857): 162.

63. Information from Richard Fosdick's diaries from Warder H. Cadbury. I think Warder Cadbury for this and much other assistance concerning the popularity of the Adirondacks for sportsmen.

64. "Henry Inman, Esq.," *The Spirit of the Times* 14 (April 6, 1844): 61. For this journal, see Norris W. Yates, *William T. Porter and the Spirit of the Times: A Study of the Big Bear School of Humor* (Baton Rouge: Louisiana State University Press, 1957). The *Spirit of the Times,* founded by Porter in New York in 1831, and the *American Turf Register,* which began in Baltimore in 1829, were the earliest American sporting journals. Porter also took over as editor of the *Register* in 1840. For Porter's friendship with Inman, and a beautiful eulogy on Inman's death, see Francis Brinley, *Life of William T. Porter* (New York: D. Appleton and Company, 1860), 205–209.

65. "Fishing in New-York," *The Spirit of the Times* 20 (June 22, 1850): 205.

66. N. Parker Willis, *The Hurry-Graphs; or, Sketches of Scenery, Celebrities and Society, Taken from Life* (New York: Charles Scribner, 1851), 80. Willis had already written about bass fishing on Cape Cod in this series of travel letters, 68. Willis documented his introduction to trout fishing in his first book, *Al' Abri, or the Tent Pitched* (New York: Samuel Colman, 1839), 39–43.

67. This scandal is described, with some relish, in the recent book by Thomas N. Baker, *Sentiment and Celebrity: Nathaniel Parker Willis and the Trials of Literary Fame* (New York and Oxford: Oxford University Press, 1999), 138–139.

68. Herbert may have been the most prolific writer on hunting and fishing in nineteenth-century America. His books dealing with angling include (under the pseudonym Frank Forester): *Frank Forester's Fish and Fishing of the United States and British Provinces of North America* (New York: Stringer & Townsend, 1850); *The Complete Manual for Young Sportsmen* (New York: Stringer & Townsend, 1856); *Fishing with Hook and Line* (New York: Brother Jonathan Office, 1858).

69. David W. Judd, *Life and Writings of Frank Forester (Henry William Herbert),* 2 vols. (New York: Orange Judd Company, 1882), vol. 1, 68–69. Herbert's first book (again written under the name Frank Forester) was *The Warwick Woodlands, or Things as they were there, ten years ago* (Philadelphia: G. B. Zieber & Co., 1845), although hunting, not fishing, is the subject of this volume.

70. Judd, *Life and Writings of Frank Forester,* 70.

71. "Sporting Expedition to Hamilton Co., N.Y.," *The Spirit of the Times* 10 (September 5, 1840): 319, courtesy of Warder Cadbury.

72. [Charles Fenno Hoffman; his authorship, as "C. F. Hoffman," was given only in the last of these articles], "Scenes at the Sources of the Hudson," *New-York Mirror,* 1837: October 7, 118–119; October 14, 124–125; October 21, 132; October 28, 140–141; December 16, 193–194; these were later published in *Wild Scenes in the Forest and Prairie,* 2 vols. (London: Richard Bentley, 1839–1840). Hoffman, who had founded the *Knickerbocker Magazine* and was an early writer on the American West, had taken over some of the editorial duties on the *Mirror* from George Pope Morris at this time.

73. J[oel] T[yler] Headley, *The Adirondack; or Life in the Woods* (New York: Baker and Scribner, 1849). Headley discussed trout fishing in chapters 1, 2, 14, 23, and 24, the last two at Raquette Lake. For Porter as the pioneer sporting figure in the Adirondacks, see Schullery, *American Fly Fishing,* 46. Murray's *Adventures in the Wilderness,* which includes the chapter "Rod and Reel," 126–140, is especially credited with the popularization of the Adirondacks, but the region had long drawn sportsmen for both fishing and hunting.

74. Goodspeed also mentioned Jerome V.C. Smith, *Natural History of the Fishes of Massachusetts* (Boston: Allen and Ticknor, 1833). While noting that "As a professed scientific treatise, the first part of this work calls for no attention here," he acknowledged that "The book was, however, in a way a landmark,

for Smith was the first American writer to make fishing the subject of even a short treatise." Goodspeed, *Angling in America*, 156.

75. Henry David Thoreau, *Walden; or, Life in the Woods* (Boston: Ticknor and Fields, 1854). See especially the sections "The Ponds," "Baker Farm," "Higher Laws," and "Brute Neighbors." One should also note Thoreau's poem "Salmon Brook" (possibly 1842) in which he asks: "When shall I look,/Or cast the hook/In your waves again?" Thoreau, *A Week on the Concord and Merrimack Rivers* (Boston: Ticknor and Fields, 1868), 372. For a discussion of Thoreau and fishing, see Gordon V. Boudveau, "Transcendental Sport: Hunting, Fishing, and Trapping in *Walden*," *Thought* 67 (March 1992): 74–87.

76. Goodspeed, *Angling in America*, 167.

77. Lanman was described in 1850 as "a young gentleman of artistic and literary tastes, who was a devoted disciple of the angler Isaak Walton." Benjamin Perley Poore, *Perley's Reminiscences of Sixty Years in the National Metropolis*, 2 vols. (Philadelphia: Hubard Brothers, 1886), vol. 1, 382.

78. See the entry by Gudmund Vigtel on this painting in *Sport in Art from American Museums*, 36. Hubard's image was engraved and published (in reverse) in Lanman's *Adventures of an Angler in Canada, Nova Scotia and the United States* (London: Richard Bentley, 1848).

79. Charles Lanman, *A Tour to the River Saguenay, in Lower Canada* (Philadelphia: Carey & Hart, 1848). The book was also published under the title *Adventures of an Angler in Canada, Nova Scotia and the United States*. Hallock, *The Fishing Tourist*, devotes a chapter to fishing the Saguenay River. Despite its remoteness, the Saguenay River was a recommended excursion in North America travel at midcentury. See [T. Addison Richards], *Appleton's Illustrated Hand-Book of American Travel* (New York: D. Appleton & Co., 1857), 29–31. Other of his books dealing, at least in print, with fishing include *Essays for Summer Hours* (Boston: Hilliard, Gray & Company, 1841); *Letters from a Landscape Painter* (Boston: James Munroe & Co., 1845); *A Summer in the Wilderness* (New York: D. Appleton & Co., 1847); *Haw-ho-noo; or, Records of a Tourist* (Philadelphia: Lippincott, Grambo & Co., 1850); *Recollections of Curious Characters and Pleasant Places* (Edinburgh: David Douglas, 1881). Lanman also frequently published articles on fishing, including "Our Finney Tribes," *American Whig Review*, November–December 1847; and "The Annals of Angling," *Galaxy* 6 (September 1868): 305–312. Lanman's collected travel works were published as *Adventures in the Wilds of the United States and British American Provinces*, 2 vols. (Philadelphia: John W. Moore, 1856). Volume 2 includes additional angling material in "A Tour of the River Restigouche," a Canadian excursion described on 9–92, and essays on fishing, including ones specifically on salmon, trout, bass, rock, and pike, 316–393. That on "The Striped Bass or Rock Fish" had appeared previously in *Southern Literary Messenger* 14 (November 1848): 682–687.

80. Lanman did not accede to Bethune's request, though, as we have seen, Henry William Herbert did provide "Trout Fishing on Long Island."

81. Charles Lanman, *Haphazard Personalities* (Boston: Lee and Shepard; New York: Charles T. Dillingham, 1886), 250–253.

82. Goodspeed, *Angling in America*, 169.

83. Preface to Lanman, *Recollections of Curious Characters and Pleasant Places*, repeated, in part, in M.L.D. Ferris, "Charles Lanman," *American Author* 1 (November 1902): 359.

84. See esp. "Our New-York Painters. By a Landscape Painter," *New World* 8 (February 10, 1844): 185–188, one of the most important documents on the New York art scene of the period. The work was reprinted in the *Southern Literary Messenger* 16 (May 1850). Lanman also wrote "On the Requisites for the Formation of a National School of Historical Painting," *Southern Literary Messenger* 14 (December 1848): 727–730, and when living in Washington, D.C., "Our National Paintings," *Crayon* 1 (February 28, 1855): 136–137. Lanman also prepared the "Catalogue of W. W. Corcoran's Gallery," 1857, Archives, Corcoran

Gallery of Art, Washington, D.C. Lanman's career as an artist has been studied by Lynn Harris Heft, "Charles Lanman: Cultural Networking in the Nineteenth Century," Ph.D. diss., Drew University, Madison, N.J., 1996. See also the article written by the artist's great-grandniece Dorothy McNeilly, "Charles Lanman," *American Fly Fisher* 11 (summer 1984): 14–19.

85. For a list of Lanman's paintings, see *Oil Sketches of American Scenery*, exh. cat. (Washington, D.C.: James Anglin & Co., 1883).

86. Lanman's *Trouting in New Hampshire* was sold at Sotheby Parke-Bernet, New York, June 1979.

87. Harry Frederick Orchard, *Charles Lanman Landscapes and Nature Studies*, exh. cat. (Madison, N.J.: Morris Museum of Arts and Sciences, 1984).

88. Charles Lanman, "An Aged Artist at Home," *Washington, D.C., Tribune*, December 23, 1883; article discussed in Heft, "Charles Lanman, Cultural Networking," 85–88. Lanman had written on Durand much earlier, comparing his art with that of Thomas Cole: Charles Lanman, "Cole and Durand," *New York Evening Post*, April 23, 1847, 2.

89. Durand's *Trouting in New Hampshire* (formerly, Jeffrey R. Brown), probably painted in 1857 around Woodstock and West Campton, New Hampshire, is quite similar to Lanman's *Salmon Fishing in Canada*, in general composition, the natural dynamics, and the envelopment of the tiny fisherman by giant rocks and a screen of evergreens, See David B. Lawall, *Asher B. Durand: A Documentary Catalogue of the Narrative and Landscape Paintings* (New York and London: Garland Publishing, 1978), 178, fig. 209.

90. The location of *The Sketcher* is unidentified, but Durand had spent the summer of 1869 in the Berkshires of Massachusetts and at Lake Placid, New York, and this work may well represent wilderness country in one of those regions.

91. The work, therefore, may also offer additional confirmation of Durand's well-established, longtime involvement in out-of-door sketching. For Durand in this context, see Eleanor Jones Harvey, *The Painted Sketch: American Impressions from Nature, 1830–1880*, exh. cat. (Dallas: Dallas Museum of Art, 1998), 33–36.

92. "Address by W. Whittredge," *Gifford Memorial Meeting of the Century* (New York: Century Association, 1880), 46.

93. James David Smillie diaries, 1865–1880, Archives of American Art, Smithsonian Institution, Washington, D.C. Smillie's 1868 watercolor of the Ausable River is in the Adirondack Museum, Blue Mountain Lake, New York.

94. G[eorge] H[enry] Smillie, "Morning on the Ausable," *Aldine* 4 (February 1872): 40.

95. For Bricher in the White Mountains, see "Fine Arts," *New York Evening Post*, October 6, 1868, 1.

96. This painting does not display the pointed mountain peak of Cole's earlier depictions of Mount Chocorua but rather the more rounded formation painted by Benjamin Champney and others, as seen from the north. This is true of Bricher's painting of *Mount Chocorua and Moat Mountain from Intervale* (private collection), which may be the painting *Mt. Chocorua* by Bricher that was exhibited at the Boston Athenæum in 1866 and again in 1868 and 1869.

97. Robert L. McGrath, *Gods in Granite: The Art of the White Mountains of New Hampshire* (Syracuse, N.Y.: Syracuse University Press, 2001), 147.

98. A[sher] B. Durand, "Correspondence," *Crayon* 2 (August 29, 1855): 133.

99. "Storm Coming On," engraved by John A. Rolph, in Henry William Herbert, ed., *The Magnolia for 1837* (New York: Bancroft & Holley, 1837), opp. 146, accompanying Herbert's poem "The Summer Storm." That Inman's *Landscape* is the same image as *Storm Coming* is clear from the reviews of the exhibition. See, for instance, "Editor's Table," *Knickerbocker* 8 (July 1836): 115.

100. Lee M. Edwards, "The Life and Career of Jerome Thompson," *American Art Journal* 14 (autumn 1982): 10.

101. Thompson exhibited another painting, *The Trout Brook*, at the National Academy of Design annual in 1871.

102. With the exception of two works by the obscure Portland, Maine, painter, John Greenleaf Cloudman, which were included in the exhibition *Young America: Children and Art* (Sandwich, Mass.: Heritage Plantation of Sandwich, 1985), 15, I have not found references to or images of fishing in the literature specifically devoted to children in American art. In an internet search for this subject, the most frequent references are to Hiram Powers's *Fisher Boy* sculpture of 1841–1844, a youthful nude "Apollino" whose distinctive identity is confined to the conch shell pressed to his ear, some shells in the sand at his feet, and the net-covered boat rudder behind him, which acts as the sculptural support. While fisher boys are numerous, fisher girls are not. An illustration of a *Fisher Girl* accompanied a poem of that title by the Philadelphia poet Charles West Thomson in the gift book *The Violet: A Christmas and New Year's Present, 1840* (Philadelphia: Carey and Hart, 1840), 122. Thomson had previously published the poem "The Fisher-Boy's Song," which appeared in another gift book, *The Gift: A Christmas and New Year's Present for 1837* (Philadelphia: E. L. Carey and A. Hart, 1837), 83–84, with an illustration of a *Fisher Boy;* both gift books were edited by Eliza Leslie. The Currier & Ives lithograph *"Hush! I've a Nibble"* features a little girl fishing by a stream, accompanied by two boys.

103. This work was painted, in part, to be engraved by George B. Ellis for *The Atlantic Souvenir for 1830:* in this case, the short essay "The Fisher Boy" appears to have been written to accompany the illustration, rather than vice versa. It is possible that Inman was inspired to essay this subject by the appearance at the first annual exhibition held at the Boston Athenæum in 1827 of *Young Angler*, a painting by the celebrated British artist Thomas Miles Richardson. This was one of two works by that artist owned by Boston's preeminent collector, Thomas Handasyd Perkins.

104. The author has discussed this work previously in William H. Gerdts, "Henry Inman: Genre Painter," *American Art Journal* 9 (May 1977): 35–38.

105. Shepard Alonzo Mount's (1804–1868) *Boy Fishing* was shown at the National Academy annual in 1835 and Stuart Watson's (fl. 1834–1858) *Boys Fishing* was shown at the same venue in 1839. Charles Loring Elliott (1812–1868), who would become Inman's successor as New York's most acclaimed portrait painter, had painted a copy of Inman's *The Young Fisherman* from the George Ellis engraving, probably soon after it was published in 1830. Charles Edward Lester, "Charles Loring Elliott," *Harper's New Monthly Magazine* 38 (December 1868): 45. Thomas Augustus Cummings (1823–1859), the son of Inman's friend and one-time partner, the miniaturist Thomas Seir Cummings, exhibited a *Young Angler* at the American Art-Union in 1847. The year before, Thomas Le Clear's (1818–1882) *Boys Fishing* appeared with the Art-Union, as did Edwin White's (1817–1877) *Fisher Boy*, while William Tylee Ranney (1813–1857) had a *Fisher Boy* shown there in 1848. In 1850 William Sanford Mason (1824–1864) showed a *Fisher Boy* at the annual exhibition of the Pennsylvania Academy of the Fine Arts; Christian Schussele (1824–1879) exhibited a *Fisher Boy* at the same venue in 1853; and William Winner (ca. 1815–1883) a *Fisher Boy* there in 1857. In addition, Luther Terry (1813–1869), who had expatriated to Italy in 1837, showed an *Italian Fisher Boy* at the National Academy annual in 1845. For a study of several later-nineteenth-century images by the Bangor, Maine, artist Jeremiah Pearson Hardy, *The Smelt Seller* (Farnsworth Art Museum, Rockland, Maine) and *The Fisher Boy* (Bangor Public Library, Maine), painted in the 1870s, see Molly Mulhern Gross, "Jeremiah P. Hardy's *The Smelt Seller* Genre Painting in Bangor," *Maine Historical Society Quarterly* 36 (summer–fall 1996): 18–37.

106. "National Academy of Design," *Knickerbocker* 23 (June 1844): 596. My appreciation to Dr. Margaret Conrads, Curator at the Nelson-Atkins Museum of Art, for her assistance in regard to this painting.

107. References are too extensive to list here, but see esp. the discussion of the painting by Karen M. Adams, "The Black Image in the Paintings of William Sidney Mount," *American Art Journal* 7 (November 1975): 55–58.

108. Theodore A. Green, "The Hart-Sells Connection," in *William Sidney Mount: Family, Friends, and Ideas* (Setauket, N.Y.: Three Village Historical Society, 1999), 63–64, which contains an extended discussion of eel spearing in the region. It may be no more than coincidence that the fishing here, not by line but by spear—here wielded by the "Other" (African-American; woman)—finds its only significant counterpart in this period in the paintings by Seth Eastman and George Catlin of fish spearing by another "Other" (Native American).

109. William Sidney Mount to Charles Lanman, November 17, 1847, New-York Historical Society.

110. Alfred Frankenstein, *William Sidney Mount* (New York: Harry N. Abrams, 1975), 106–126; letter concerning Long Island fish, written September 15, 1847, on 120.

111. [Charles Lanman], "Our New-York Painters. By a Landscape Painter," *New World* 8 (February 10, 1844): 186–187, republished by Lanman a year later in his book *Letters from a Landscape Painter*, 243–246; Lanman, *Haphazard Personalities; Chiefly of Noted Americans* (Boston: Lee and Shepard; New York: Charles T. Dillingham, 1866), 168–180. Mount was one of only three artists discussed in this book (Emanuel Leutze and John Trumbull were the other two).

112. Clonney is the subject of the fine study by Lucretia H. Giese, "James Goodwyn Clonney (1812–1867): American Genre Painter," *American Art Journal* 11 (October 1979): 4–31.

113. Early in his career, Clonney probably had contact with Thomas Doughty, for he created lithographs for the first two volumes of the Doughtys' *Cabinet of Natural History and American Rural Sports*.

114. David Park Curry, *American Dreams: Paintings and Decorative Arts from the Warner Collection*, exh. cat. (Richmond: Virginia Museum of Fine Arts, 1997), 33.

115. "Clonney—Is not less devoted to his art than formerly, and has produced several of his *happiest* subjects during the past year, much better chosen, and decidedly in better taste, and more appropriately within the scope of his pencil, than that exhibited by him last season." "Art and Artists," *New Mirror* 1 (April 29, 1843): 65. Elizabeth Johns, *American Genre Painting: The Politics of Everyday Life* (New Haven and London: Yale University Press, 1991), 108–114, deals with Clonney's denigration of the African-American in both his fishing and nonfishing paintings, though her implication that each picture was linked to specific slavery issues does not appear to find contemporary justification.

116. It has been suggested that this work may have provided inspiration for Herman Melville's 1854 story "The Happy Failure: A Story of the River Hudson." See John M.J. Gretchko, "An Incisive Analogue to 'The Happy Failure,'" *Melville Society Extracts* 86 (September 1991): 9.

117. Heade's *Sleepy Fisherman* was acquired for distribution by the American Art-Union in 1847, the only acquisition of that artist's work that the Art-Union ever made; Ranney's *The Lazy Fisherman* was with the American Art-Union in 1850, described as "'an elderly gentleman' dosing [sic] beside a 'murmuring stream', with a book in his hand, and a rod lying on the ground." *American Art-Union Bulletin* 3 (December 31, 1850): 174. I have not been able to identify the figure in Heade's *Sleepy Fisherman*; the *Literary World*, October 30, 1847, 303, merely commented that it was a "well-drawn figure, lost by the little attention given to the light and shade." Heade subsequently introduced fishermen (and hunters) occasionally in his New England marsh scenes, such as one of the finest of these, *Sunrise on the Marshes* (1863; Flint Institute of Arts, Flint, Michigan), where the appearance of a small, languid fisherman only adds to the evocative silence characteristic of the artist's luminist landscapes. Heade's marsh subjects have received abundant scholarly attention, but almost none of this has been directed toward the human activity therein.

118. Michael Edward Shapiro, "The River Paintings," in *George Caleb Bingham*, exh. cat. (Saint Louis: Saint Louis Art Museum, 1990), 159.

119. There were complaints about ". . . the so-called sport of fishing through the ice, each hole equipped with a stick or small furze bush as an indicator so that one man on skates could tend to as many as one hundred holes." This practice was condemned more as a concern for an enormous catch than for the sport of angling. John Allen Krout, *Annals of American Sport* (New Haven: Yale University Press, 1929), 96.

120. Warder H. Cadbury, *Arthur Fitzwilliam Tait: Artist in the Adirondacks* (Newark: University of Delaware Press; London and Toronto: Associated University Presses, 1986), 36, 45. This is the definitive study of Tait, with a checklist by Henry F. Marsh. I wish to acknowledge Cadbury for all his assistance in this and other projects in which I have been involved over many years.

121. Cadbury, *Arthur Fitzwilliam Tait*, 67.

122. Headley, *The Adirondack*, 205.

123. Cadbury, *Arthur Fitzwilliam Tait*, 67, 76.

124. In addition to Cadbury, *Arthur Fitzwilliam Tait*, passim, see "A. F. Tait in Painting and Lithograph," *Antiques* 24 (July 1933): 24–25.

125. Almost half the Currier & Ives fishing prints are specifically devoted to trout. See Fred J. Peters, *Sporting Prints by N. Currier and Currier & Ives* (New York: Antique Bulletin Publishing Co., 1930), 15–42; Walton Rawls, *The Great Book of Currier & Ives' America* (New York: Abbeville Press, 1979), 325–363; and H[olman] J. Swinney, "Fishing," with illustrations, in John Lowell Pratt, ed., *Currier & Ives Chronicles of America* (New York: Promontory Press, 1968), 216–223. See also Georgia B. Barnhill, *The Adirondack on Paper: Wild Impressions*, exh. cat. (Blue Mountain Lake, N.Y.: Adirondack Museum; Boston: David R. Godine, 1995), esp. the section "Promotion: Prints in the Service of Tourism," 15–39.

126. Murray, *Adventures in the Wilderness*, see esp. the chapter "Rod and Reel," 126–140; S[eneca] R[ay] Stoddard, *The Adirondacks: Illustrated* (Albany: Weed, Parsons & Co., 1874).

127. A collection of twenty woodcuts from *Gleason's Pictorial* were gathered and published as a separate portfolio in *The Sportsman's Portfolio of American Field Sports* (Boston: M. M. Ballou, 1855).

128. Henry Smith Mount's art has received little attention; see the section on him in *A Loan Exhibition of Paintings, Sketches, Manuscripts, Memorabilia, Henry Smith Mount, A.N.A., 1802–1841, Shepard Alonzo Mount, N.A., 1804–1868, William Sidney Mount, N.A., 1807–1868*, exh. cat. (New York: Suffolk Museum at Stony Brook, 1947), 17–19. Fish still lifes seldom gained any critical attention, for still lifes had continually been deemed the least worthy theme of artistic accomplishment. See [Samuel F.B. Morse], "Review. The Exhibition of the National Academy of Design, 1827," *United States Magazine and Literary Gazette* 2 (July 1827): 244.

129. Shepard exhibited a *Shell Fish* painting even later, in 1867. He also showed a *Boy Fishing* (unlocated) at the National Academy in 1835, one of the earliest paintings of this subject following Inman's *The Young Fisherman* of 1829–1830; another painting, *Boy with a Line of Fish*, of 1841, is in a private collection.

130. Shepard Alonzo Mount to William Sidney Mount, September 19, 1847, in a series of fifty-six articles by Edward P. Buffet, "William Sidney Mount: A Biography," *Port Jefferson Times*, December 1, 1923–June 12, 1924, chap. 27. Photocopies from the Archives of the Museums of Long Island, Stony Brook, New York.

131. "National Academy of Design. Twenty-third Annual Exhibition. Eighth Visit," *New York Evening Post*, June 21, 1848, 2.

132. See esp. Lanman's letter of April 25, 1850, to William Sidney Mount, quoted in Alfred Frankenstein, *William Sidney Mount* (New York: Harry N. Abrams, 1975), 124. Shepard's fishing still lifes are admirably and fully discussed by Deborah J. Johnson in *Shepard Alonzo Mount: His Life and Art*, exh. cat. (Stony Brook, N.Y.: Museums at Stony Brook, 1988), 18–23.

133. Quinn, *Angling in Art*, 76–78.

134. In 1865 several of Walter Brackett's paintings of a string of fish were advertised as "Elegant Dining Room Pictures." See "Fine Arts," *New York Evening Post*, March 20, 1865, 2, courtesy of Merl M. Moore Jr.

135. I want to thank Warder Cadbury for his suggestion here, based in part on his examination of homes where work by Arthur Tait were originally hung. I had considered the study in private homes as the most likely male preserve for the display of sporting still lifes, but Cadbury suggests that the study may be a later development within domestic architecture. The library was also a male domain but probably not as "restricted" as the game room, usually complete with billiard table, and where the gentlemen also went to smoke.

136. Pieter A. Scheen, *Lexicon Nederlandse Beeldende Kunstnaars, 1850–1950*, 2 vols. ('s-Gravenhage, 1969–1970), vol. 2, 627.

137. "In the Picture Galleries," *Forest and Stream* 2 (March 26, 1874): 105; H[enry] W. French, *Art and Artists in Connecticut* (Boston: Lee and Shepard; New York: Charles T. Dillingham, 1879), 150.

138. Goodspeed, *Angling in America*, 214–215. For the club, see Reuben G. Allerton, *Brook Trout Fishing. An Account of a trip of the Oquossoc Angling Association to northern Maine, in June, 1869* (New York: R. G. Allerton, 1869); Oquossoc is the Indian name for the lake now called Rangeley. See the appropriately titled article on Steele by C. Stuart Johnson, "With Brush and Rod," *Munsey's Magazine* 12 (March 1895): 577–580.

139. "Necrology," *American Art Review* 2, pt. 2 (1881): 90.

140. S[amuel] A. Kilbourne, text by G. Brown Goode, *Game Fishes of the United States* (New York: Charles Scribner's Sons, 1879; reprint, New York: Winchester Press, 1972).

141. Ralph Greenwood, "A Sportsman and Artist," *Shooting and Fishing* 15 (December 21, 1893): 169–171; I thank Patricia Junker for locating and sharing this important article. See also "Walter M. Brackett, the Fish Painter," *Wisdom* 2 (September 1902): 319.

142. The earliest mention of this series that I have located is "Fine Arts—Music—Drama," *New York Tribune*, March 4, 1872, 5.

143. "At the Crystal Palace," *Art-Journal* (London) 73 (1873): 223.

144. Greenwood, "A Sportsman and Artist," 169; "Walter M. Brackett, the Fish Painter."

145. "The Fine Arts. Mr. Walter M. Brackett's Reception," *Boston Daily Advertiser*, May 28, 1875, 4.

146. It should not escape notice, however, that Brackett's four-part series offers a naturalistic, late-nineteenth-century analogy with the romantic concepts imbedded in Thomas Cole's 1840 *Voyage of Life* (Munson-Williams-Proctor Arts Institute, Museum of Art, Utica, New York). Brackett's series is also, of course, a Darwinian "voyage of (piscatorial) life"—Darwinian because the protagonist is subject, not to God as in Cole's series, but to a higher order of life (and death)—man.

147. "Fish and Dog Pictures," *Forest and Stream* 20 (May 3, 1883): 262.

148. "Walter M. Brackett, the Fish Painter."

149. Probably referencing a picture similar to this, a San Francisco critic wrote: "S. M. Brookes has at his studio a very powerful and truthful painting of our large river salmon, life-size—the models for which weighed respectively 18 and 35 pounds. They are suspended by the gills, partly lying on a bit of matting and

are painted with wonderful vigor and truth. . . . As an illustration of the way it works, we mention that in executing the picture just noticed he used up 160 pounds of salmon, having to buy his models several times over. No market in the world offers facilities equal to ours for this branch of still life." "Local Pictures," *San Francisco Bulletin*, March 5, 1872, 3. Given the popularity and fame of Brookes's paintings of the catch, it is puzzling that no painters in the first decades of San Francisco's growing, thriving art culture appear to have painted fishing landscapes. Thomas Hill, who became one of California's most celebrated landscape painters, later painted fishing scenes in the mountains and lakes of the state, but those he painted before 1875 were set in New England.

150. For Brookes, see the detailed and perceptive study of his art and career in Janice T. Driesbach, *Bountiful Harvest. 19th-Century California Still Life Painting*, exh. cat. (Sacramento: Crocker Art Museum, 1991), 12–37.

151. For a consideration of Stearns's procedure in painting this picture, see Lance Mayer and Gay Myers, "Bierstadt and Other 19th-Century American Painters in Context," *Journal of the American Institute for Conservation* 38, no. 1 (1999): 55–67.

152. Mark Edward Thistlethwaite, "Picturing the Past—Junius Brutus Stearns's Paintings of George Washington," *Arts in Virginia* 25, nos. 2–3 (1985): 12–23.

153. Millard F. Rogers Jr., "Fishing Subjects by Junius Brutus Stearns," *Antiques* 98 (August 1970): 246–250. For Stearns, see also Richard C. Randt, "The Discovery of the Portrait of Grahams Polley," *Polley Pointers* 3 (June 1996): 22–24; and Randt, "Junius Brutus Stearns (1810–1885) American Artist. A Biographical Sketch and Genealogy," 1993, incomplete. I want to thank Mr. Randt for making his splendid work on Stearns available to me.

154. Scott, *Fishing in American Waters*, frontispiece. Brackett's two illustrations are on 147 and 290.

155. This may be the painting *Striped Bass with Creel*, dated 1848, private collection.

156. "I give my best fishing rod to Junius B. Stearns, Junior, and all my other fishing tackle to my sons Michael Angelo and Raphael C., in consideration of their services as executors of this will to be divided between them; the large Star Reel to one, the other two reels to the other as they may agree. . . ." Last Will and Testament of Junius B. Stearns, Sr., dated June 12, 1882; probated October 13, 1885; King's County Surrogate's Court, Brooklyn, New York, in Randt, "Junius Brutus Stearns," 6.

157. A painting of a *Youthful Fisherman* by Stearns was sold at Sotheby Parke-Bernet in 1947. *Children Fishing*, of 1850, was sold at Sotheby Parke-Bernet, New York, in 1970. *Two Children Fishing*, of 1878, was sold by Phillips Auctioneers, New York, June 12, 1997. A comic version of this theme, *The Old Story*, by Sol Eytinge Jr., had already appeared as *Trout Fishing—Nature Versus Art*, in *Harper's Weekly*, May 19, 1877, 393. *The Old Story* is in the collection of The Art Museum, Princeton University.

158. *Trout Fishing* was sold with The Congoleum Corporate Collection, Christie's, New York, January 27, 1987, lot 29. *A Fishing Party off Long Island* is in the collection of the Minneapolis Institute of Arts. *A Fishing Party in a Catboat on Great South Bay, Long Island New York* is in the collection of the New-York Historical Society.

159. "Domestic Art Gossip," *Crayon* 5 (March 1857): 88; "Sketchings," 5 (June 1858): 176.

160. Henry T. Tuckerman, *Book of the Artists. American Artist Life* (New York: G. P. Putnam & Son, 1867), 632. Stearns's painting was included in the McGuire estate auction, though in the catalogue the portraits were said to have been painted by Elliott. See *Catalogue of the Collection of Paintings, Statuary, Bronzes, &c., Belonging to the Estate of the Late James C. McGuire* (Washington, D.C.: Thomas Dowling, 1890?), 13, no. 45.

161. [Lewis Gaylord Clark], "Editor's Table," *Knickerbocker* 50 (October 1857): 414–417. Clark maddeningly identifies his companions, and not all of them at

that, by their last initial, but among them is "tall E. . . . , all fisherman . . . ," 416. This was an excursion to "John Brown's Tract" in the Adirondack wilderness along the Black River and Lyons Falls, but these falls involve a precipitous drop that is not the topography here.

162. See esp. "Fine Arts. The National Academy of Design. Third and Concluding Notice," *Albion* 36 (May 8, 1858): 225.

163. "Editor's Table. Late Words Touching the National Academy Exhibition," *Knickerbocker* 52 (July 1858): 81–82.

164. *The Knickerbocker Gallery* (New York: Samuel Hueston, 1855), frontispiece and 163.

165. L[ewis] Gaylord Clark, *Knick-Knacks from an Editor's Table* (New York: D. Appleton and Company, 1852), 137.

166. Clark to H. S. Randall, April 8, 1852, in Leslie W. Dunlap, ed., *The Letters of Willis Gaylord Clark and Lewis Gaylord Clark* (New York: New York Public Library, 1940), 155. This was probably Henry Stephens Randall, an authority and writer on sheep husbandry.

167. "Studios of American Artists," *Home Journal*, February 9, 1856, 1. My thanks to Merl M. Moore Jr. for this information.

168. Letter fragment, ca. 1882, owned by Mrs. Frederic W. Loeser, great-granddaughter of Stearns. Randt, "Junius Brutus Stearns," 3.

169. *Catalogue of the Collection of Paintings Belonging to the Late Charles L. Elliott* (New York: George A. Leavitt & Co., Auctioneers, December 7–8, 1876), no. 19.

170. "The Late J. B. Stearns," *Brooklyn Union*, September 16, 1885.

171. "In a Collision," *Brooklyn Daily Eagle*, September 18, 1885, 6.

172. "Doesn't Want the Title," *Brooklyn Daily Eagle*, July 5, 1895, 2. The Oceanus Boat Club was also a political association; in addition to Mayor Kalbfleisch, it numbered among its membership Hugh McLaughlin, the Brooklyn Democratic party boss for over four decades. My thanks to Lai Jin Wong of the Brooklyn Public Library, and Cynthia Sanford, Curator at the Brooklyn Historical Society, for unearthing information on this organization.

173. "At Snedicor's, in Broadway. . . . Stearns shows his study for the "'Fishing Party,' painted for Mr. Hone." "Art Gossip," *Cosmopolitan Art Journal* 4 (December 1860): 183. My thanks to Merl M. Moore Jr. for this source. Philip Hone, former mayor of New York and a major art patron of the early nineteenth century, had died in 1851, and his collection was auctioned the following year. It is possible that this was a typographical error and meant to refer to Robert Hoe, a major New York collector of the period, although Hoe's preferences ran to landscapes and to slightly more sophisticated art.

174. "In a Collision," "Death of J. B. Stearns," *New-York Times*, September 19, 1885, 1.

175. Charles Dudley Warner, "The Adirondacks Verified. III. A Fight with a Trout," *Atlantic Monthly* 41 (March 1878): 343. This was reprinted in Warner's *In the Wilderness* (Boston: Houghton, Mifflin and Company, 1878), 41–53.

176. "Mr. Homer's Water Colors. An Artist in the Adirondacks," *New York Tribune*, February 26, 1890, 6. I want to thank Abigail Booth Gerdts for bringing this trenchant article to my attention.

Works in the Exhibition

All works are by Winslow Homer

1. *Rising to the Fly,* 1861
Watercolor on paper, 6 ⅜ × 9 ¾ in.
Lower left: *Homer 61*
Museum of Art, Rhode Island School of Design,
    Providence. Given anonymously (48.156)
Ill. p. 39

2. *Crossing the Pasture,* 1871–1872
Oil on canvas, 26 ¼ × 38 ⅛ in.
Amon Carter Museum, Fort Worth, Texas (1976.37)
Ill. p. 20, detail p. 12

3. *The Angler,* [1874]
Oil on canvas, 23 ½ × 16 in.
Lower left: *Homer*
Private collection
Ill. p.43

4. *Waiting for a Bite,* 1874
Oil on canvas, 12 × 20 in.
Lower left: *WINSLOW HOMER 1874*
The Cummer Museum of Art and Gardens, Jacksonville,
    Florida. Bequest of Ninah M.H. Cummer (C.119.1)
Ill. p. 35

5. *Fishing,* 1879
Oil on canvas. 7 ½ × 9 ¼ in.
Lower left: *HOMER/1879*
Museum of Art, Rhode Island School of Design,
    Providence. Bequest of Isaac C. Bates (13.935)
Ill. p. 15

6. *Camp Fire,* [1877]/1880
Oil on canvas, 23 ¾ × 38 ⅛ in.
Lower right: *HOMER/'80*
The Metropolitan Museum of Art, New York. Gift of
    Henry Keney Pomeroy (27.181)
Ill. p. 25

7. *Thornhill Bar,* 1886
Watercolor over graphite on paper, 14 × 20 in.
Lower left: *W.H. 1886*
Museum of Fine Arts, Boston. Gift of Mrs. Robert B.
    Osgood, 1939 (39.620)
Ill. p. 167

8. *Casting, "A Rise,"* 1889
Watercolor on paper, 9 × 20 in.
Lower left: *Homer 89*
The Adirondack Museum, Blue Mountain Lake, New
    York (67.058.01)
Ill. p. 78

9. *Casting in the Falls,* 1889
Watercolor over graphite on paper, 14 × 20 in.
Upper left: *Winslow Homer/1889*
Dallas Museum of Art, Texas. Dallas Art Association
    Purchase, 1961 (1961.11)
Ill. p. 36

10. *Fishing in the Adirondacks,* 1889
Watercolor over graphite on paper, 14 × 20 in.
Lower left: *Winslow Homer/1889*
Private collection
Ill. p. 101

11. *A Good One,* 1889
Watercolor over graphite on paper, 12 ¼ × 19 ½ in.
Lower left: *Winslow Homer;* lower right: *Winslow Homer 1889*
The Hyde Collection Trust, Glens Falls, New York
    (1971.68)
[Exhibited in Fort Worth only]
Ill. p. 56, detail p. 32

12. *Jumping Trout,* 1889
Watercolor over graphite on paper, 13 ¹⁵⁄₁₆ × 19 ¹⁵⁄₁₆ in.
Upper left: *HOMER/89*
Brooklyn Museum of Art, New York, in memory of Dick
    S. Ramsay (41.220)
Ill. p. 118

13. *Leaping Trout,* 1889
Watercolor over graphite on paper, 14 ¹⁄₁₆ × 20 ¹⁄₁₆ in.
Lower right: *Winslow Homer 1889*
Portland Museum of Art, Portland, Maine. Bequest of
    Charles Shipman Payson (1988.55.7)
Ill. p. 81

14. *A Quiet Pool on a Sunny Day,* 1889
Watercolor over graphite on paper, 13 × 20 in.
Lower right: *Winslow Homer 1889*
Karen and Kevin W. Kennedy Collection, courtesy
    James Graham & Sons Gallery, New York
Ill. p. 100

15. *Sunrise, Fishing in the Adirondacks,* 1889
Watercolor over graphite on paper, 14 × 21 in.
Lower right: *HOMER*
Fine Arts Museums of San Francisco, Achenbach
    Foundation for Graphic Arts. Mildred Anna Williams
    Collection (1966.2)
Ill. p. 120, detail p. 94

16. *Trout Breaking [Rise to a Fly],* 1889
Watercolor over graphite on paper, 13 ⅞ × 19 ⅞ in.
Lower left: *HOMER 89/HOMER 1889;* reverse:
    Homer/1889
Museum of Fine Arts, Boston. Bequest of John T.
    Spaulding (48.729)
Ill. p. 119

17. *Two Trout*, 1889
Watercolor over graphite on paper, 19 ½ × 13 ¼ in.
Lower right: *Winslow Homer/1889*
Private collection
Ill. p. 64

18. *An Unexpected Catch [A Disappointing Catch]*,
1889–1890
Watercolor over graphite on paper, 10 × 20 in.
Lower left: *HOMER 90*
Portland Museum of Art, Portland, Maine. Bequest of
Charles Shipman Payson (1988.55.9)
Ill. p. 112

19. *Fly Fishing, Saranac Lake*, 1889/1890
Etching and aquatint on paper, plate 17 ½ × 22 ⅝ in.;
sheet 19 ⅞ × 27 ⅛ in.
Lower left, in plate: *Winslow Homer S^c 1889 copyright*;
lower left in margin: *Winslow Homer*; lower right, in
margin: *#42*
Amon Carter Museum, Fort Worth, Texas. Purchase with
funds provided by the Council of the Amon Carter
Museum (2002.3)
Ill. p. 45

20. *Netting the Fish*, 1889–1890
Watercolor over graphite on paper, 14 × 20 in.
Lower right: *Winslow Homer 1890/Copyright—1889*
The Art Institute of Chicago. Gift of Annie Swan
Coburn to the Mr. and Mrs. Lewis L. Coburn
Memorial Collection (1933.526)
Ill. p. 44

21. *St. John's River, Florida*, 1890
Watercolor over graphite on paper, 13 ½ × 19 ⅞ in.
Lower right: *HOMER 1890*
The Hyde Collection Trust, Glens Falls, New York
(1971.70)
[Exhibited in San Francisco only]
Ill. p. 170, frontispiece detail

22. *Two Trout*, 1891
Watercolor over graphite on paper, 18 ⅞ × 13 ⅜ in.
Lower right: *To J. Ernest Yalden/with compts of Winslow
Homer/1891*
Private collection
Ill. p. 62

23. *A Brook Trout*, 1892
Watercolor over graphite on paper, 13 ¾ × 19 ¾ in.
Lower right: *HOMER 1892*; upper right: *HOMER/1892*
Private collection
Ill. p. 91

24. *Boy Fishing*, 1892
Watercolor over graphite on paper, 15 ⅛ × 21 ½ in.
Lower left: *Winslow Homer 1892*; lower right: *Homer 1892*
San Antonio Museum of Art, Texas. Purchased with
funds provided by the Robert J. and Helen Kleberg
Foundation and Friends of the San Antonio Museum
of Art (86.130)
Ill. p. 115, cover

25. *Canoeing in the Adirondacks*, 1892
Watercolor over graphite on paper, 15 ½ × 20 in.
Lower left: *HOMER 1892*
James and Frances McGlothlin
[Exhibited in Fort Worth only]
Ill. p. 105

26. *Casting the Fly [Casting, Number Two]*, 1894
Watercolor over graphite on paper, 15 × 21 ⅜ in.
Center right, on boat stern: *HOMER 1894*
National Gallery of Art, Washington, D.C. Gift of Ruth
K. Henschel in memory of her husband, Charles R.
Henschel (1975.92.2)
Ill. p. 73

27. *Playing Him [The North Woods]*, 1894
Watercolor over graphite on paper, 15 ⅛ × 21 ½ in.
Reverse: *This is not so bad/W-H-*; reverse: *Homer/1894*
The Currier Gallery of Art, Manchester, New
Hampshire. Gift of Mr. and Mrs. Frederic Haines
Curtiss (1960.13)
[Exhibited in San Francisco only]
Ill. p. 89

28. *The Rapids, Hudson River, Adirondacks*, 1894
Watercolor over graphite on paper, 15 ⅛ × 21 ½ in.
Lower left: *Hudson River/June 1894 W.H.*
The Art Institute of Chicago. Mr. and Mrs. Martin
Ryerson Collection (1933.1250)
Ill. p. 107

29. *Canoe on a Canadian Lake*, 1895
Watercolor over graphite on paper, 11 ¾ × 20 in.
Lower left: *Winslow Homer/P.Q. Canada 1895/W.H.*
Private collection
Ill. p. 144

30. *A Good Pool, Saguenay River*, 1895
Watercolor over graphite on paper, 9 ¾ × 18 ⅞ in.
Lower left: *HOMER/1895*; lower right: *Ouananiche*
Sterling and Francine Clark Art Institute, Williamstown,
Massachusetts (1955.1492)
[Exhibited in San Francisco only]
Ill. p. 48

31. *The Guide*, 1895
Watercolor over graphite on paper, 13 ½ × 19 ⅝ in.
Lower right: *Winslow Homer/1895*
The James W. Glanville Family Partnership
Ill. p. 60

32. *The Guide*, 1895
Watercolor over graphite on paper, 16 ¼ × 14 in.
Lower left: *W.H. 1895*
Private collection
Ill. p. 61

33. *Log Cabin, Tourilli Club*, 1895
Watercolor over graphite on paper, 14 × 20 in.
Lower left: *W.H. 1895*
Private collection
Ill. p. 131

34. *Montagnais Indians [Indians Making Canoes]*, 1895
Watercolor over graphite on paper, 14 × 20 in.
Lower left: *HOMER/Roberval 1895/P.Q.*
Henry E. Huntington Library and Art Gallery, San
Marino, California. Gift of the Virginia Steele Scott
Foundation (83.8.24)
Ill. p. 127

35. *Trout Fishing, Lake St. John, Quebec*, 1895
Watercolor over graphite on paper, 11 × 20 in.
Lower left: *HOMER 1895*
Museum of Fine Arts, Boston. Warren Collection.
William Wilkins Warren Fund (99.29)
Ill. p. 145

36. *Two Men in a Canoe*, 1895
Watercolor over graphite on paper, 13 ⅛ × 19 ⅜ in.
Lower right: *Winslow Homer. P.Q. Canada/Sept. 1895*
Portland Museum of Art, Portland, Maine. Bequest of
Charles Shipman Payson (1988.55.12)
Ill. p. 143

37. *Under the Falls, the Grand Discharge, Lake St. John,
P.Q.*, 1895
Watercolor over graphite on paper, 13 ⅞ × 19 ¹⁵⁄₁₆ in.
Lower right: *Homer 1895/Ouananiche Fishing*
Brooklyn Museum of Art, New York. Bequest of Helen
B. Sanders (78.151.2)
Ill. p. 146

38. *Canoe in the Rapids,* 1897
Watercolor over graphite on paper, 13 ⅝ × 20 ½ in.
Lower left: *HOMER/1897*
Harvard University Art Museums (Fogg Art Museum),
Cambridge, Massachusetts. Purchase, Louise E. Betten
Fund (1924.30)
Ill. p. 150

39. *End of the Portage,* 1897
Watercolor over graphite on paper, 14 × 21 in.
Lower left: *HOMER '97*
Brooklyn Museum of Art, New York. Bequest of Helen
B. Sanders (78.151.1)
Ill. p. 137

40. *Entering the First Rapid, Grand Discharge,* 1897
Watercolor over graphite on paper, 13 ½ × 20 ½ in.
Lower left: *HOMER 1897. Grand Discharge P.Q.*
Private collection
Ill. p. 28

41. *Guide Hiding a Canoe,* [1897]
Watercolor over graphite on paper, 14 × 21 in.
Private collection
Ill. p. 138

42. *Ouananiche, Lake St. John,* 1897
Watercolor over graphite on paper, 13 ½ × 20 ½ in.
Lower left: *W.H. '97*
Private collection
Ill. p. 149

43. *The Portage [The Return up the River],* 1897
Watercolor over graphite on paper, 13 ¾ × 20 ½ in.
Lower right: HOMER/*1897*
Yale University Art Gallery, New Haven, Connecticut.
Bequest of Doris M. Brixey (1984.32.17)
Ill. p. 139

44. *Bass,* [1900]
Watercolor over graphite on paper, 13 ¾ × 21 in.
Arizona State University Art Museum, Nelson Fine Arts
Center, Tempe, Arizona. Gift of Oliver B. James
(53.138)
Ill. p. 63

45. *Fish and Butterflies,* 1900
Watercolor over graphite on paper, 14 ½ × 20 ¹¹⁄₁₆ in.
Lower left: *HOMER. 1900.*
Sterling and Francine Clark Art Institute, Williamstown,
Massachusetts (1955.775)
[Exhibited in San Francisco only]
Ill. p. 55

46. *The Rise,* 1900
Watercolor over graphite on paper, 13 ¾ × 20 ¾ in.
Lower right: *HOMER 1900*
National Gallery of Art, Washington, D.C. Gift of Ruth
K. Henschel in memory of her husband, Charles R.
Henschel (1975.92.14)
Ill. p. 79

47. *Canoes in Rapids, Saguenay River [Against the Shoal],*
1902
Watercolor over graphite on paper, 13 ¼ × 21 ¾ in.
Upper right: *HOMER/1902*
Private collection
Ill. p. 59

48. *Fishing the Rapids, Saguenay River,* 1902
Watercolor over graphite on paper, 13 ½ × 20 in.
Lower right: *HOMER/1902*
Private collection
Ill. p. 152, detail p. 124

49. *Shooting the Rapids,* 1902
Watercolor over graphite on paper, 13 ⅞ × 21 ¾ in.
Lower right: *HOMER/1902*
Brooklyn Museum of Art, New York. Museum
Collection Fund and Special Subscription (11.537)
Ill. p. 151

50. *Channel Bass, Florida,* 1904
Watercolor over graphite on paper, 11 ¹⁄₁₆ × 19 ⅛ in.
Lower left: *Channel Bass/W.H. 1904*
The Metropolitan Museum of Art, New York. George A.
Hearn Fund, 1952 (52.155)
Ill. p. 87, detail p. 70

51. *Homosassa Jungle in Florida,* 1904
Watercolor over graphite on paper, 13 ⅝ × 21 ⁷⁄₁₆ in.
Lower left: *Homer 1904*
Harvard University Art Museums (Fogg Art Museum),
Cambridge, Massachusetts. Gift of Mrs. Charles S.
Homer, in memory of the late Charles S. Homer and
his brother, Winslow Homer (1935.50)
Ill. p. 176

52. *Red Shirt: Homosassa, Florida,* 1904
Watercolor over graphite on paper, 14 × 19 ¾ in.
Lower right: *HOMER 1904*
National Gallery of Art, Washington, D.C. Gift of Ruth
K. Henschel in memory of her husband, Charles R.
Henschel (1975.92.13)
Ill. p. 177

53. *Spotted Weakfish (Sea Trout), Homosassa, Florida, for
Mrs. R. A. Watts,* 1905
Watercolor over graphite on paper, 6 ⅜ × 15 ³⁄₁₆ in.
Lower left: *Winslow Homer 1905;* center right to lower
right side: *This sketch presented to Mrs. R. A. Watts—
with sincere appreciation*
Collection of Graham D. Williford
Ill. p. 84

Selected Bibliography

Angling, Outdoor Sport, and Sporting Art

MANUSCRIPT SOURCES

Adirondack Preserve Association. Club House Register of the Adirondack Forest Preserve (North Woods Club), April 1887–April 1968. Collection of the North Woods Club, Minerva, New York. Microfilm copy, The Adirondack Museum, Blue Mountain Lake, New York.

Brock House, Enterprise, Florida. Registers, 1875–1878, 1884–1902. West Volusia Historical Society, DeLand House, DeLand, Florida.

BOOKS AND EXHIBITION CATALOGUES

Adler, Jeanne Watson. *Early Days in the Adirondacks: The Photographs of Seneca Ray Stoddard.* New York: Harry N. Abrams, 1997.

Aflalo, Frederick G. *A Fisherman's Summer in Canada.* Toronto: McClelland & Goodchild; London: Witherby, 1911.

Barbour, George M. *Florida for Tourists, Invalids, and Settlers.* New York: D. Appleton and Company, 1884.

Boy's Treasury of Sports, Pastimes, and Recreations. Philadelphia: Lea and Blanchard, 1847.

[Brown, John J.]. *The American Angler's Guide.* New York: Burgess, Stringer & Co., 1845.

Brumley, Charles. *Guides of the Adirondacks: A History.* Utica, N.Y.: North Country Books, 1994.

Call of the Wild: A Sportsman's Life. Exh. cat. New York: Hirschl & Adler Galleries; Houston: Meredith Long & Co., 1994.

Chambers, E[dward] T[homas] D[avies]. *The Angler's Guide to Eastern Canada, Showing Where, When, and How to Fish for Salmon, Bass, Ouananiche, and Trout.* Rev. ed. Quebec: Chronicle Printing Co., [1903].

—. *The Ouananiche and Its Canadian Environment.* New York: Harper & Brothers, 1896.

Cleveland, Grover. *Fishing and Shooting Sketches.* New York: The Outing Publishing Company, 1904.

Comstock, Edward, Jr., ed. and comp. *The Adirondack League Club, 1890–1990.* Old Forge, N.Y.: The Adirondack League Club, 1990.

Davidson, James Wood. *The Florida of To-day: A Guide for Tourists and Settlers.* New York: D. Appleton and Company, 1889.

Dawson, George. *Pleasures of Angling.* New York: Sheldon & Co., 1876.

Donaldson, Alfred L. *A History of the Adirondacks.* 2 vols. 1921. Reprint. Port Washington, N.Y.: Ira J. Friedman, 1963.

Doughty, John, and Thomas Doughty. *The Cabinet of Natural History and American Rural Sports, with Illustrations,* 2 vols. Philadelphia: J. and T. Doughty, 1830–1833.

Gilborn, Craig. *Adirondack Camps: Homes Away from Home, 1850–1950.* Blue Mountain Lake, N.Y.: The Adirondack Museum, 2000.

Goode, George Brown. *Game Fishes of the United States.* Illustrations by S. A. Kilbourne. New York: Charles Scribner's Sons, 1878–1881. Facsimile edition. New York: Winchester Press, 1972.

Goodspeed, Charles Eliot. *Angling in America: Its Early History and Literature.* Boston: Houghton Mifflin Company, 1939.

Gould, Arthur Corbin, ed. *Sport; or Fishing and Shooting.* Boston: B. Whidden, 1889.

Hallock, Charles. *The Fishing Tourist: Angler's Guide and Reference Book.* New York: Harper & Brothers, 1873.

Harris, William C., ed. and comp. *The Angler's Guide Book and Tourist's Gazeteer of the Fishing Waters of the United States and Canada.* New York: The American Angler, 1885.

—. *The Fishes of North America that are Caught on Hook and Line.* Illustrations by J. L. Petrie. New York: The Harris Publishing Co., [1891]–1898.

Headley, J[oel] T[yler]. *The Adirondack; or, Life in the Woods.* New York: Baker and Scribner, 1849.

Henderson, Robert W., comp. *Early American Sport.* New York: A. S. Barnes & Co., 1953.

Henshall, James. *Book of the Black Bass.* Cincinnati, Ohio: Robert Clarke, 1881.

—. *Camping and Cruising in Florida.* Cincinnati, Ohio: Robert Clarke, 1884.

—. *Favorite Fish and Fishing.* New York: Outing, 1908.

Herbert, William Henry [Frank Forester]. *Fishing with Hook and Line.* New York: Brother Jonathan Office, 1858.

—. *Frank Forester's Fish and Fishing of the United States and British Provinces of North America.* London: R. Bentley, 1849.

Higginson, Alexander Henry. *British and American Sporting Authors, Their Writings and Biographies.* Berryville, Va.: Blue Ridge Press, 1949.

Hoffman, Charles Fenno. *Wild Scenes in the Forest and Prairie.* 2 vols. London: Richard Bentley, 1839; first American edition, 1 vol. New York: Colyer & Co., 1843.

Holberton, Wakeman. *The Art of Angling.* New York: Dick & Fitzgerald, [ca. 1887].

Holliman, Jennie. *American Sports (1785–1935).* Durham, N.C.: Seeman Press, 1931.

Johnson, Frank Mackie. *Forest, Lake and River: The Fishes of New England and Eastern Canada.* 2 vols. Boston: Printed for Subscribers, 1902.

Kaiser, Harvey. *Great Camps of the Adirondacks.* Boston: D. R. Godine, 1982.

Lanman, Charles. *Adventures in the Wilds of North America.* London: Longmans, Brown, Green and Longmans, 1854.

—. *A Summer in the Wilderness.* New York: Appleton, 1847.

—. *A Tour to the River Saguenay.* Philadelphia: Carey & Hart, 1848.

Marbury, Mary Orvis. *Favorite Flies and Their Histories.* Boston and New York: Houghton Mifflin & Co., 1892.

Mather, Fred. *Men I Have Fished With.* New York: Forest and Stream, 1897.

—. *My Angling Friends.* New York: Forest and Stream, 1901.

Mayer, Alfred M., ed. *Sport with Gun and Rod in American Woods and Waters.* New York: The Century Co., [1883].

McCarthy, Eugene. *The Leaping Ouananiche: What It Is, Where, When and How to Catch It.* New York: Forest and Stream Publishing Co., 1894.

—. *A Tale of Lake St. John: Comprising a Bit of History, a Quantity of Facts, and a Plentitude of Fish Stories.* Montreal: Desbarats & Co., 1903.

Murray, William Henry Harrison. *Adventures in the Wilderness;* or, *Camp-Life in the Adirondacks.* Boston: Fields, Osgood, & Co., 1869. Reprint, edited by William K. Verner, introduction and notes by Warder H. Cadbury. Syracuse, N.Y.: Syracuse University Press for the Adirondack Museum, 1970.

Norris, Thaddeus. *The American Angler's Book.* Philadelphia: E. H. Butler & Co., 1864.

Orvis, Charles, and Albert N. Cheney. *Fishing with the Fly: Sketches by Lovers of the Art, with Illustrations of Standard Flies.* Manchester, Vt.: J. J. Little and Co., 1883.

Phillips, John C. *A Bibliography of American Sporting Books.* Boston: Edward Morrill, and Son, 1930.

Piscatorial Pictorials of America: A Private Collection. Exh. cat. Montclair, N.J.: Montclair Art Museum, 1973.

Popkin, Susan A., and Roger B. Allen. *Gone Fishing: A History of Fishing in River, Bay, and Sea.* Philadelphia: Philadelphia Maritime Museum, 1987.

Prosek, James. *The Complete Angler: A Connecticut Yankee Follows in the Footsteps of Walton.* New York: HarperCollins, 1999.

—. *Trout: An Illustrated History.* New York: Knopf, 1996.

Quinn, Tom. *Angling in Art.* London: The Sportsman's Press, 1991.

Rhodes, Reilly, ed. *Sport in Art from American Museums.* New York: Palgrave, 1991.

Roosevelt, Theodore. *A Book-Lover's Holidays in the Open.* New York: Charles Scribner's Sons, 1916.

Rosenbauer, Tom. *Fly Fishing in America.* New York: Universe Publishing, 1996.

Samuels, Edward A. *With Fly-Rod and Camera.* New York: Forest and Stream Publishing Co., 1890.

Schmitt, Victorian Sandwick. *Four Centuries of Sporting Art: Selections from the John L. Wehle Collection, Gallery of Sporting Art, Genesee County Museum.* Mumford, N.Y.: Genesee County Museum, 1984.

Schneider, Paul. *The Adirondacks: A History of America's First Wilderness.* New York: Henry Holt and Co., 1997.

Schullery, Paul. *American Fly Fishing: A History.* New York: Lyons & Burford Publishers, 1987.

Scott, Genio C. *Fishing in American Waters.* New York: Harper & Brothers, 1869.

Shooting and Fishing in Art. Exh. cat. Baltimore: Baltimore Museum of Art, 1958.

Sparrow, Walter Shaw. *Angling in British Art.* London: John Lane/The Bodley Head, 1923.

Sport in American Art. Exh. cat. Boston: Museum of Fine Arts, Boston, 1944.

"*Sportscapes": Hunting, Fowling, Angling.* Exh. cat. Southampton, N.Y.: Parrish Art Museum, 1959.

Walton, Izaak. *The Compleat Angler; or, the Contemplative Man's Recreation. Being a Discourse on River, Fish-Ponds, Fish, and Fishing.* (1653). Edited by John Burton, introduction by John Buchan. Oxford and New York: Oxford University Press, 1982.

Warner, Charles Dudley. *In the Wilderness.* 1878. Reprint. Syracuse, N.Y.: Syracuse University Press for the Adirondack Museum, 1990.

Wessels, William L. *Adirondack Profiles.* Lake George, N.Y.: Adirondack Resorts Press, 1961.

Wetzel, Charles McKinley. *American Fishing Books: A Bibliography from the Earliest Times up to 1948, Together with a History of Angling and Angling Literature in America.* Newark, Del.: privately printed, 1950.

Wilson, Leila Fosburgh. *The North Woods Club, 1886–1986: One Hundred Years in the Adirondack Wilderness.* Minerva, N.Y.: privately printed, 1986.

JOURNALS

American Angler. Vols. 1–30. October 15, 1881–1900. Edited by William C. Harris. New York: The Angler's Publishing Company.

Forest and Stream. A Journal of Outdoor Life, Travel, Nature Study, Shooting, Fishing, Yachting. Vols. 1–100, 1873–1930. Vols. 1–12 edited by Charles Hallock. New York: Forest and Stream Publishing Co.

Lanman, Charles. "The Annals of Angling." *Galaxy* 6 (September 1868): 308.

McCarthy, Eugene. "Ouananiche Fishing." *Outing: The Gentleman's Magazine of Sport, Travel, and Outdoor Life* 23 (October 1893): 37–39.

McNeilly, Dorothy. "Charles Lanman." *The American Fly Fisher* 11, no. 3 (1984): 14–19.

Rod and Gun and American Sportsman. Vols. 1–10, October 1871–April 28, 1877. October 1873–March 7, 1874 edited by Arnold Burges. March 14, 1874–July 1875 edited by W. F. Parker. July 1875–April 1877 edited by William Humphreys. West Meriden, Conn.: Parker Bros., 1871–1874; New York: Rod and Gun Association, 1874–1877.

Sandys, Edward W. "Where the Ouananiche Is Waiting." *Outing: The Gentleman's Magazine of Sport, Travel, and Outdoor Life* 34 (June 1899): 237–244.

Shooting and Fishing: A Weekly Journal of the Rifle, Gun, and Rod. Edited by A. C. Gould. Boston; Shooting and Fishing Publishing Co., 1886–1895; New York: Shooting and Fishing Publishing Co., 1895–1906.

Winston, N. B. "Fishing à la Tourilli." *Outing: The Gentleman's Magazine of Sport, Travel, and Outdoor Life* 20 (September 1892): 488–492.

Winslow Homer and American Art

MANUSCRIPT SOURCES

Clarke, Thomas B. Letters. Archives of American Art, Smithsonian Institution, Washington, D.C. Gift of Joyce Tyler and purchased with funds provided by the Joseph Coudon VII memorial fund, established by Katherine Coudon, in memory of her son.

Doll & Richards Gallery, Boston. Records. Archives of American Art, Smithsonian Institution, Washington, D.C. Gift of Jeanne and Paul Sylva and gift of Wendell Zoehler.

Evans, William T., III. Letters. Archives of American Art, Smithsonian Institution, Washington, D.C. Transfer from the Smithsonian American Art Museum.

Goodrich, Lloyd. The Lloyd Goodrich and Edith Havens Goodrich/Whitney Museum of American Art Record of Works by Winslow Homer. Abigail Booth Gerdts, Director. New York.

Homer, Winslow. Papers and Family Memorabilia. Bowdoin College Museum of Art, Brunswick, Maine. Gift of the Homer family. Microfilm copies, Archives of American Art, Smithsonian Institution, Washington, D.C., lent by the Bowdoin College Museum of Art.

M. Knoedler & Co. Archives, New York. Copies of Homer material in Archives of American Art, Smithsonian Institution, Washington, D.C., lent by M. Knoedler & Co.

Macbeth Gallery Records, ca. 1890–1964. Archives of American Art, Smithsonian Institution, Washington, D.C. Gift of Robert G. McIntyre and of his estate, and gift of Phoebe C. and William Macbeth II.

Prang, Louis. Letters. Archives of American Art, Smithsonian Institution, Washington, D.C. Gift of Charles Feinberg, via Castano Galleries.

BOOKS AND EXHIBITION CATALOGUES

Beam, Philip C. *Winslow Homer at Prout's Neck.* Boston and Toronto: Little, Brown and Company, 1966.

—. *Winslow Homer's Magazine Engravings.* New York: Harper & Row, 1979.

—. *Winslow Homer Watercolors.* Exh. cat. Brunswick, Maine: Bowdoin College Museum of Art, 1983.

Burns, Sarah. *Inventing the Modern Artist: Art and Culture in Gilded Age America.* New Haven and London: Yale University Press, 1996.

Catalogue of a Loan Exhibition of Paintings by Winslow Homer. Exh. cat. New York: The Metropolitan Museum of Art, 1911.

Century Loan Exhibition as a Memorial to Winslow Homer by the Prout's Neck Association. Exh. cat. Prout's Neck, Maine: Prout's Neck Association, 1936.

Cikovsky, Nicolai, Jr. *Winslow Homer.* New York: Abrams, in association with the National Museum of American Art, Smithsonian Institution, 1990.

—. *Winslow Homer Watercolors.* New York: Macmillan Publishing Co., 1991.

—, ed. *Winslow Homer: A Symposium.* Washington, D.C.: National Gallery of Art, 1990.

Cikovsky, Nicolai, Jr., and Franklin Kelly. *Winslow Homer.* With contributions by Judith Walsh and Charles Brock. Exh. cat. New Haven and London: Yale University Press in association with the National Gallery of Art, 1995.

Conrads, Margaret C. *Winslow Homer and the Critics: Forging a National Art in the 1870s.* Exh. cat. Princeton, N.J.: Princeton University Press in association with the Nelson-Atkins Museum of Art, 2001.

Cooper, Helen A. *Winslow Homer Watercolors.* Exh. cat. New Haven and London: Yale University Press for the National Gallery of Art, 1986.

Davis, Melinda Dempster. *Winslow Homer: An Annotated Bibliography of Periodical Literature.* Metuchen, N.J.: Scarecrow Press, 1975.

Downes, William Howe. *The Life and Works of Winslow Homer.* 1911. Reprint. New York: Dover Publications, 1989.

Ferber, Linda S., and Barbara Dayer Gallati. *Masters of Color and Light: Homer, Sargent, and the American Watercolor Movement.* Exh. cat. Washington, D.C., and London: Smithsonian Institution Press in association with the Brooklyn Museum of Art, 1998.

Flexner, James Thomas. *The World of Winslow Homer.* New York: Time, [1966].

Fosburgh, James W. *Winslow Homer in the Adirondacks: An Exhibition of Paintings.* Exh. cat. Blue Mountain Lake, N.Y.: Adirondack Museum, 1959.

Gardner, Albert Ten Eyck. *Winslow Homer, American Artist: His World and His Work.* New York: Clarkson Potter, 1961.

—. *Winslow Homer: A Retrospective Exhibition.* Exh. cat. Washington, D.C.: National Gallery of Art, 1958.

Goodrich, Lloyd. *American Watercolor and Winslow Homer.* Exh. cat. Minneapolis: Walker Art Center, 1945.

—. *The Graphic Art of Winslow Homer.* Exh. cat. New York: Museum of Graphic Art, 1968.

—. *Winslow Homer.* New York: Macmillan, for the Whitney Museum of American Art, 1944.

—. *Winslow Homer.* New York: G. Braziller, 1959.

—. *Winslow Homer.* Exh. cat. New York: Whitney Museum of American Art, 1973.

—. *Winslow Homer Centenary Exhibition.* Exh. cat. New York: Whitney Museum of American Art, 1936.

—. *Winslow Homer in New York State.* Exh. cat. New York: Storm King Art Center, 1963.

—. *Winslow Homer's America.* New York: Tudor, 1969.

Goodrich, Lloyd, and Abigail Booth Gerdts. *Winslow Homer in Monochrome.* Exh. cat. New York: Knoedler, 1986.

Hannaway, Patti. *Winslow Homer in the Tropics.* Richmond, Va.: Westover Publishing Co., 1973.

Hendricks, Gordon. *The Life and Work of Winslow Homer.* New York: Harry N. Abrams, 1979.

Hoopes, Donelson F. *Winslow Homer Watercolors.* Exh. cat. New York: Watson-Guptill Publications in association with the Brooklyn Museum of Art and the Metropolitan Museum of Art, 1969.

Junker, Patricia, et al. *Winslow Homer in the 1890s: Prout's Neck Observed.* Exh. cat. New York: Hudson Hills Press in association with the Memorial Art Gallery of the University of Rochester, 1990.

Kelsey, Mavis Parrott, and David Tatham. *Winslow Homer Graphics: From the Mavis P. and Mary Wilson Kelsey Collection of Winslow Homer Graphics.* Exh. cat. Houston: The Museum of Fine Arts, Houston, 1977.

Kern, Stephen. *The Culture of Time and Space, 1880–1918.* Cambridge, Mass.: Harvard University Press, 1983.

Kushner, Marilyn S., Barbara Dayer Gallati, and Linda S. Ferber. *Winslow Homer: Illustrating America.* New York: George Braziller in association with the Brooklyn Museum of Art, 2000.

Lanman, Charles. *Letters from a Landscape Painter.* Boston: James Munroe & Co., 1845.

Laughton, Rodney. *Images of America: Scarborough.* Dover, N.H.: Arcadia Publishing, 1996.

Lears, T. J. Jackson. *No Place of Grace: Antimodernism and the Transformation of American Culture, 1880–1920.* Chicago: University of Chicago Press, 1994.

Libby, Gary R., ed. *Celebrating Florida: Works of Art from the Vickers Collection.* Gainesville: University Press of Florida, 1995.

Mandel, C. F. *Fair Wilderness: American Paintings in the Collection of the Adirondack Museum.* Blue Mountain Lake, N.Y.: The Adirondack Museum, 1990.

Marzio, Peter. *A Democratic Art: Chromolithography, 1840–1900.* Boston: David R. Godine, in association with the Amon Carter Museum of Western Art, 1979.

Mayer, A. Hyatt, and Mark Davis. *American Art at the Century.* New York: Century Association, 1977.

McSpadden, J. Walker. *Famous Painters of America.* New York: T. Y. Crowell & Co., 1907.

Murphy, Alexandra. *Winslow Homer in the Clark Collection.* With contributions by Rafael Fernandez and Jennifer Gordon. Exh. cat. Williamstown, Mass.: Sterling and Francine Clark Art Institute, 1986.

Reed, Sue Welsh, and Carol Troyen. *Awash in Color: Homer, Sargent, and the Great American Watercolor.* Exh. cat. Boston: Bulfinch Press, in association with the Museum of Fine Arts, Boston, 1993.

Reynolds, Jock, Susan C. Faxon, and Paul Metcalf. *Winslow Homer at the Addison.* Exh. cat. Andover, Mass.: Addison Gallery of American Art, 1990.

Rubin, Stephen. *American Watercolors from the Metropolitan Museum of Art.* Exh. cat. New York: Harry N. Abrams, in association with the American Federation of Arts, 1991.

Schlageter, Robert W. *Winslow Homer's Florida, 1886–1909.* Exh. cat. Jacksonville, Fla.: The Cummer Gallery of Art, 1977.

Spassky, Natalie. *Winslow Homer: A Selection of Watercolors, Drawings and Prints from the Metropolitan Museum of Art.* Exh. cat. New York: The Metropolitan Museum of Art, 1972.

—, et al. *American Paintings in the Metropolitan Museum of Art. Vol.2. A Catalogue of Works by Artists Born between 1816 and 1845.* Princeton, N.J.: Princeton University Press in association with the Metropolitan Museum of Art, 1985.

Steadman, William E. *Yankee Painter: A Retrospective Exhibition of Oils, Water Colors, and Graphics by Winslow Homer.* Exh. cat. Tucson: University of Arizona Art Gallery, 1963.

Stepanek, Stephanie Loeb. *Winslow Homer.* Exh. cat. Boston: Museum of Fine Arts, Boston, 1977.

Tatham, David. *Winslow Homer and the Illustrated Book.* Syracuse, N.Y.: Syracuse University Press, 1992.

—. *Winslow Homer in the Adirondacks.* Syracuse, N.Y.: Syracuse University Press, 1996.

—. *Winslow Homer in the 1880s: Watercolors, Drawings, Etchings.* Exh. cat. Syracuse, N.Y.: Everson Museum of Art, 1983.

Tatham, David, Hallie E. Bond, and Tom Rosenbauer. *Fishing in the North Woods: Winslow Homer.* New York: Universe Publishing for the Museum of Fine Arts, Boston, 1995.

Tuckerman, Henry T. *Book of the Artists: American Artist Life.* 1867. Reprint. New York: James F. Carr, 1966.

Van Rensselaer, Marianna (Mrs. Schuyler). *Six Portraits.* Boston: Houghton Mifflin, 1889.

Water Colors by Winslow Homer Loaned to the Brooklyn Institute. Exh. cat. New York: Brooklyn Institute, 1915.

Wilmerding, John. *Winslow Homer.* New York: Praeger Publishers, 1972.

—. *Winslow Homer: The Charles Shipman Payson Gift to the Portland Museum of Art, Portland, Maine.* Exh. cat. New York: Coe Kerr Gallery, 1981.

Wilmerding, John, and Linda Ayres. *Winslow Homer in the 1870s: Selections from the Valentine-Pulsifer Collection.* Exh. cat. Hanover, N.H.: The University Press of New England for the Art Museum, Princeton University, 1990.

Wilmerding, John, and Elaine Dee. *Winslow Homer, 1836–1910: A Selection from the Cooper-Hewitt Collection, Smithsonian Institution.* Exh. cat. Washington, D.C.: Smithsonian Institution Press, 1972.

Winslow Homer. Exh. cat. Williamstown, Mass.: Sterling and Francine Clark Art Institute, [1961].

Winslow Homer at Prout's Neck. Exh. cat. Brunswick, Maine: Bowdoin College Museum of Art, 1966.

Winslow Homer's Sub-Tropical America. Exh. cat. Coral Gables, Fla.: Lowe Art Museum, 1968.

Yarnall, James, and William H. Gerdts, comps. *The National Museum of American Art's Index to American Art Exhibition Catalogues, from the Beginning through the 1876 Centennial Year.* 3 vols. Boston: G. K. Hall & Co., 1986.

Zbornik, Matthew. *Winslow Homer: Water and Light, Selected Watercolors, 1874–1897.* Exh. cat. Miami, Fla.: Center for the Fine Arts, 1991.

JOURNALS

Beam, Philip Conway. "Winslow Homer's Father." *The New England Quarterly* 20, no. 1 (March 1947): 51–74.

Cox, Kenyon. "The Art of Winslow Homer." *Scribner's Magazine* 56 (September 1914): 377–388.

—. "The Watercolors of Winslow Homer." *Art in America* 6 (October 1914): 404–415.

Downes, William Howe, and F. T. Robinson. "Some Living American Painters, Winslow Homer, N.A." *Art Interchange,* May 1894; 136–138.

Fosburgh, Pieter W. "Winslow Homer, Painter of Fishes and Fishermen." *The Conservationist,* April–May 1972; 4–7.

Johnston, Patricia Condon. "Winslow Homer." *Sporting Classics* 5, no. 3 (May–June 1986): 42–51.

May, Stephen. "The Artist as Angler." *Fly Rod and Reel,* May–June 1996; 12–13.

—. "The Artist as Angler: Winslow Homer in Florida." *Florida Naturalist: The Magazine of the Florida Audubon Society* 70, no. 2 (summer 1997): 13–15.

—. "Winslow Homer: An Adirondack Aficionado." *New York Outdoors,* July–August 1996; 16–17, 26.

—. "Winslow Homer: Artist and Bassmaster." *Bassmaster Magazine,* July–August 1996; 54–58.

Morse, Margaret. "Winslow Homer: The Adirondack Years." *New York Alive* [bimonthly journal of the Business Council of New York State] 9, no. 5 (September–October 1989): 32–37.

O'Brien, Peggy. "Shurtleff." *Adirondack Life,* November–December 1979; 40–43.

Poole, Robert M. "Winslow Homer: American Original." *National Geographic,* December 1998; 75–100.

Sleeper, Frank, and Robert Cantwell. "Odyssey of an Angler." *Sports Illustrated* 37, no. 26 (December 25, 1972): 62–73.

Tatham, David. "Paddling at Dusk: Winslow Homer and Ernest Yalden." *Porticus* [Journal of the Memorial Art Gallery of the University of Rochester] 9 (1986): 16–19.

—. "Trapper, Hunter, and Woodsman: Winslow Homer's Adirondack Figures." *American Art Journal* 22, no. 4 (1990): 41–67.

—. "*The Two Guides:* Winslow Homer at Keene Valley, Adirondacks." *American Art Journal* 20 (1988): 20–34.

—. "Winslow Homer at the North Woods Club." In *Winslow Homer: A Symposium,* edited by Nicolai Cikovsky Jr., 114–130. *Studies in the History of Art* 26. Center for the Advanced Study in the Visual Arts, Symposium Papers XI. Washington, D.C.: National Gallery of Art, 1990.

—. "Winslow Homer's Library." *American Art Journal* 9, no. 1 (May 1977): 92–98.

Teitelbaum, Gene, ed. *Winslow Homer: An Annual.* Vols. 1–7, 1985–1992. New Albany, Ind.: the editor.

Weinberg, H. Barbara. "Thomas B. Clarke: Foremost Patron of American Art from 1872 to 1899." *American Art Journal* 8, no. 1 (May 1976): 52–83.

DISSERTATION

Mackle, Elliott James, Jr. "The Eden of the South: Florida's Image in American Travel Literature and Painting, 1865–1900." Ph.D. diss., Emory University, 1977.

Index

Page numbers in boldface refer to illustrations.

Produced by the Publications Department of the Fine Arts Museums of San Francisco,
in collaboration with the Amon Carter Museum, Fort Worth, Texas
Project Manager: Ann Heath Karlstrom, Director of Publications and Graphic Design,
Fine Arts Museums of San Francisco

Copy Editor: Fronia W. Simpson, Bennington, Vermont
Book and cover design: Michael Sumner, Santa Fe, New Mexico
Typeset in Adobe Garamond

Printed on Furioso matt, 150 gsm, at Snoeck-Ducaju & Zoon, Ghent, Belgium